Troubleshooting Local Area Networks

Preproduction Copy

Troubleshooting
Local Area Networks

Othmar Kyas
Thomas Heim

INTERNATIONAL THOMSON PUBLISHING

I(T)P An International Thomson Publishing Company

London • New York • Bonn • Boston • Madrid • Melbourne • Mexico City • Paris • Singapore
Tokyo • Toronto • Albany, NY • Belmont, CA • Cincinnati, OH • Detroit, MI

Troubleshooting Local Area Networks

International Thomson Publishing
  Commissioning Editor: Samantha Whittaker
  Editorial Assistant: Jonathan Simpson
Van Nostrand Reinhold
  Sponsoring Editor: Neil Levine

I(T)P A division of International Thomson Publishing Inc.
The ITP logo is a trademark under licence

Made in Logotechnics C.P.C. Ltd., Sheffield
  Project Management: Sandra M. Potestà
  Production: Hans-Dieter Rauschner + Team
  Artistic Direction: Stefano E. Potestà
  Cover Illustration: William Smith

First printed 1995

International Thomson Publishing   Van Nostrand Reinhold
Berkshire House   115 Fifth Avenue, 4th Floor
168–173 High Holborn   New York, NY 10003
London WC1V 7AA

ISBN (ITP UK)   1-850-32122-1
ISBN (Van Nostrand Reinhold) 0-442-01999-8

British Library Cataloguing-in-Publication Data
A catalogue record for this book is available from the British Library

Library of Congress Cataloging-in-Publication Data
A catalog record for this book is available from the Library of Congress

Contents

Forward   vii

1   The nature of problems in local networks   1

   1.1   Behaviour of complex structures - catastrophe theory   2

      1.1.2   Fault categories and their frequency   4

   1.2   The cost of network failures   5

      1.2.1   Sudden failure of all or part of the network   5

      1.2.2   Under-utilisation of available network infrastructure   8

      1.2.3   Reducing network failure costs   8

2   **Strategic fault-tracing in LANS**   **11**

   2.1   Some first thoughts on faults-tracing   11

   2.2   Interpreting reports of faults   12

   2.3   Breaking down complex fault structures   13

   2.4   Problem analysis in general   15

       2.4.1   Familiarity with systems in use   17

       2.4.2   Methodical treatment of facts and assumptions   17

       2.4.3   Methodical fault-tracing   18

   2.5   The many faces of trouble-shooting   19

       2.5.1   Cable test   20

       2.5.2   Active response and echo tests   22

       2.5.3   Statistics   31

       2.5.4   Data analysis   36

       2.5.5   Automatic analyses   37

3   **LAN-WAN coupling**   **39**

   3.1   Linking a number of LANs via a Wide-Area Network   39

   3.2   Connection-orientated vs. connectionless   40
         protocols in the WAN section

   3.3   Useful protocols for a WAN link   41

   3.4   Effective planning to avoid potential bottlenecks   42

   3.5   Diagnostic methods   43

3.6   Sumary   43

4   **Operating a network**   **45**

4.1   The development of LANs and the problems encountered   45

4.2   The health check   47

4.3   Summary   50

5   **Diagnostic aids for lcal networks**   **51**

5.1   Protocol analysers   51

5.1.1   Software-based analysers   52

5.1.2   Software and hardware-based analyers   52

5.1.3   Dedicated analyser systems   53

5.2   The multi-protocol PC   54

5.3   Distributed monitoring units   54

5.4   Diagnostics at the physical level   55

5.4.1   Multimeters   56

5.4.2   Cable testers   56

5.4.3   Spectrum Analysers   56

5.4.4   Oscilloscopes   57

6   **Transfer media**   **59**

6.1   Coaxial cable   60

6.1.1   Structure and connection of coaxial cables   60

6.1.2   Coax cable problems and their causes   61

6.1.3   Isolation of fault sources   62

6.2   Twisted-pair cable   66

6.2.1   Problems with Twisted-Pair Cables and their causes   67

6.3   Optical Fibre Cables   68

6.3.1   Problems with optical fibre and their causes   69

7   Network interface cards, MAUs and concentrators   71

7.1   Network interface cards   72

7.1.1   Problems with Ethernet interface cards   72

7.1.2   Problems with token Ring interface cards   73

7.1.3   Operating statistics for network interface cards   74

7.2   MaUs (Media Access Units) and AUIs (Attachments   75
Unit Interfaces) in Ethernet networks

7.2.1   Inserting and removing AUI cables and MAUs   76

7.2.2   Trouble-shooting equipment   76

7.2.3   Symptoms of faulty MAUs/AUIs   77

7.2.4   Diagnosing faulty MAUs   77

7.3   Concentrators in Token Ring networks   78

7.3.1   Trouble-shooting equipment   78

7.3.2   Symptoms of concentrator problems   79

7.3.3   Diagnosing concentrator problems   79

8   Repeaters and hubs (star couplers)   81

    8.1   Repeater problems   81

          8.1.1   Repeaters in Ethernet   81

          8.1.2   Repeater functions   82

          8.1.3   Problems in Ethernet networks with repeaters   83

          8.1.4   Token Ring and FDDI   87

    8.2   Problems with star couplers   87
          (multi-port repeaters)

          8.2.1   Optical star couplers without repeater functions   87

          8.2.2   Star couplers with repeater functions   88

          8.2.3   Problems with star couplers in Ethernet networks   89

9   Bridges and routers   91

    9.1   Types of bridge   91

    9.2   Linking networks of different types   92

    9.3   Critical bridge parameters   92

          9.3.1   Throughput capacity and throughput rate   92

          9.3.2   Loss of data packets   93

          9.3.3   Buffering   93

          9.3.4   Data packets too long   93

          9.3.5   Changes to packet sequence   94

          9.3.6   Address tables   94

9.3.7   Filter table   94

9.3.8   Spanning tree and source routing   95

9.3.9   Wrong mode: Ethernet V.2.0 vs. IEEE 802.3   97

9.3.10 No packet length limit   97

9.3.11 Differences in protocol implementation   97

9.3.12 Problems with remote bridge cables   97

9.3.13 Wrong ring speed (Token Ring)   97

9.4 Functions of the various types of network   98

9.4.1   Bridge from Ethernet to Ethernet   98

9.4.2   Bridge from Token Ring to Token Ring   98

9.4.3   Bridge from FDDI to FDDI   98

9.4.4   Bridge from Ethernet to Token Ring   99

9.4.5   Bridge from Token Ring to Ethernet   99

9.4.6   Bridge from Ethernet to FDDI   99

9.4.7   Bridge from FDDI to Ethernet   100

9.4.8   Bridge from Token Ring to FDDI   100

9.4.9   Bridge from FDDI to Token Ring   101

9.5 Routers   101

9.5.1   Vector Distance (Bellman-Ford) Routing   101

9.5.2   Link State or Shortest Path First Routing   101

9.5.3   Problems with routers and their causes   102

10   Network problems: symptoms - causes - actions   105

10.1 Layer 1: the physical layer   106

    10.1.1 Coaxial cable   106

    10.1.2 Twisted pair cable   107

    10.1.3 Optical fibre links   109

10.2 Ethernet   109

10.3 Token Ring   120

    10.3.1 Faults endemic to the system   120

    10.3.2 Token ring fault symptoms - causes - action   122

10.4 Fault symptoms in FDDI networks - causes - action   135

11   The standards   141

11.1 ANSI/IEEE 802.2/iso 8802-2 Logical Link Control   143

    11.1.1 The LLC data format   144

    11.1.2 The LLC protocol   146

    11.1.3 Timers   153

11.2 The IEEE 802.3/ISO 8802-3 standard for local networks   153

    11.2.1 Design and Function   154

    11.2.2 Structure of MAC Frames   155

    11.2.3 Functional Model of CSMA/CD   158

    11.2.4 Physical Signalling (PLS) and AUI Specifications   161

    11.2.5 Specifications for MAUs, repeaters and cables   165

11.2.6 Characteristics of Coax Cable   168

11.3 The IEEE 802.5/ISO IS 8802-5 standard   170
      or local networks: Token Ring access method

      11.3.1 Data format   171

      11.3.2 MAC frames   177

      11.3.3 Timers   181

      11.3.4 Flags   182

      11.3.5 Registers and Stacks   182

      11.3.6 The Latency Buffer   183

      11.3.7 The Token Ring Protocol   183

      11.3.8 Signalling Specifications   186

      11.3.9 The Physical Level   187

      11.3.10 Attachment of Cables   191

11.4 ANSI ASC X329.5/ISO 9314 FDDI: THE FIBRE   191
      DISTRIBUTED DATA INTERFACE

      11.4.1 Encoding   193

      11.4.3 PHY Functions   198

      11.4.4 PData Formats   203

      11.4.5 Operation of the MAC Layer   210

      11.4.6 The Media Interface Connector (MIC)   212

      11.4.7 Signal Characteristics   213

      11.4.8 Testing Methods   215

11.4.9 SMT draft for FDDI   215

11.4.10   (Entity Co-ordination Management)
217

11.4.11   PCM (Physical Connection Management)
217

11.4.12   CEM (Configuration Element Management)

11.4.13   Ring Management (RMT)

11.4.14   The SMT Agent

12   Network Performance   225

12.1 IEEE 802.5 Token Ring   226

12.2 IEEE 802.3 CSMA/CD   228

Appendix   233

Foreword

This book sets out to provide practical help in tracing, correcting and preventing problems in local networks.

The book demonstrates systematic approaches to fault-tracing. A chapter on diagnostic tools describes how they can be put to successful and effective use. A list of common fault symptoms and typical causes for them offers tips on where to look for potential sources of problems. And finally, an Appendix provides reference tables of important parameters and the main address assignments. This removes the need for time-consuming and inefficient trouble-shooting methods such as 'Reset All' or 'Binary Search'.

The technical terms used in the book have in most cases been left in the English original, to avoid confusion arising from unfamiliar German translations.

The term 'Ethernet' is used for both IEEE 802.3 CSMA/CD and Ethernet V2.0 networks. Only in cases where it is necessary to make a distinction will the full name be given. 'Token Ring' and 'FDDI' mean IEEE 802.5 networks and ANSI ASC X329.5/ISO 9314 networks respectively.

Lists of manufacturers are given in alphabetical order.

To encourage the reader into the right frame of mind, here is a relevant quotation from Confucius, who considered that there were 'three ways to act wisely':

The first way, by thinking, is the noblest.
The second way, by imitation, is the easiest.
The third way, through experience, is the bitterest.

Munich, May 1993

Othmar Kyas
Thomas Heim

1

The nature of problems in local networks

As more and more computer systems are linked together in networks, the reliability of local networks has become a central factor determining the performance of computer infrastructure. In 1989, for example, only one out of every five business PCs was connected to a network; now it is one in two. In 1993/94, some 58 million PCs and 7 million workstations worldwide will operate within networks (Figure 1.1). Further to this growth in the size and spread of networks, new technologies with higher capacities (FDDI) have come into service and existing networks have been linked together, so that hybrid network topologies will occur ever more frequently.

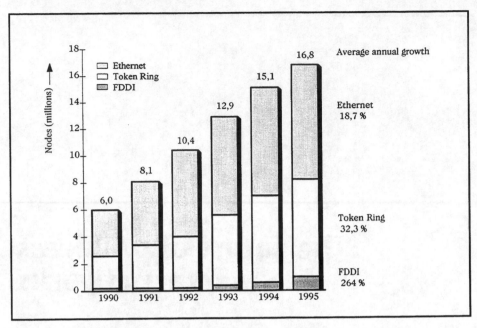

Figure 1.1   Network nodes installed annually worldwide.

1.1   Behaviour of complex structures – catastrophe theory

The greater the complexity of a structure and the number of parameters it is affected by, the harder it becomes to predict its behaviour. One way of describing the behaviour of complex structures like LANs, especially where the – usually non-linear – faults we are interested in occur, is offered by catastrophe theory (René Thom, 1975). It supplies a qualitative description, rather than quantitative statements, of the behaviour of structures of this type. That is, it is able to say, for example: 'In front of us there is a river, with a hill behind it.' But it cannot tell us anything about the depth of the river or the height of the hill.

The theory itself is based on seven elementary catastrophes, in which the behaviour of the system is determined not by the nature of the parameters affecting it, but solely by their number. The behavioural model for catastrophes determined by two parameters is known as a 'cusp catastrophe graph' and shows a three-dimensional surface with an upper side representing states of equilibrium and an underside representing unstable maximum values (singularities). This model is used to characterise the behavioural patterns of a wide range of processes, and will serve as a basis for our Ethernet example.

Two of the most interesting parameters in Ethernet networks – slot time and system load – will be the variable parameters. The slot time (which equals twice the transit time required for a signal to travel between the two stations furthest apart) is determined by the components which create delays in the signal – that is, additional cabling, repeaters, star couplers etc. If we now keep all other variables constant – variables such as the average packet length, the number of stations etc. – we arrive at the behavioural chart for data throughput shown in Figure 1.2.

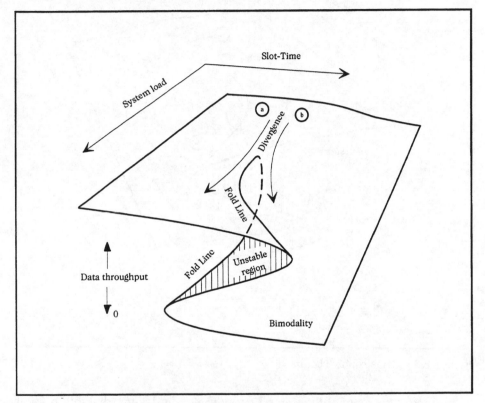

Figure 1.2   Catastrophe Theory 1.

An increase in the system load, starting from a specified slot time a, moves the working point of the network across the surface of the cusp catastrophe graph in the direction of the x axis. Data throughput increases accordingly. However, the same increase in system load, starting from a larger slot time b, drastically reduces the efficiency of the network. All these trends are played out on the surface of the graph, and are thus linear (Figure 1.2).

Now, if, for example, we start at operating state a and increase the system load, and then, on reaching state c, we increase the slot time, the result is that the equilibrium state is abandoned abruptly at point d in

favour of the fastest available route to point e, which represents a new
stable state, but this time with a stable minimum data throughput. The
abrupt transition from d to e is referred to as a catastrophe (Figure 1.3).

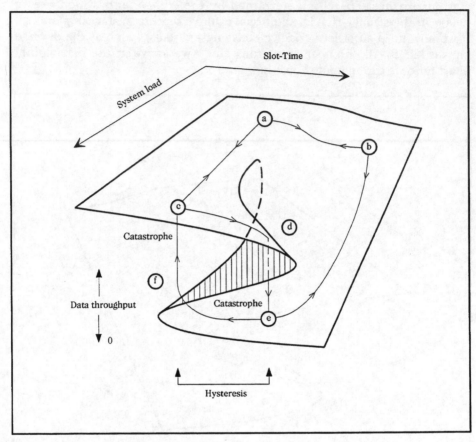

Figure 1.3   Catastrophe Theory 2.

Catastrophe theory illustrates how complex and unpredictable a local
network can be. Symptoms of faults can usually be traced to a number of
causes. One event triggers another, which in turn sets off yet another.
Feedback can amplify or reduce the effect.

When a fault eventually makes itself felt, it may be in quite another place
and in a totally different form, triggered by something apparently quite trivial.

1.1.2 Fault categories and their frequency

Experience shows that approximately 4/5 of all network problems are
hardware-related. Network problems can be divided into five groups.

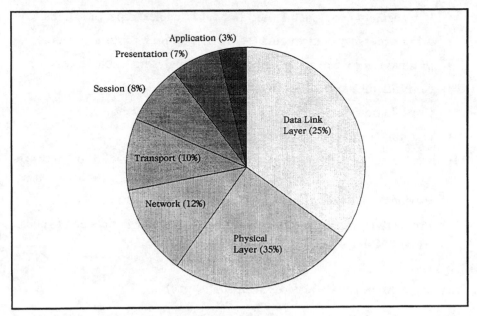

Figure 1.4   Frequency of faults (OSI 7 layer model).

Figure 1.4 illustrates the frequency of different classes of fault, arranged according to the OSI 7-layer model. This shows that 60% of all problems occur in the two lowest OSI layers, and we will be concentrating especially on these in the following chapters.

1.2   The cost of network failures

This section will demonstrate how a quick estimate of the costs of network problems can be made, sufficiently exact for most applications.

1.2.1   Sudden failure of all or part of the network

Sudden failures are network faults which make the network, or parts of it, inoperative from one minute to the next. The costs arising from this can be classified as follows:

Immediate costs (costs arising within 48 hours)

(a) Direct costs (costs directly connected with the network problem and its removal):

- Replacement components (network cards, cables, repeaters, hubs, ...),
- other necessary components (additional bridges, routers, servers ...),
- purchase or hire of equipment (network analysers, cable testers ...),
- Consultancy services by (external) network specialist,
- Consultancy services by hardware/software manufacturer,
- Overtime in networking department.

(b) Indirect costs (costs arising as a result of reduced/lost work by network users):

- Productivity losses by staff using computer workstations,
- Productivity losses in production lines, purchasing and sale of goods, warehousing, automatic racking systems etc.

Derivative costs (costs arising after 48 hours)

(a) Direct costs:

- Re-planning of parts of the network (restructuring of servers, bridges ...),
- Checking of other segments of the network for possible faults similar to those experienced,
- Documentation of fault.

(b) Indirect costs:

- Delayed completion of projects and consequential expenses (product development, production etc.),
- Delayed completion of services and consequential expenses (in accounting, tendering, invoicing, etc.).

The following example illustrates how an estimate may be drawn up for the derivative costs of a network failure in an average service operation:

- Down time: 4 hours.
- Network: Token ring, 6 segments connected by bridges.
- Segments affected: CAD department CAD-1, with 15 workstations on the network; accounting department A-1, with 20 PCs on the network.

Direct costs:

- External network specialist (0.5 day): £500
- Overtime in networking department: £150
- Total: £650.

Indirect costs:

The calculation of the indirect costs is shown in the table below, and is initially based on the cost to the company per employee per hour. If an employee's workstation goes down, his or her productivity will suffer.

Employee	Number	Hourly rate	Network down time	Of which lost	Productivity loss
CAD-1 dept.					
Engineer	6	£80	3 hrs	1.5 hrs	£720
CAD artist	9	£50	3 hrs	2.5 hrs	£1125
A-1 dept.					
Accountant	2	£50	4 hrs	1.5 hrs	£150
Senior					
admin. clerk	18	£25	4 hrs	3.0 hrs	£1350
				Total	£3345

This has to take into account the degree to which a given activity depends on the use of the computer (in per cent) and whether there is any alternative work which can be usefully done in the meantime.

A senior administrative clerk, whose main task involves sitting at a workstation and keying in or analysing data, will lose more time when the

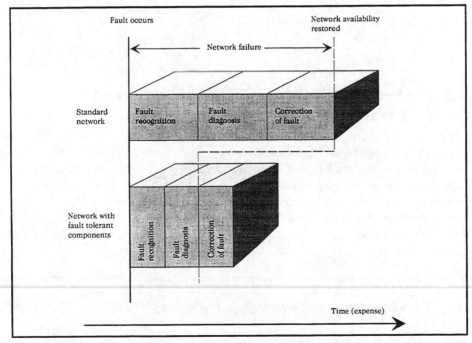

Figure 1.5   Direct and indirect costs

network goes down (3 hours if the failure lasts 4 hours) than a development
engineer who can temporarily turn to other work for which he does not
need access to a computer.

As Figure 1.5 shows, the indirect costs mount up to several times the
size of the direct costs. Reducing the Mean Time to Repair (MTTR) by
increasing the direct costs (e.g. by giving staff specialist training or by
buying analyser systems) will therefore pay off very quickly.

An independent study of network failures investigated 66 companies
with local networks, averaging 468 network nodes. The study showed that a
typical network (or parts of a network) fails on average 20.28 times per
year, losing 39.8 users 3345 hours' work annually.

- Average size of network:
  468 nodes

- Failures per year:
  20.28

- Users affected by each failure:
  39.8

- Working hours lost per failure:
  165

- Working hours lost per year:
  3345

1.2.2   Under-utilisation of available network infrastructure

Cost factors which should not be under-estimated are inadequate planning,
persistent uncorrected faults and under-utilised network components. In
such cases, a performance analysis of the network can work wonders. A
planned conversion of a 4 Mbps token ring to 16 Mbps may suddenly turn
out to be completely unnecessary, or it may show there is little to be gained
from the envisaged new server. This is covered more fully in Section 4.2: A
LAN health check.

1.2.3   Reducing network failure costs

The costs entailed by a network failure can be reduced either by reducing
the Mean Time to Repair (MTTR) or by increasing the network's fail-safe

characteristics. Both of these will achieve an increase in the availability of the network.

Availability = MTBF / MTTR + MTBF

- The Mean Time Between Failures (MTBF) is the average length of time between occurrences of a network fault.
- The Mean Time to Repair (MTTR) is the time lost between the occurrence of a fault and its correction.

Given a MTBF of 18 days, or 432 hours, and a MTTR of 6 hours, the availability is calculated as

---

Availability = 432/(432+6) = 98.63%

An increase in the system availability can be achieved in the following ways:

Increasing the MTBF

- Use of redundant network structures (back-up ring in token ring, dual ring in FDDI, self-reconfiguring hubs ...),
- Use of mirrored disks in servers,

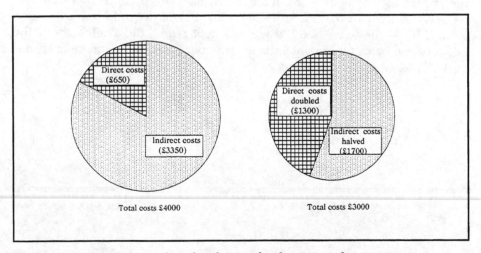

Figure 1.6   Down time with and without redundant network structures

- Use of uninterruptible power supplies (UPS).

Where the network uses fault-tolerant components, which are capable of reconfiguring themselves in the event of a fault, or at least isolating the source of the fault so that most of the network is largely unaffected, fault diagnosis is deferred until after the operation of the network has been restored (Figure 1.6). An intelligent multi-port repeater, after all, will very quickly spot a fault in a sub-segment and automatically isolate it (auto-partitioning). The other network users will not be aware of this. After this automatic, temporary 'fault clearance', the diagnostics can start. The same kind of thing is done by an intelligent concentrator in a token ring network, using the back-up ring, or a DAS (Dual-Attached) concentrator in FDDI. A line problem is recognised and the system is immediately reconfigured to the back-up ring. It is then possible to track down the fault itself.

Reducing the MTTR

- Use of network analysis and monitoring systems (*see* Chapter 5: Measuring equipment and methods),
- Training in-house network specialists,
- Stocking 'vital components',
- Regular 'health checks' on the network.

A reduction in the MTTR can usually be carried out much more cheaply than the relatively expensive route of increasing MTBF. Thus, for example, in a token ring network a stock of concentrators can measurably increase the availability of the network. If a concentrator fails and no replacement is on hand, at least 12 to 24 hours will be lost before the order for a new one is met. If, on the other hand, a spare is kept ready, the availability of the network can be restored in as little as two hours (diagnosis and installation) in the absence of complications.

2

Strategic fault-tracing in LANs

2.1 Some first thoughts on fault-tracing

Tracing faults in a network can to some extent be compared with hunting down the infamous needle in the legendary haystack. It can be a trivial matter to trace a fault if it is obvious. But trickier faults call for a trouble-shooting expert, with the methodical thinking and logical approach of a Sherlock Holmes. In a network environment, a methodical and systematical approach is an absolute necessity. Interim findings need to be checked and re-checked at every stage to make sure nothing has been accidentally overlooked. A dash of intuition coupled, of course, with experience of the behaviour of systems in a computer network, and anyone can be a Sherlock Holmes. But we must not forget that Holmes had his helpers, who supplied him with additional information. Even specialists need to obtain extra information. There is no set recipe for fault-tracing in a network, any more than there was for Sherlock Holmes' masterpieces of detection.

A computer network – and the 'net' in 'network' perfectly describes the structure and arrangement of this type of system, that is, frequently highly interlocking – is not something that anyone can know in all its details. The only exceptions to this are small networks of 5 to 20 stations, connected by just one cable (coax or token ring) and accessing just one file server or similar component. In these cases, of course, we can hardly speak of an interlocking structure. But in the end, what is needed for systematic trouble-shooting in a large network is not much different from the elements of trouble-shooting in a small network.

Often the only answer is to reduce a large network to smaller logical and physical structures for the purpose of trouble-shooting. It is in the nature of human thinking processes that we are unable to fully comprehend complex structures. Simplifying intricate and involved structures is frequently an automatic response. But caution is advised here: an inexperienced mind tends intuitively to exclude unfamiliar factors in this reducing process, as it is unable to evaluate and assess the unfamiliar, or judge its importance for the fault-tracing process. But there is nothing for it: a complex system has to be simplified if the problem is to be tracked down. Even mathematical descriptions, called in elsewhere to describe processes of every sort, make use of simplification when the task becomes complex.

Sometimes this is the only way we can explain or represent something. However, the assumptions made for the purpose of tracking down the problem must be borne in mind when assessing the result, in case a given assumption is not universally applicable. But let's not allow ourselves to be side-tracked: in this section we are describing the steps involved in systematic fault-tracing.

2.2   Interpreting reports of faults

The first step has to be to take stock of the problem or the situation resulting from a fault. Here again, caution is advised: very often, the situation is characterised or described as 'incredibly slow' or 'everything's stopped working' or the like. Information of this sort should not be taken at face value.

An example will make this clear. The statement, 'The car is moving fairly slowly' is only valid in a relative sense. It may be an objective judgement, or it may be a subjective impression. On the one hand, you can certainly take it that the speaker has known it to go faster – and this applies equally where networks are concerned. In the context of a longish period of collected experience, the statement can indeed be considered objective.

But suppose the speaker has just turned off the motorway, where he has been cruising at 120 mph (wherever this may still be possible – on some German autobahns, perhaps), and suddenly has to content himself with a modest 80.

Just how much this is a subjective impression is clear at once when we consider that an American driver would describe this speed, compared with the legal maximum of 65 mph in the USA, as 'pretty fast' – a description any German motorist would greet with scorn.

This trivial and mundane example serves to underline that statements of this sort must be approached with care. We can all imagine the questions we would want to ask when confronted with a simple statement such as: 'Hardly anything's working on the network today.' Here are some possibilities:

- What isn't working?

- Nobody else has complained.

- What are you trying do to and what was happening before?

- If nobody else has complained, it's not too likely there's anything wrong.

Reactions of this sort come naturally to a member of a network support team, confronted with a statement like this.

This means that the first step in trouble-shooting must be rephrased as: collect information from all sides to put together a picture of the situation, interpreting the fault reports correctly. There's no option but to find out for yourself what is happening and what the actual situation is. Get some comparison data by running similar applications, or tests, at another point in the network. This will provide you with a set of data which can be important in evaluating the problem. This should also include historical information – the little details that somehow never get quite the attention that they should. They may seem to have nothing to do with the symptom in question, but they may still be part of the jigsaw puzzle and help to complete the final picture. No expert, and certainly no expert system, however much time and money has been lavished on its design, can afford to overlook this information.

2.3   Breaking down complex fault structures

Although the first step was a simple one, and however obvious it may seem to most of us, it needed to be made clear before we go further.

From here on, describing a systematic fault analysis becomes a more difficult task, because it is more abstract: it is only if the fault situation and the structure of the network are relatively simple that we can progress by means of simple YES/NO answers to the various questions.

A YES/NO answer, or rather, decision, leaves no room for the kind of interpretation expressed by words like 'possibly', 'fairly' or 'ish'. These expressions will not fit into a YES/NO structure. It would be marvellous if we could just draw up a set of questions, a decision tree for all known situations, and be given the answers. But life is not that simple in the world of networks, even though some cases can be presented and solved in that way. This can be seen in another example:

> User:
>
> 'There's nothing on the screen, nothing's happening.'
>
> Support:
>
> 'Is the screen completely blank or can you see some letters or figures?'
>
> User:
>
> 'Well, there are some numbers at the top and a sort of message thingy.'
>
> Support:
>
> 'What does the message say?'
>
> User:
>
> 'Server not available.'
>
> Support:
>
> 'Is this just affecting you, or has everyone else got the same problem?'
>
> User:
>
> 'Only me, and all I've done is switch the computer on, the same as I do every morning.'
>
> Support:
>
> 'Have you checked whether the network cable is still connected at the back of the computer, or whether it's worked loose?'
>
> Pause.
>
> User:
>
> 'The cable was loose. I've pushed it in again, and everything's all right now.'

We may smile when we read this conversation, but it is only a brief version of a situation which crops up again and again. If a 'non-expert' draws up a decision tree the first time he meets it, he will recognise it the next time it happens and be able to home in on the problem immediately.

But suppose the cable was not the cause. It could also be the configuration of the computer, a bridge, a router, a faulty interface card or simply an overloaded server causing the software to 'time out' and stop. In most cases, the error message will be exactly the same and tell you nothing. This makes the decision tree for the problem (Figure 2.1) immensely more complex.

It goes without saying that an expert will approach fault analysis with all these other possibilities in mind as well, and refer to an existing database, which amounts to the experience amassed by him or her over a period of time. All sorts of information and comparable situations will be stored in

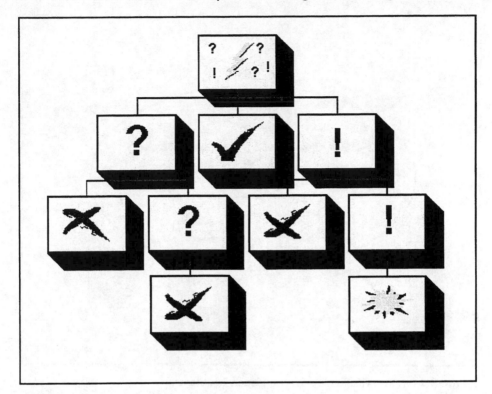

Figure 2.1   The classical decision tree

his or her head. But something more essential also has its part to play: intuition. An expert will reach a decision not only on the basis of experience, but will also rely on intuition to close in on the solution to a complex fault.

A decision tree does not provide for intuitive leaps to another branch. An expert will evaluate every piece of known information and compare it with his or her experience. A vast range of 'what if' situations will be thought through and applied to the problem, well beyond anything that could be covered by a simple rule. The word 'maybe' is important here: all mental models are automatically subject to an evaluation which will in the end be expressed as a probability (in per cent) of certain components, programs etc. having failed or being involved.

2.4   Problem analysis in general

As a rule, there will be no expert on hand to take over the trouble-shooting; and this does not exactly make it easier to track down the trouble. The lack

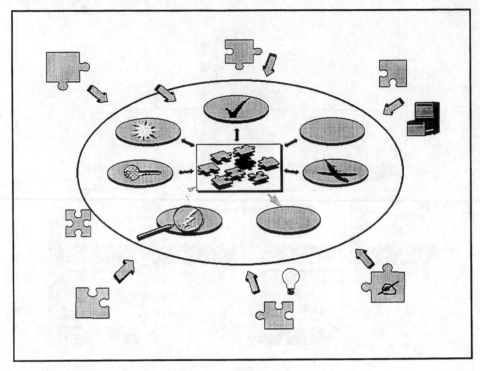

Figure 2.2   A knowledge base as a collection of objects

of knowledge and the problems encountered during the search can be roughly classified as follows:

- No fault-tracing technique is known.

- There is no familiarity with the network or the likely faults.

- The available tools and equipment are only being put to partial use, or there is insufficient knowledge of how to use them.

- The available data and test results cannot be interpreted.

As we said before, there is no universal recipe for trouble-shooting in a network; and the above pages will have made this quite clear. But we would not wish to discourage anyone at this stage by suggesting that a specialist is needed in every case. After all, where would they come from if there were not methods through which you can become one? It took the first specialists a long time to collect their experience; but today there a number of analytical methods enabling even a 'non-specialist' to track down faults, or at least to narrow them down. The experience gained from this may then help when the next fault occurs.

Experienced trouble-shooters know that it is a 'must' to approach fault-tracing in a methodical and disciplined way. This means that gaps in knowledge can often be compensated by methodology. Although this technique cannot make up for a lack of knowledge, it is most certainly an important element in the overall process of fault analysis. But even the experts cannot agree on the 'correct' approach to trouble-shooting.

Some swear by a purely scientific and analytical approach, others prefer to trust in their experience and intuition. Individual preferences for a particular technique naturally play a prominent role in deciding on the best way to solve a problem. But very often a technique is used which has been selected at random rather than because it is particularly suited to the problem in hand.

There are reasons aplenty for this, including a lack of familiarity with the type of problem, inadequate training etc. And as a result, the true causes and problems can very easily lie undiscovered, or it may take an unnecessarily long time to find the fault and correct it. In the end, however, what is right and what is wrong is of course something for the individual to decide.

Investigation will confirm the choice of approach, or else the the search will be continued using another method. However, many specialists have amassed a considerable breadth of experience covering a wide range of situations they can draw on to solve even the most complex problems.

2.4.1 Familiarity with systems in use

A good knowledge of the components and systems used in the network is vital and indispensable in tracing faults and analysing symptoms. Without it, no one will be able to assess the variety of symptoms encountered and search for accompanying signs of a fault. Here again, experience is a major factor. This is what enables a specialist to decide which parameters are central to tracing the fault and how the individual items of data relate to each other and/or affect each other. Unfortunately, today's networks use an increasing variety of hardware, protocols and technologies, so that it is less and less common for one person to command a knowledge of the entire network and all the situations that might possibly occur.

2.4.2 Methodical treatment of facts and assumptions

Sherlock Holmes would be pleased to see that, in the modern world, his methods are still as valid as ever. But the fact that he constantly mocked the police for failing to spot obvious pieces of evidence should make us stop and think. Very often, network operators or managers find themselves in the same position. Modern technology provides any number of tools: there is hardly a single area on which information is not now readily available.

Unfortunately, using the hardware is a science in itself, so it is hardly surprising that, even where there is a whole array of diagnostic systems and/or network management systems, a lack of knowledge means that their potential is barely used.

A further point should be mentioned here. The systems in use may pour out a flood of information and results. Not many people are capable of interpreting the data and making the right connections with other information. Only a few of the analytical systems currently available are able to present the test results in a simple and readily understandable way, so that anyone can follow them. Possessing a protocol analyser is a step in the direction of fault analysis, though not the only one. Setting up the analyser correctly, so that it lists the particular data needed to solve the problem and presents it in an accessible manner, is probably the most difficult part. Deciding what data are important is a question of experience (there it is again).

Which of us has not looked on in amazement at the simple tools used by experienced engineers to obtain information on a problem and find a solution, without falling back on more complicated new systems?

To take an example: what is the use of a computer if there are no programs available for it, or the few that exist are not properly tailored for the specific situation? In the same way, it is little help having a stack of different programming languages covering every eventuality. If, when the need arises, there is neither the time to do the programming, nor the ability or interest, even the fastest and most flexible computer is useless.

Exactly the same could be said of the available diagnostic systems. They should be simple to use, so that the cause of a fault can be traced quickly without the need for training on their operation and adjustment (if an oscilloscope is badly set up and wrongly adjusted, it is guaranteed to give the wrong results).

2.4.3   Methodical fault-tracing

However complicated the above outline may seem, it has shown that the basic mechanisms for a systematic fault analysis are certainly available. In principle, it is a matter of feeling one's way towards the seat of the problem, making use of a number of indicators and symptoms which can provide a closer description of the problem. These are checked for specific faults, and the process is then repeated in a different place. But what do we need? First of all, of course, more information on the fault and the network in general. This is where Sherlock Holmes' little helpers come in: these providers of information include wide-ranging statistical programs, active tests and protocol analysis.

And this is where we take the next step in systematic fault-tracing. Depending on the nature of the fault, we need to know how and where this information was obtained so that we can assess its significance properly. Often, computer-oriented statistics or programs will be all we need. Depending on the size of the network and the knowledge base, data analysers can offer integrated test environments to provide all the necessary information, such as statistics, active tests and protocol analysis. Systems of this sort can be used almost anywhere: in the simplest case, it may be no more than a specialised program costing relatively little, which will run on practically any PC with a LAN card (*see* Chapter 5).

The analytical systems and tools that are chosen will depend in the first instance on what is known about the technologies and products in use, how much time can be provided for network support, the level of network availability required, the size of the network and, last but not least, the type of problem faced when an emergency arises.

For trouble-shooting purposes, fault symptoms can be classified into various categories. Here are some of the possible areas:

- Total failure of a component.

- Total failure of a network or of a sub-network or segment.

- Several users affected, not all accessing the same server.

- Several users affected, all accessing the same server.

- One station restricted in its use.

- The fault is not always apparent, but occurs intermittently.

The total failure of a single component is relatively simple to fix. Where a fault is intermittent, trouble-shooting becomes more complex, as it can sometimes be very difficult to collect the necessary information on the cause of the fault. Simulations, intended to imitate a typical day's work, are time-consuming to install and frequently fail to give the desired result. Sometimes there is only one way out – to collect as much information as possible over a long period and make repeated comparisons. The available ways of obtaining information are described in the following sections.

2.5   The many faces of trouble-shooting

Where insufficient information is directly available for fault-tracing, and therefore for the correction of the fault – whether as a result of the nature of the error itself, or because the error messages in the system in question are not precise enough or not understood – there is nothing for it but for the systems engineer to take a hand on the spot and personally track down the information needed. There are special 'tools' for this, enabling you to find out practically all you need to know about a computer and a communications network. The various types of information on a network required for fault-tracing can be roughly classified as follows:

- cable tests,

- packet decoding,

- statistics,

- automatic analyses and evaluations,

- simulation/response tests.

2.5.1   Cable test

A cable test is required to check the network infrastructure and connections. It is worth mentioning once again at this point that tidy and precise documentation of the cabling is a vital necessity for troubleshooting. This includes records of tests carried out after installation. This may not seem terribly important for an individual segment; but as soon as faults occur which could be related to the cabling this sort of information is worth its weight in gold, if only because of the time it can save (and time is money). These test records are especially important when it comes to coaxial segments: excessively long cable runs can quickly develop, as the users only know about the section which is more or less visible in their own department, and not the entire system. It is very easy for another foot or two of cable to be inserted in the network, and it is only by using reference documentation that these locations can be discovered.

Any change that has been made since installation may have something to do with the fault situation. There are fixed limits of tolerance for any system: although those specified by Ethernet, IEEE 802.3, Token Ring and FDDI (ANSI) are only guidelines, all suppliers of computer systems or network components will invoke these values to refuse support if they are exceeded. True, in any individual case these recommendations are only relevant to maximum values, but even these can be set too high for certain operating conditions – which means that a practical check is never a bad idea.

To take an example: a 10Base-T cable is sharing a cable duct with the telephone installation. Where the phone system is still using pulse dialling, this can lead to problems in data communications.

Sometimes, active cable tests are the only way of finding out what the actual transfer parameters are. Analog checks with cable testers, along with level tests, will guarantee that a proper basis for data transfer exists. A specialised active test is the only of finding out how a transmission route behaves in operation. However, this always requires two pieces of equipment, located at the furthest points and sending random data streams to be checked for errors by the unit at the opposite end of the cable. The results can then be analysed quite simply by reference to statistics of transfer and error rates.

One example from the real world will suffice for this: a 'Thick LAN' cable (Yellow Cable) has been laid the full length of a 200-metre long production shop inside a cable duct. Along the wall of the building, at a distance of about 5m from the wall, there are some 20 NC lathes at which the work is carried out. The other side of the building is taken up by an arc-welding section, positioned about 30m from the cable route and thus from the LAN cable. When tested with a TDR (Time-Domain Reflectometry) meter, the coax cable shows no faults. The cable was laid without damage and no taps are installed anywhere along its length. Despite this, a terminal server at one end of the cable would not function.

The obvious question is: Why not? The segment of cable was tested by means of two protocol analysers. For this, both analysers were loaded with a statistical program to generate data loads while running in the background. The reason for this is that the measurements had to be based on known values, so that a verdict on the data transfer characteristics could be obtained. When the program was run, both units generated a basic load of 30%, equivalent to around 470 frames/sec at an average frame size of 777 bytes (the program generated frames between 64 and 1512 bytes). This put a total load of 60% = 940 frames/sec on the cable – not entirely a typical workload for the segment, admittedly, but better in terms of gaining meaningful results from the test.

The statistical analysis of the network loading did not at first show up any faults. But after a time the utilisation fell to around 45%. At the same time, the error rate rose sharply; these were all FCS and misaligned errors, and affected above all the longer data frames. This was also the reason why the terminal server would not boot up properly.

But what was causing these errors? From the brief presentation of this example it will be simple enough to see. The route of the cable run, even though it was not laid directly alongside the power supply line, resulted in interference during normal operation. On top of this, there were the interference fields from the NC lathes – not forgetting the arc-welders.

All together, these made it impossible for any useful data to be transferred for any significant period of time. There was only one sensible alternative: the coaxial cable was replaced by a fibre optics cable.

This example, which is representative of many others, demonstrates that in practice active testing is very useful and necessary.

Needless to say, judging the situation before cables are laid requires some experience. But in medium-sized businesses and above all in large companies, this is the way the problems are now being attacked, and the sum of experience is continually being added to. It is no surprise, therefore, that in some areas of production the maximum cable length laid is only 100 metres, as tests show that anything longer cannot be relied upon.

2.5.2 Active response and echo tests

Another aid to localising faults is an active response test. This uses a simulation frame to prompt an end system for a response. These active tests can be employed in many areas of communication technology.

One example is the procedure for cable testing described above. It makes no difference whether the data transfer is tested on the cable itself or across a repeater, star coupler, bridge or router/gateway. However, it must be remembered that some tests will require two pieces of hardware, as it is the link between the test locations that is under investigation. These tests enable connections to be made between the cabling infrastructure, the components used and possible faults, problems or difficulties in using a network. But one point needs to be made at this juncture, and cannot be repeated often enough:

An active test on a network should always, as far as possible, emulate real data communication.

All this means is that a measurement is of no practical use if the reality is different from the conditions of the test. This means that there is no point running response tests over a weekend if the network has a very light workload outside the working week, or testing the response time as far as a bridge or a router if the communication link involves further coupling elements beyond them. In a case of this sort, the only useful delay value is one for the entire link, taking in all the segments, bridges and routers involved.

Returning, however, to the use of active tests in fault-tracing: these can be roughly assigned to three categories. On the one hand, there is active testing of a network using specialised hardware such as protocol analysers. Then there are the tests that can be carried out directly from a terminator node or an analyser. These include all response tests, such as a ping in a TCP/IP network. The following pages describes some of the tests that can be carried out.

Finally, a special case comprises the active tests used to find out the transfer parameters of lines, bridges and routers, the last of which will be of particular interest to manufacturers of the units.

2.5.2.1 Tests in MAC and LLC Layer 2

It is important, of course, whenever an active test is being carried out, to have decided what the test is meant to show or what information is required. These active response tests, as we will call them here, can provide a wide spread of information. It is possible, for example, to test for the presence of an interface or the time response of higher network protocols.

For Level 1 of the OSI model, the following test sequences can be sent:

- Ethernet CTP (Configuration Test Packet):
  very often used in DECnet installations,

- 802.2 LLC Test Frame,

- 802.2 LLC XID (Exchange Identification) Frame.

This test (test frames are shown in Figure 2.3) will always require an analyser or specialist software loaded on the computer. The test frames have a variety of structures. First, we are dealing with Ethernet and IEEE 802.2 frames, and even between these two types the structure of the frame is different. The contents also have a different significance, which we will not deal with here. Needless to say, there will always be a difference between Ethernet and IEEE protocols; and PCs, printers and other smaller systems will generally only work with one protocol, either Ethernet or

```
┌─                     802.3 / Ethernet Detailed Decode
│Control │Config │Actions │Format │Other displays │Print │Help
│    Frame: 2           Time: Apr 06@15:03:06.3453153   Length: 64
│Field                  Value                Description
│Destination address    Cisco Router         Individual, global
│Source address         LAN-Analyser         Individual, global
│Type                   90-00                Loop Back
│> Data size            46
│Frame check sequence   9E-5F-90-B2
│
│    Frame: 3           Time: Apr 06@15:03:06.3457240   Length: 64
│Field                  Value                Description
│Destination address    LAN-Analyser         Individual, global
│Source address         Cisco Router         Individual, global
│Type                   90-00                Loop Back
│> Data size            46
│Frame check sequence   1D-96-81-D0
```

Figure 2.3a   Ethernet CTP loop-back (response time: 408.7 μs)

IEEE. Unix workstations or file servers are capable of handling both protocols in parallel. This only applies, of course, for CSMA/CD networks.

In a token ring there will only be MAC or 802.2 LLC frames. What interface reacts to which frame will depend on the design of the interface card at hardware level (implemented by the manufacturer) or the network software that has been loaded. Information on what has and has not been implemented can be obtained from the suppliers of the systems. If it is not

```
   Frame: 1          Time: Nov 230 6:06:11.8550021  Length: 74
Field                    Value                   Description
Destination SAP          00                      Null address
Source SAP               00                      Null address
Command/Response         ....-...0               Command
Type                     ....-..11               Unnumbered
Poll                     ...0-....
Modifier                 111.-00..               Test
User Data:
   00-01-00-00-00-00-40-00 00-00-00-00-8C-00-00-00
   00-00-00-02-00-00-00-00 B0-04-00-00-00-00-EE-05
   00-00-00-00-00-00-00-00 00-00-5A-BD-00-00-00-00
   00-00-00-00-00
> New address

   Frame: 2          Time: Nov 230 6:06:11.8553541  Length: 74
Field                    Value                   Description
Destination SAP          00                      Null address
Source SAP               01                      Null address
Command/Response         ....-...1               Response
Type                     ....-..11               Unnumbered
Final                    ...0-....
Modifier                 111.-00..               Test
User Data:
   00-01-00-00-00-00-40-00 00-00-00-00-8C-00-00-00
   00-00-00-02-00-00-00-00 B0-04-00-00-00-00-EE-05
   00-00-00-00-00-00-00-00 00-00-5A-BD-00-00-00-00
   00-00-00-00-00
> New address
```

Figure 2.3b   802.2 LLC TST Command/Response Frames (response time 352 µs)

```
! Frame: 1          Time: Nov 24017:51:09.3040640  Length: 64
Field                    Value                   Description
Destination SAP          00                      Null address
Source SAP               00                      Null address
Command/Response         ....-...0               Command
Type                     ....-..11               Unnumbered
Poll                     ...1-....
Modifier                 101.-11..               eXchange IDentification
Identifier               0000-0000               Unrecognized format
Type/Class               ...0-0000               Error: Unknown class
Reserved                 ....-.000-0...-....
Receive Window           0
> New address

! Frame: 2          Time: Nov 24017:51:09.3043230  Length: 64
Field                    Value                   Description
Destination SAP          00                      Null address
Source SAP               01                      Null address
Command/Response         ....-...1               Response
Type                     ....-..11               Unnumbered
Final                    ...1-....
Modifier                 101.-11..               eXchange IDentification
Identifier               1000-0001               IEEE basic format
Type/Class               ...0-0001               Error: Unknown class
Reserved                 ....-.000-0...-....
Receive Window           0
> New address
```

Figure 2.3c   802.2 XID Command/Response Frames (response time 259 µs)

possible to obtain the necessary information, a test can always be run to find out which computer is reacting to which test frames, and in what way.

This is easily done using a short test program. The listing of results can be filed for future reference.

These test data only address the interface at the specific destination. This makes it possible to measure minimum delay times for a transfer. But please remember: the time measured will include the propagation time for the transfer in both directions.

A measuring accuracy of 1 ms is usually good enough, as the shortest response times are typically around 3 ms for a PC. However, a UNIX system can achieve values down to 0.2 ms. If a test of this sort is performed over

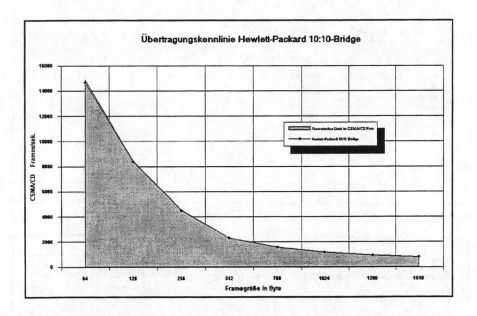

Figure 2.4   Average response times for a HP9000/705 with and without bridges in the data path

an extended period, it is even possible to deduce the degree of loading on a server by reference to the response times.

This information depends, of course, on the number of frames processed. The chart in Figure 2.4 illustrates how the response time changes if the interface to the computer has extra data to process.

The data flow in the application was around 20 frames/sec and the 802.2 LLC XID test generated a further 2400 frames/sec (a UNIX interface is very fast). Despite this, the response times are in the region of 250 ~s, an impressive time. The second curve shows the results of the same test on a larger network. The effect on the response time can be seen quite clearly, and is mainly attributable to the bridges included in the network. However, these tests can only be used within a logical network as far as bridges, as a router is unable to process a Level 2 test frame to a target system, since it contains no network addresses. The usefulness of this test is that the graph of propagation times provides a direct picture of response times on the network under realistic conditions.

```
 Frame: 2          Time: Nov 24@16:59:32.3690647  Length: 64
Field                      Value             Description
Exclusion Address Count    00                Diagnostic Request Packet
Additional Fields          00
  IPX:
Checksum                   FFFF
IPX Length                 31
Transport Control          00
Packet Type                4                 PEP
Destination Network        00000000
Destination Node           080009328E24
Destination Socket         0456              Diagnostic Packet
Source Network             00000000
Source Node                0000C6001022
Source Socket              4001
> Data size                2
  802.3 / Ethernet:
Destination address        HP-------32-8E-24 Individual, global
Source address             HP-INO---00-10-22 Individual, global
Length                     32                IPX
> Data size                32
Padding:
      00-00-00-00-00-00-00-00  00-00-56-A6-20-D4
Frame check sequence       0D-C7-4A-9E
```

Figure 2.5a   802.3 IPX Diagnostic Request Packet

```
                        XNS Stack Detailed Decode
 Control Config Actions Format Other displays Print Help
 Frame: 1          Time: Apr 15@15:18:33.6759411  Length: 84
Field                      Value             Description
  IDP:
Checksum                   FFFF
IDP Length                 66
Transport Control          00
Packet Type                2                 Echo
Destination Network        00000002
Destination Node           080020062AAF
Destination Socket         0002              Echo
Source Network             00000002
Source Node                080009000A2A
Source Socket              0002              Echo
> Data size                36
  802.3 / Ethernet:
Destination address        SUN Workstation   Individual, global
Source address             LAN-Analyser      Individual, global
Type                       06-00             XNS-IDP
> Data size                66
Frame check sequence       B8-0A-BE-63
```

Figure 2.5b   Ethernet XNS Echo Packet

```
┌─────────────────────────────────────────────────────────────────────────┐
│ ▀                          ARPA Stack Detailed Decode                     │
│ Control │Config │Actions │Format │Other displays │Print │Help             │
│   Frame: 1              Time: Nov 24@16:58:22.3040640  Length: 67         │
│ Field                     Value              Description                   │
│  ICMP                                                                     │
│ Type                      08                 Echo request                 │
│ Code                      0                                               │
│ Checksum                  51-6D                                           │
│ Identifier                0                  ID to match echos and replies│
│ Sequence number           32005              Seqnum to match echos and repl│
│ > Data size               21                                              │
│ > New address                                                            │
│   IP                                                                     │
│ Version                   4                                               │
│ Internet header length    5                  (32 bit words)              │
│ Precedence                000.-....          Routine                      │
│ Delay                     ...0-....          Delay normal                 │
│ Throughput                ....-0...          Throughput normal            │
│ Reliability               ....-.0..          Reliability normal           │
│ Reserved                  ....-..00                                      │
│ Total Length              49                                              │
│ Identification            2932                                            │
│ Reserved                  00..-....                                      │
│ May / Do Not Fragment     .0..-....          Fragmentation allowed        │
│ Last / More Fragments     ..0.-....          Last fragment                │
│ Offset                    0                                               │
│ Time To Live              255                                             │
│ Next Protocol             1                  ICMP                         │
│ Checksum                  2F-50                                           │
│ Source                    192.80.0.53        OPENVIEW Station             │
│ Destination               192.80.0.50        MAIL Server                  │
│ > Data size               29                                              │
│   802.3/Ethernet                                                         │
│ Destination address       HP-------32-8E-24  Individual, global           │
│ Source address            HP-INO---00-10-22  Individual, global           │
│ Type                      08-00              IP                           │
│ Frame check sequence      CB-B1-14-F3                                     │
└─────────────────────────────────────────────────────────────────────────┘
```

Figure 2.5c   802.3 IP/ICMP Ping

2.5.2.2 Tests on Network Layer 3

One level higher in the OSI model, there are also loop-back tests, of course, which provide similar useful results to those described above. However, in this case we are faced with response times of a quite different magnitude, as the test frames are now being processed not by the interface itself, but by the network software (Figure 2.5).

In almost 99% of cases it is the internal system processor which runs this software, so the response times will be a direct representation of the available CPU capacity. If the computer is not under load, so that the processor is available, it can work very quickly. But the greater the computer's workload, the less time is left for communication. A test of this sort will thus reveal any bottlenecks in the servers. As there is a vast number of different protocols for Network Level 3, the test frames need to be specified precisely for each protocol. Probably the best-known test is the 'ping' test in a TCP/IP network, which can be run by any computer with TCP/IP software. However, only limited response time tests are possible with this, as the routines frequently send only one test frame per second, although the general trend can certainly be followed up. For tests over

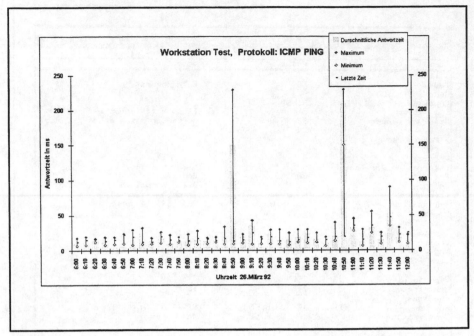

Figure 2.6   PING test

longer periods, protocol analysers or other intelligent stations can again be used.

Figure 2.6 shows response times to a local computer and via a complex network. Once again, the differences are clearly visible. The spread of values for each measurement is an aggregate of the transfer delays and the residence time inside the target computer. This test again provides information on the extent of typical delays on the network. Problems such as aborted connections and slow transfer rates may arise from timing faults generated by the protocols in use. This test allows the values configured to be checked.

2.5.2.3 Finding transfer parameters for bridges and routers

Occasionally it is useful to know about the behaviour of network coupling elements such as bridges and routers. Certainly, data in this area are very important for the manufacturers of the systems; end users can only gain limited value from them. When testing a bridge it is not enough to simply generate a heavy data flow and monitor how it is received: we need to include the widest possible range of addresses on both sides of the bridge, as the most important factor where a bridge is concerned is not the throughput so much as the filter rate.

When only a single address is used, there is no need for the bridge to refer to a look-up table to see what is supposed to happen to the data frame: it is simply passed on. And there is another reason why this test is now rarely used: modern bridges are capable of working to the fastest transfer speeds, where older systems broke down at around 2000 to 5000 frames/sec. All bridges now on the market work at transfer rates in the 'media speed' range, which means, for a CSMA/CD ethernet system, a data rate of around 14,800 frames per second.

Filter rates are much higher, and are quoted by some manufacturers at up to 29,000 frames/sec. This is because most manufacturers use a RISC processor of the AMD 29000 type, which achieves a performance of around 17 mips. Bridge-related delays arise because a bridge has to receive a complete data frame before confirming whether there is an FCS error. In

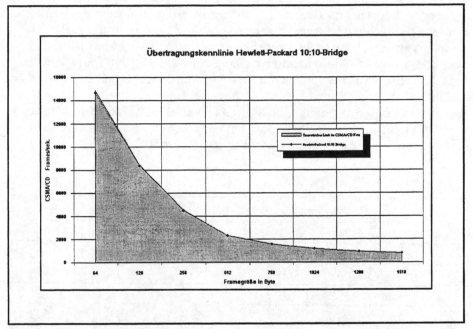

Figure 2.7   Test on an HP bridge

the meantime, the processor will already have indicated whether the frame should be forwarded or not. The delay involved in using a bridge is nearly always the time required to receive a complete data frame; these times range between approximately 51 µs (CSMA/CD 640 bytes) and 10 ms (16 Mbit [sic] token ring, maximum frame length). Any delays on top of this are barely measurable.

Figure 2.7 shows a test on a CSMA/CD bridge, carried out using Wandel & Goltermann's DA30 protocol analyser. The bridge tested was Hewlett-Packard's, which is marketed as a 'media speed' bridge. The test confirms that the description 'media speed' paints a true picture, apart from the fact that, at 14,862 frames/sec, 1% of the 446,000 frames sent (i.e. 7300 frames) were lost.

A verdict on how good or bad a bridge is, however, does not depend solely on its transfer characteristics. These are meaningless in practice if things work out differently in reality. There is no point, for example, testing a bridge at its top speed of 14,000 frames/sec if the expected workload will only amount to 500 to 1000 frames/sec and there is no likelihood of its growing beyond that. There are simpler and cheaper bridges which can cope with this. This is not to say an active bridge test should never be carried out, as it will always be useful and provide important data. It's simply that no one would think of testing the cornering of a family car at 120 mph and comparing it against a Formula 1 racer, when it will only ever be driven in town.

Very often, however, the actual operating values are compared with theoretical figures, and this sort of comparison is not a great deal of help. But let's get back to the transfer values we will encounter in the real world.

It is very rarely that data rates of above 5000 frames/sec will be met over a long period. The maximum on an Ethernet of 14,800 frames/sec can only be achieved if the data are in 64-byte frames and no other station is sending. Test conditions of this sort never exist in reality, and in 99% of cases it will be good enough for a bridge to achieve a data throughput of 2,000 frames/sec. If a 50-Kbyte data buffer is also provided, to take care of large quantities of data, hardly anything can go wrong.

Channel Access Test				Response Test in ms	
Time in µsec	# tries	# resets	# collisions	XID	Novell
0	1000	0	0	7	98
0	1001	0	0	8	123
< 1	998	0	0	7	121
1	1000	0	2	46	532
40	1001	1	1	11	218
86	999	2	0	9	80
825	1000	1	9	351	1320
89	1000	2	1	65	423
174	999	4	0	23	312
357	1001	0	4	193	846
532	999	2	3	138	963
280	1001	1	2	36	234

Figure 2.8   Comparative values for c.a. time, XID test, Novell test

Testing a router is not much different. Here again, the router's transfer parameters will be far above average data rates.

Although a router (*see* Chapter 6) operates at network level, delays are again minimal at worst:

Today's multi-protocol routers can handle transfer rates of 7,000 to 2,000 [sic] frames/sec for routing and a matching 2,000 to 14,000 frames/sec in bridge mode.

2.5.2.4 Summary of active tests and analysis

Active tests can have a major influence on how a problem is assessed. In some cases, there is no alternative. However, it takes a little experience to interpret the results, so the reference figures for a problem should be found out first.

Where there are problems with transmission over long routes – that is, via bridges and routers – the total transfer time should be measured and then compared with the configuration parameters in the computer. If the two values are close to each other, we can say with certainty that we have found the cause of the problem. Measurements from individual sections of the route will not as a rule provide realistic or usable results. The table in Figure 2.8 will give an idea of the sort of actual values measured when investigating a problem with a server. The 'channel access time' is the time taken for the analyser to send one data frame.

2.5.3   Statistics

As the last few sections showed, statistics provide an excellent survey of the behaviour and activity on the network.

However, this information is not only important for fault-tracing, but also provides a targeted analysis of specific areas of the network which can be useful in planning an expansion of the system.

2.5.3.1 Statistics as information summaries

When planning an expansion of the network, it is vital to know its current condition and the existing characteristics. More than once it has happened that bridges or routers have been bought which turned out afterwards to be an unnecessary or even wasted investment.

The table in Figure 2.9 lists the parameters which are most important and most relevant for planning decisions. However, this list is also useful to trouble-shooters, as the figures will provide an excellent reflection of activity on the network, and the errors that crop up will also show in the results.

Transmission parameters – Planning and Fault tracing		
Applying to all types of transmission		
Data frame size in bytes per frame Data rate in frames/sec Stations with most faults Number of active nodes Statistics of all nodes in the network in summary by node Server statistics for the most active users, with frames/sec sent and received Top-rating network users 'Distribution and quantity': broadcast and multicast frames Distribution of frame types		
Ethernet/IEEE.802.3	**Token ring**	**FDDI**
Collisions	Beaconing rate	Beaconing rate
Misaligned errors	Purge rate	Token errors
RUNT errors	Soft error rate	Lost frame errors
FCS errors	Burst errors	'E-bit set' rate
Jabber errors	'Claim token' rate	'Claim token' rate
	'Receiver congestion' errors	'Stripped frame' rate
	Abort errors	Illegal code
	Access/Control errors	Preamble too short
	Lost frame errors	Frame too long
	Line errors	Token rotation time
	Token rate	Token rate
	Token rotation time	MAC frames and bytes
	MAC frames and bytes	LLC frames and bytes
	Source routing:	SMT frames and bytes
	local–local, local–remote,	
	remote–local,	
	remote–remote	

Figure 2.9 :

Which particular values are most important at the planning stage will of course depend on the nature of the expansion under consideration. The frame size and the utilisation of capacity in % will be of minor importance.

The table in Figure 2.10 provides a brief survey of which values can be used for what. Obviously, this list can make no claims to completeness, as there are more sides to requirements planning than there are pages in this book – and, in principle, the values found in testing can be used to cover just about any planning need.

Planning for	Priority 1	Priority 2	Priority 3	Priority 4
New segment	Mean and maximum data rate in frames/sec	Number of active notes on local segment		
Bridge when installed to increase the maximum distance between computers	Mean and maximum data rate in frames/sec	Mean and maximum broadcast rate in frames/sec	Mean and maximum multicast rate in frames/sec	Server statistics: which stations access how intensively!
Bridge when installed for load separation	Mean and maximum data rate in frames/sec	Mean and maximum broadcast rate in frames/sec	Mean and maximum multicast rate in frames/sec	! INFO ! Servers should not be permanently accessed via the bridge in this case!
Bridge when installed for data protection purposes	Mean and maximum data rate in frames/sec	Mean and maximum broadcast rate in frames/sec	Mean and maximum multicast rate in frames/sec	! INFO ! Servers should not be permanently accessed via the bridge in this case!
Router Local	Summary of use of various network protocols	Mean and maximum data rate in frames/sec		

Figure 2.10 :

2.5.3.2 Statistics for fault-tracing

Anyone who thinks an unknown fault can be tracked down by listing all the data flows using a protocol analyser so that they can be analysed for the causes afterwards (at 1000 frames/sec, it certainly can't be done in real time!) will need a great deal of time and even more patience. It is as good as impossible to trace a fault at a stroke by approaching it this way. Just a glance at the orders of magnitude of the frames carried on a network will immediately dispel any such ideas.

To take an example: an Ethernet/802.3 network with a utilisation of around 5% and some 20 active stations has an intermittent problem with a server, with file transfer and sometimes with printers. Sometimes connections are broken, and sometimes there are delays in data transfers. The fault is difficult to reproduce and occurs two or three times a day. A protocol analyser is connected to record the data frames, with 2 Mbytes of memory. After about 8 minutes, with an average frame size of 120 bytes, there are 34,000 (!) data frames in memory. Finding out what is wrong in these frames is a practically impossible task. Mindless recording of data, then, is not always the last word in wisdom. The work can be made a good deal easier by first making a study of the network.

For this, statistics can come in useful: by studying the characteristics, it is often possible to spot very quickly what is not quite right. There are all sorts of parameters which it can be useful to investigate and which can be used in fault analysis. The information that can be drawn from the statistics will of course depend on the nature of the fault, that is, the

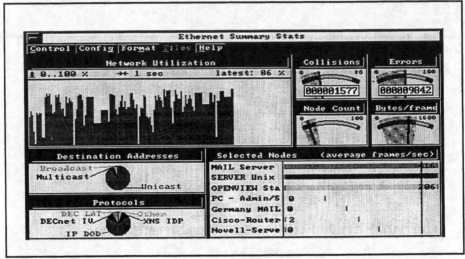

Figure 2.11   Statistical summary of the main network parameters

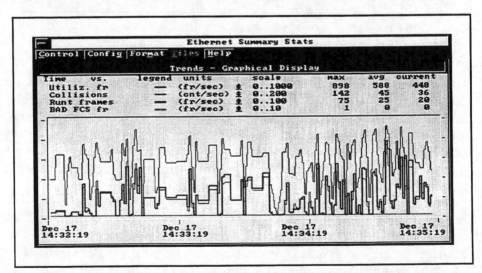

Figure 2.12   Characteristics of errors shown correlated with error rate and collisions

symptoms. All that is then needed is a reference value to enable the test figures to be compared and assessed.

Another example will show how statistical information can be used in tracing faults. Users are complaining that it sometimes takes a very long time to get a response from the mail server. This is a typical description of a fault. Follow-up enquiries reveal only that this occurs in various departments, irrespective of the sub-network used, but always in connection with the local mail server. As the server is only connected to one network, global statistics are examined to *see* how the network is behaving generally.

Figure 2.11 shows how this looks. The error rate and collision rate on the network are both very high, and practically all the activity is on the IP node. The MAIL server is sending data at up to 416 frames/sec. The Unix server also has a high data rate.

The question that naturally arises is: what sort of errors are they? Another chart (Figure 2.12), detailing information on the errors in

Netzwerk MAIL Server					
Control Config Format Help					
Bar Chart Display Format					
Count frames: TO or FROM MAIL Server					
Node	Frms Xmt	Frms Rcv	Bytes Xmt	Bytes Rcv	Broadcast
Network Total	451712	451712	413387574	413387574	706
MAIL Server	211482	140210		13183893	706
OPENVIEW Station	60526	227984	4300768	335964916	0
Cisco-Router	40242	41627	6322038	4075934	0
SERVER Unix NOV	38363	38648	2456714	57924363	0
LaserJet III	439	439	41420	40823	0
PC - Office4	39	39	4217	3794	0
Germany MAIL-HUB	37	37	4110	3589	0
Kunden Support01	34	34	3726	3286	0
CAD Workstation4	34	34	3642	3217	0
CAD Workstation3	34	34	3648	3217	0
PC - Office3	34	34	3688	3258	0
Multiuser Workst	34	34	3690	3255	0
PC - Office5	34	34	3498	3182	0
Unix CAD Raum10	31	31	3322	2952	0
Unix Comm-System	26	26	3334	2816	0
FAX-Server	24	23	2177	1953	0
HP-LanProbe	21	13	1470	1101	0
HP-CAD Demo	20	20	1576	1630	0
PC - All. Raum23	20	20	1614	1668	0
HP----124A8E	20	20	1614	1668	0
Run started on Dec 17, 1992 @ 13:12:58				0 frames lost	

Figure 2.13   Data rates to and from the MAIL server

correlation with the workload and the collisions, shows that the errors are 'runt' frames, and that these nearly always appear when a collision occurs. This behaviour is very typical of local networks when there is a multi-port repeater, a hub or a star coupler in the network and a large number of collisions occur. As the charts show that only three stations are handling unusually high data rates, a third chart is brought in to provide a summary of the 20 most active nodes and their error rates. This is shown in Figure 2.13.

The cause of the errors was almost certainly the collisions and the hubs in the network, which means that the network itself has been operating normally. The only ususual aspect was the high data rates in the MAIL server. A check showed that a database file transfer had been run by the server and had generated a network load of almost 86%.

This example shows how a fault can be narrowed down without the need to examine the data frames individually. That would have been totally unnecessary here in any case, as the protocols in use did not contain any errors and the trouble was that one station had become overloaded.

2.5.4 Data analysis

In some situations, it will usually be necessary to analyse the data frames individually as well as looking at the overall statistics. The conventional protocol analysers on the market are capable of decoding nearly all the data communication protocols available and used in operational systems. But the name 'protocol analysers' should not be taken at face value: not one of these units actually performs an analysis. They are more like protocol decoders, and the analysis is left up to the user. The only thing these 'analysers' explicitly indicate and identify are errors in the data transfer, such as FCS errors, short data frames etc.

The reason they have been given the name 'analyser' can be traced to the history of the device. Ten years ago, when the first protocol decoders appeared, for use with serial lines and with integrated protocol decoding, they were a major step forward, making it no longer necessary to decode the individual bits and bytes by hand. This analysis was carried out by the new 'analyser'. With today's technology, we can expect more of the hardware; but additional functions for the higher-level protocols are only supplied by a very few of the models on the market. Most are limited to showing the control information, and errors are identified solely by text. Only one model marks data frames in addition to the faulty ones, if there is important and relevant information to be drawn from the control data in the frame headers. This vastly simplifies things for the user, as it removes the need to examine every frame to see whether there is some important item of information hidden in it. The interpretation has thus already been carried out automatically by the system. Along with details of the control information, a data decoding also shows the sequence of communication and the time response.

An accuracy of 1 ms is good enough for this, as no one is able to achieve synchronisation with external hardware more precise than this. However, if the response times of a station are to be checked, it is desirable and sometimes necessary to resolve the times down to bit level. The control information holds all the data relevant to the communication process; however, no one can be familiar with all the network protocols on the market, which means that using data decoding is not always easy for a non-specialist. The profitable use of a protocol decoding demands precise knowledge of the protocols, the operation and sometimes the actual behaviour of the computer systems involved. With sometimes up to five or more different types of protocol and associated user applications active on any one network at the same time, it's easy to understand why even experts are liable to break out in a cold sweat.

2.5.5   Automatic analyses

Further simplification is achieved by automatic processing and presentation of the information mentioned above. Certain processes within protocols are easy to follow. For a practised and experienced specialist, it is relatively simple to seek out the useful information from the mass of data produced, provided the protocol is a familiar one. All that is needed as a rule is a large amount of recorded data or the use of a data filter in the recording process to ensure that only data relevant to him is stored in memory. However, it is more difficult working out what data is important and what is not if the protocol that is being investigated is less familiar..

This is where analysis programs come in, carrying out this analysis automatically along with the standard data search in an analyser. These programs can also get through the work far faster than a human brain ever could. The information that has been gathered is then entered in a table as an event or displayed directly on screen. As these systems are fully automatic there is no need to deal with them more fully here: they are simply mentioned for the sake of completeness.

3

LAN–WAN coupling

3.1 Linking a number of LANs via a Wide-Area Network

More and more networks are now being linked together to make a single large network out of any number of different local networks. This is often done in response to the demands of top management, who are likely to be quite unaware of the problems involved in fulfilling this sort of request. Apart from the wide variety of network addresses, which have to be converted and adapted, there are also a vast range of network protocols, some of which cannot be used at the same time on the same network (at least as far as the older software versions are concerned).

However, this is the stage networking has reached today, and most problems occur in this area. The rest result from linking up different local networks via the currently available WAN connections. Hardly any of the protocols used in LANs take into account the fact that a link may be made via a relatively slow WAN connection.

The existing time limits, as well as the structure and the protocol overhead, were originally designed for local communication at high transfer rates. As soon as a slow connection is included in the data path the trouble starts. The ratio of LAN to WAN speeds is generally between 5:1 and 100:1.

We don't need to dwell on the fact that this is obviously going to cause problems. The end node configurations must be set up with this in mind. Very often, however, no one really knows what quantities of data will be handled, and bad planning based on mistaken estimates of the actual requirements can result in delays in transmission, which are in turn reflected in loading and transmission problems.

3.2   Connection-oriented vs. connectionless protocols in the WAN section

Today, then, connections between greatly differing LANs via WAN lines are a likely cause of a wide variety of network problems. This is due not only to the grotesquely wide differences in transmission speeds, but as much or more to the fundamentally different protocols used in LANs and WANs.

Classical WAN protocols trace their origin to the world of long-distance links, that is, serial telephone circuits. In the past, these were always more prone to interference than local links. When data communication was in its infancy, error rates of 10^4 were not uncommon; and even today the best error rates guaranteed for point-to-point connections are in the order of 10^6.

It is for this reason that protocols were developed, including of course IBM's SDLC protocol, which were able to detect immediately the errors occurring during data transfer at what is now Layer 1 of the OSI model, and to correct them. This naturally made these protocols slower than was necessary for a direct link, as they were usually 'connection-oriented'.

This type of communication begins by setting up a logical connection between the two communicating parties. This connection is constantly monitored by means of the protocols, so that errors in the transmission can be corrected via the protocol, in a transparent process as far as the higher transmission layers are concerned. Needless to say, these functions call for extensive control mechanisms in the protocols. At data transfer rates of 9600 bits/sec, however, it was better to put up with this control overhead than be faced with repeated sending of large quantities of data. A transmission error will always be noticed in the end, and all the data transmitted and received up to the time when the error is noticed will be useless. For this reason, communication via WAN links to this day is as a rule carried out via 'connection-oriented' circuits.

However, the more advanced digital networks which have been set up by telecommunications operators round the world now allow considerably higher transfer speeds; and error rates have also improved by one to two orders of magnitude. In the wake of this technological advance, more appropriate transmission protocols and systems are now coming into use, which can benefit from the improved infrastructure and offer noticeably better transfer characteristics. An example of this is the frame relay system.

The situation with LAN systems was different from the start. The first LANs were set up between 1976 and 1981, and interference on coaxial cables was and remains very rare. Error rates, by order of magnitude, are in the range 10^9 to 10^{12}. This means that an error caused by the transmission and cable structure will occur at the earliest after 1,000,000,000 bits have been sent. As a rule, the error rate will not even be measurable. The developers of this system did not consider that there was any need to use a connection-oriented protocol, and this is why, with only a few exceptions, all protocols used in LANs today are 'connectionless' protocols.

'Connectionless' simply means that a data frame is sent without any confirmation of receipt. At this level, the sender has no control facility. Any interference on the line will result in the frame arriving at the receiver with an FCS error, with the result that it will be ignored. Transmission errors are only detected in higher protocol layers, as data will suddenly turn out to be missing. The protocol layer which first detects the data loss will initiate a repeat transfer of the data. This procedure has proved to be far more effective, as even in the worst case it is only every two-millionth data frame or thereabouts which is faulty (at an average frame size of 500 bytes).

3.3   Useful protocols for a WAN link

After this excursion into communications theory, let's return to the requirements for coupling up LANs via WANs. It will be clear by now that we cannot use the same protocol mechanisms for communication over a WAN route. It would make sense if the coupling systems we chose used a connection-oriented protocol. Simply transferring the LAN protocols to a WAN environment is certainly not a good idea.

Unfortunately, a number of older coupling elements are still on the market which were designed without taking into account the differences in transmission behaviour between LAN and WAN routes, and used a connectionless transfer protocol. On top of that, a few of the older systems worked in 'half-duplex' operation, which is also a LAN standard and means that only one of the parties in communication can send data at a time, while the other end waits for a turn. When using a slow WAN connection – and, compared with 4, 10 or 16 Mbits, 64 kbits is slow – this effectively halves the data rate which is physically and technically possible. Later systems operate on the HDLC protocol or similar bit-oriented protocols, which allow them to use 'full duplex'. This irons out any bottlenecks.

Finally, there is still the serious difference between the LAN and WAN transmission speeds. Even the most sophisticated methods, such as data compression, frame relay protocols and the like, cannot eliminate this speed difference, which therefore makes considerable demands on the planning of these links.

Here again, detailed statistics can be very important, as this is the only way vital information can be obtained. Unlike LANs, however, the data frame size needs to be considered as well as the frame rate, as large frames will affect the loading of a WAN route much more than for a LAN. In the considerably higher transfer bandwidths of a LAN link, the sizes of the data frames are less important.

A good many coupling elements, including remote bridges and routers, provide internal information on the loading, and above all on overloading of the system. Sometimes this information can not only be called up on a connected terminal, but also accessed remotely via integrated network management functions. (A book on the subject has been written by Petra Borowka: ~Brücken und Router~, DATACOM-Verlag 1992).

3.4   Effective planning to avoid potential bottlenecks

Thoughtful planning can avoid not only the coupling problems mentioned above, and the speed differences entailed, but also a good many problems and faults in later operation. A very important class of information will of course relate to the type of data streams to be carried. Bridges, because of the way they work, will transfer all broadcast and multicast addresses unless a special configuration prevents it.

Statistics will supply information on the broadcast and multicast rates occurring during normal operation, and a simple calculation giving the total number of data bits will provide an idea of whether 1%, 10% or as much as 50% of the transmission capacity of the WAN route needs to be made available for these special data frames. Depending on the protocol used, it may be necessary to use the more intelligent routers.

If the network includes stations which are completely dependent on the multicast frames, which will generally mean stations in DECnet systems, bridges or routers must not under any circumstances filter them out. This must of course be considered at the planning stage, as it could result in serious transfer bottlenecks later. For routers, the routing table is of prime importance. Where the router cannot determine the data routing dynamically and independently by reference to the routing protocols, there will always be static routing tables on hand. If these tables are not precisely planned and constantly checked, minor local problems could build up into a failure of the network coupling. A far greater problem for router networks is supplied by duplicate network addressing and the use of incorrect sub-network addresses. These mean that neither the router nor the destination node can tell what address is intended, or that the stations involved may misinterpret the values sent. As a result, it will be totally impossible to set up a connection.

3.5   Diagnostic methods

Measurements in WAN links mainly involve the more intelligent tools. All this means is that there is not much to be achieved by looking at the two sides of the coupling element using two analysers, because it will sometimes be necessary to work through not just 1 x 200 frames/sec but 2 x 200 = 400 frames/sec. This will keep you occupied for quite a while.

In an intricate network including routers, what is more, it could easily happen that, just at the moment when the test is being run, Murphy's Law comes into effect and a short-duration overload persuades the router network to send the observed data by quite a different route. A router, remember, has more than two interfaces, which means that there is no certainty that one direct configuration will be set up so that the data travel by the route where the test equipment is waiting. And this means that there is no way that realistic fault-tracing can be guaranteed. For intermittent faults, in particular, it may take an age before the fault reappears. Unknown causes cannot be tracked down by including added imponderables in the test. Direct measurements on either side of the WAN link are excluded simply by the physical distance; so it will be simpler and wiser to approach router problems by turning to the error mechanisms provided in a network protocol to obtain the information required. With an active test and a data filter relating to these data frames (IP=ICMP), all the routing problems and time-out problems will soon be tracked down.

3.6   Summary

WAN connections linking together LAN networks are a fact of life in the network world of today. However sophisticated the technology, these links demand extreme care. Tiny planning errors or errors in the configuration can result in the most unpleasant surprises. And as the WAN lines almost invariably belong to a telecommunications operator, there is no way of improving the quality of the line or quickly switching to a different route.

Furthermore, if X.25 links are being used, a new configuration, taking into account the special characteristics of the transmission protocols, may result in sizeable cost savings. Conversely, the computer configurations may be adapted to the X.25 link in the communication system.

Whatever the case, WAN routes need particular attention when trouble-shooting.

4

Operating a network

For many users, operating a network will always involve an element of mysticism. Nobody really knows how it works and what lies behind the operating procedures. It is no surprise, then, that the cause of any large or small problem is first attributed to the communication network, that is, the LANs. It would be asking too much, however, to expect every user to have studied the theory and practice of the network they are using.

All the same, network operators and network managers should have a very good knowledge of the network, whether or not they actually see themselves as network specialists. Armed with this knowledge, they will be able to react much more quickly and effectively.

4.1 The development of LANs and the problems encountered

Most LANs operated today, whether based on Ethernet/802.3, Token Ring, ARCNet or FDDI, are seen by their users as being generally free of problems. Most users may consider a few breakdowns every month, perhaps only a few per year, very annoying, but probably unavoidable. And yet, quite apart from the annoyance, the resulting losses in production can be quite considerable. The reasons for the introduction and installation of a computer network are usually based on organisational measures or moves towards rationalisation.

In the period immediately after starting work with a computer system of this sort, which generally involves not just the network but also new applications software, long-standing users may fall back on old habits. But after at most six months the old logical structures are no longer available, and there is no option but for everyone to use the new system. A breakdown can sometimes have very far-reaching consequences and bring entire departments to a halt.

For this reason, more and more companies are choosing to divide up their computer capacity so that each computer failure does not affect the business in its entirety. For reasons of organisation and data protection, however, the computers themselves are grouped in one central location. This means, of course, that the network connecting the computers takes on particular importance – an importance which is not always given due attention. Consequently, whilst a computer may not bring the whole company to a stop when it goes down for one reason or another, it does mean that the computers cannot be accessed. It can easily happen, for example in car or aircraft manufacturing or shipbuilding, that an entire construction department has to twiddle its collective thumbs until the computer is available again. In a bank, breakdowns can be even more serious: the losses can quickly mount up into five or six figures, quite apart from the damage to the bank's reputation. In addition, the pressure of competition in international markets means that unavoidable stoppages have to be kept very short, and there are other imponderables which have nothing to do with computers and networks.

Needless to say, the effect of a breakdown will depend to a very great extent on the circumstances of the individual case. It is fair to say, however, that the first line of defence lies in the principles and design of the network itself.

And yet, even today a computer network is very often regarded as being no more than a physical transfer medium – and a cable, after all, does not snap just like that. So it is understandable that network managers are frequently at a loss when they encounter intermittent faults on their network. But it would be wrong to claim that there is always a way of avoiding these failures.

There are, however, a variety of different ways by which the risk of a breakdown can be reduced or possibly, in some cases, avoided. Just as computers themselves are duplicated in some sensitive areas, a network can be installed in duplicate form, so that if one network goes down the work will automatically carry on with the back-up network. In some cases, this will be the only sensible answer.

This is not necessary in every case, of course, as there are other alternatives. Over the last few years, experience has shown that day-to-day problems are very rarely due to the complete failure of a component. What the user of a computer faces is as a rule a case of the application or the systems (printer, server etc.) becoming unavailable. But the problem can rarely be simply attributed to the network. The interconnections on a computer network are a good deal more complicated than that, especially as the technologies available today very quickly result in a mixed bag of a network environment. As a result, and as the systems become increasingly interlocked, the problems could be said to be programmed in.

There is a lot to consider in a network. Problems and errors on a network may not be evident to everyone. Present-day networks have impressive transfer capacities at their disposal, even though these are occasionally not enough. The transfer bandwidths run from 4 Mbit/sec to 16 Mbit/sec, and in FDDI up to 100 Mbit/sec. As a rule, the actual speeds will be nothing like these theoretical maximum values, and a typical load in an office environment and in the data processing area will be around 10 to 25%, which in turn implies a data frame rate of 500 to 1000 frames/sec. Exceptions to this, however, are diskless workstations and CAD terminals, which frequently achieve loadings of 50 to 70%.

4.2   The health check

Networks provide such high transfer capacities that faults in a cable nearly always go unnoticed. It has even happened (and not just occasionally) that an Ethernet system has had a load of 15% and in addition there have been around 20% of faults on the cable. In everyday operation this was not noticed, as it added up to a figure of 35% so that the network was only working at one-third of its theoretical load. But if the network had been expanded and subjected to a greater workload this could very well have become a noticeable problem. The least that can be said is that under such conditions a system will not be working at its best. But fans of Token Ring networks should not gloat: in these systems, cable problems are a major factor in any undiscovered problem, and the relationship between faults and loading capacity is often much the same. By itself, however, the error rate can usually be tolerated. It is when a fault needs to be tracked down, perhaps because the application is running too slowly or the server is suddenly unavailable, that permanent faults of this sort pile on the problems.

In the initial analysis, of course, it is impossible to tell whether the faults discovered in tests on the network have any connection with the symptom that has set off the search. This makes fault correction more difficult and more time-consuming, and supplies a few reasons for finding out how the network operates and knowing at least the main characteristics. These characteristics should reflect the normal state of a network – so it is important to discuss characteristics at this point. A single figure, such as 15.5% load or 0.5% errors, is no use whatsoever, as it could refer to either a mean over an undefined period or a one-off measurement. Surveys of the network should therefore be carried out (to collect statistics) on a continuous basis. Once a characteristic has been recorded, later measurements can be compared against it.

It therefore makes a good deal of sense to record these statistics at regular intervals and file them so that they are available for reference.

But there are other reasons for periodical, if not continuous observation. Note that this does not mean recording actual data, which would eventually use up all the memory capacity and would also conflict with data protection provisions. Faulty components are frequently indicated by rising error rates in a network. It is very rare that a network component fails completely.

Where this is the case, fault-tracing will then be a relatively simple matter. Observing network characteristics, then, enables trends to be spotted so that proactive measures can be put into effect and potential trouble avoided. This does not mean that all faults can be detected at an early stage, but experience shows that it applies in some 50% of cases. A further way these statistics can be used is in planning the expansion of existing networks. With known characteristics to hand, planning need not be based on conjecture but can be built on realistic assessments of loading and traffic so that, for example, bottlenecks can be resolved and avoided for the future. With information on the nature of the data streams, routers can

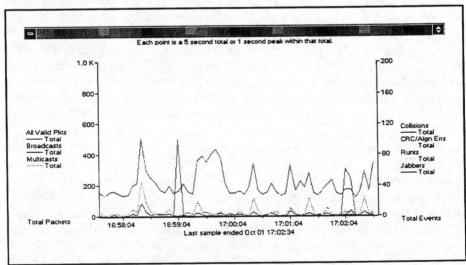

Figure 4.1   Ethernet statistics showing the main parameters

be configured effectively, saving considerable expense. A 'LAN health check', as we might call it, can thus be very useful.

Whether this is done with a system specifically designed for the measurements required or using a readily available protocol analyser is not so important. What matters is that it must be possible for the data to be presented as graphics and printed out. It is never easy to make out trends in long columns of figures.

Figure 4.1 shows an example of a statistical summary taken from an Ethernet network.

What information do we need for an analysis? The basic principle to go by is probably: the more and the more varied the better. Frequently, this is limited by the memory capacity of the hardware used: the data volumes can be very large, depending on the number of parameters sampled and the time spent on the survey. Interest will primarily be directed to the network parameters, however, which can also be used in planning decisions. And the statistics should always include data on the servers, otherwise it will be difficult afterwards to evaluate the situation realistically. Figure 4.2 shows a frame of statistics enabling the nodes with the highest error rates to be picked out. From this, a defective interface will be obvious at once, if it is only one node that keeps sending faulty data frames (although the user will be completely unaware of it).

If the existing network topology is taken into account, the same statistics can also point to a faulty repeater, bridge or router. In this case, the data frames from nearly all the stations or nodes in the affected sub-network will show faults, and this will be visible in the high error rate for the nodes or stations in the respective segment.

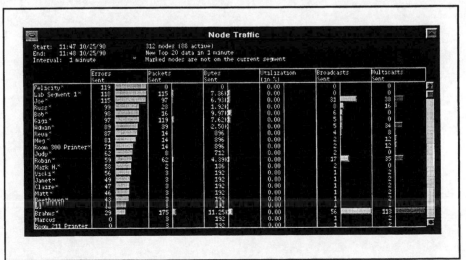

Figure 4.2   Nodes with the highest error rates

As it is highly unlikely that more than one transceiver or attachment unit (MAU) will break down at the same time, the obvious conclusion is that the fault is being caused by a coupling element.

4.3 Summary

Operating a medium-to-large network without an occasional check on the transfer parameters is not a wise course. Periodical inspection is always advisable, to avoid nasty surprises at some unknown time in the future.

It does not take much time or effort, and if automatic systems are used to record the information it will always be available for reference. If the network has already had network management systems installed, it would be foolish not to make use of the functions they provide and have periodical checks carried out automatically.

5

Diagnostic aids for local networks

Effective and efficient monitoring of a local network calls for a range of diagnostic aids. This chapter will introduce all the important items of equipment needed for successful trouble-shooting or for achieving optimum performance. A description of the platforms for network management systems has deliberately been excluded: firstly, because there is already plentiful literature on the subject and secondly, because it is our intention here to deal with what are probably the two most important aspects of network management, namely network performance management and fault management.

5.1   Protocol analysers

Protocol analysers are without doubt one of the most essential tools for fault-tracing in a local network. Not only can they – as the name suggests –

analyse protocols, but they can also provide statistical analyses of the data traffic as well as generating their own network loads. In addition, it is often possible to record faulty packets or fragments of packets, which will in some cases allow conclusions to be reached about the cause of the fault.

Protocol analysers come in all types and across a range of prices. Which model and what facilities are needed will depend on the size and complexity of the network to be monitored. As a general rule of thumb, it can be said that the number and frequency of problems on a network begin to rise noticeably once a network reaches the size where it has 80 to 100 users.

Protocol analysis systems can be divided into three basic classes.

5.1.1   Software-based analysers

These range from (sometimes astonishingly powerful) public-domain programs, available to anyone via the Internet, to more lavishly designed software products, and are suitable for smaller networks with system loads up to 15%. These software packages are installed on a 'standard' network node fitted with a network interface card designed to detect and receive the data packets addressed to it, but to ignore the rest of the data traffic on the network (hence the limitation of reliable test results to network loads of approximately 15%). Nevertheless, this software can also be useful in larger networks: if certain statistical measurements are required simultaneously from a number of segments in a network, three or four of these software packages can be installed at strategically important points and valuable data can be gathered.

The price of these software analysers is between 0 and £2,000.

Examples (alphabetically by manufacturer):

- ETHMON 2.0:   Chevin Software Ltd.;
- Ethernet Monitor: Black Box;
- LAN Command Advanced: Dolphin Networks;
- LAN Watch: FTP Software Inc.

5.1.2   Software and hardware-based analysers

These more powerful systems comprise specially adapted network interface cards with their own purpose-developed user interface. The analyser card and software are best installed in a laptop or a 'lunchbox' (a portable computer with up to five free card slots), and can give reliable results at network loads of up to 50%. The price range of these systems is between £4,000 and £15,000.

Examples (alphabetically by manufacturer):

- TokenRing: Scope Azure;
- LANVista: Digilog;
- Sniffer: Network General;
- LANalyzer: Novell;
- Spider Analyzer: Spider Systems.

5.1.3 Dedicated analyser systems

This most powerful and most expensive group of products is based on purpose-developed hardware platforms. Network loadings of up to 100% can be not only analysed and recorded with considerable precision, but also generated. Hardware-oriented filter modules guarantee that the desired filter conditions will be maintained whatever the network loading. A recent trend is the use of software applications based on expert systems, such as Hewlett Packard's 'Fault Finder' or Network General's 'Expert Sniffer'. These products are able to compare network problems they encounter with an existing knowledge base. If the fault scenario encountered is in the database, the system will give the possible cause along with tips on curing the fault.

Some systems also support what are known as Dual Port Applications – examples being the K 1100 by Siemens or the DA 30 by Wandel und Goltermann. These enable components such as bridges and routers to be checked for performance. Here, one interface generates data packets (as many and as short as possible, to achieve maximum loading of the components to be tested), and the other module – running at the same time – counts the number of packets lost. This application naturally does not come cheap, and will be mainly of interest to manufacturers of network components.

Those who feel that the luxury of two Ethernet modules is beyond their means but would still like the benefit of dual-port diagnostics could order an IDA (Intelligent Dual-Port Analysis) cable from the Munich company NETCOR GmbH for around £80. This is in fact simply an AUI cable spliced on to two DB 15 plugs, with the two transmit pins connected to the left-hand plug and the two receive pins to the right. The network components to be tested are connected to either end using two MAUs, and when a load is generated the analyser's display will show the packets transmitted by the bridge.

Prices for this third group of analysers start at around £15,000 and rise to £40,000.

Examples (alphabetically by manufacturer):

- Network Advisor: Hewlett Packard;
- K110:   Siemens AG;
- DA30:   Wandel und Goltermann.

5.2   The multi-protocol PC

In addition to a protocol analyser, it is often very useful to have what is known as a multi-protocol PC in the trouble-shooter's portfolio. This is simply a portable PC with one or more network interface cards as required and with all the relevant network operating systems installed – for example, an Ethernet card and a Token Ring card, and Novell Netware and TCP-IP for operating systems. Add some simple LAN monitoring software, as described in Section 5.1, and you have a fully-fledged multi-protocol PC.

When problems arise in the network, you will save the trouble of testing software configurations from network stations or replacing components 'on spec', as you will always have a model network node which you know for certain to be correctly configured. You will know precisely what has been installed, amd how, so that after you replace a problem station with your multi-protocol PC you will immediately be able to say, 'The trouble is in this station,' or 'The trouble is in the network itself, beyond the network plug.'

Multi-protocol PCs can also be used to get to the bottom of complex network performance problems, by installing one or more of them, together with bridges or routers, in the affected segments. Then, for example, a LAN statistics package can be run on one PC whilst another PC sends data packets across specific segments or initiates specific server applications. Using the protocol analyser, the reactions of the network can be monitored or additional load can be generated.

5.3   Distributed monitoring units

Distributed monitoring units can be an important aid to monitoring and fault-tracing, especially in extensive and heavily segmented networks. Here, LAN monitors – usually hardware units with no keyboard or screen – are connected to each segment of the network. These LAN monitors will then continuously collect data from your local network segment and send these to a central monitoring station at regular intervals. The entire network can now be monitored from a central computer by clicking on a mouse. If certain parameters, such as network load, collisions or the like, exceed a predetermined alarm threshold, the LAN monitor will automatically report it to the central monitoring station.

The Rolls-Royces of these systems will even react by selecting a serial back-up link if they are unable to access the management station for themselves via the network (e.g. because a bridge is overloaded or out of order). This truly creates a permanent network monitoring system which will operate whatever the operational status of the network being monitored.

When all is said and done, a network monitor which is only functional so long as the network is running perfectly is not a great deal of use in the first place.

A standard has recently been drawn up for the type and number of parameters to be checked by these LAN monitors, and for the protocol they use to pass the parameters to the central management station. The proposed protocol is SNMP (Simple Network Management Protocol) – the quasi-standard already taken as a basis by most network management platforms. The Management Information Base (MIB) in which the type and number of parameters to be scanned by SNMP are defined is the RMON-MIB (Remote Monitoring Management Information Base). So far, there are RMON-MIBs for Ethernet and Token Ring and one for FDDI is in preparation. The specification for the Ethernet RMON-MIB is defined in RFC 1271 and can be called up by anyone via the Internet. Modern monitoring systems already have this standard implemented.

Prices for LAN monitors are between £750 and £4,000 each for the hardware units, with the software adding between £4,000 and £7,500.

Examples (alphabetically by manufacturer):

- LAN Probe II (RMON-MIB):   Hewlett-Packard;

- Distributed Sniffer: Network General;

- LANtern: Novell.

5.4   Diagnostics at the physical level

Given that many of the problems occurring in local networks can be tracked down to causes at what is known as the physical level, that is, they derive from faults in the transfer medium (cables, plugs, terminating resistors, distributor boxes etc.), the importance of diagnostic aids at this level should not be overlooked.

5.4.1   Multimeters

A good multimeter will always be a help. Many a time, a simple measurement of the resistance or voltage on the network has supplied the answer to a problem. How to go about it in practice is covered in the next chapter. The price of a simple multimeter works out between £75 and £150.

5.4.2   Cable testers

Cable testers were specially developed for tests on local networks. Depending on the version, these will measure the attenuation resistance, crosstalk, reflections, signal noise and core reversal as well as the cable length. Some units will also locate cables. To do this, the cable tester feeds a special signal into the cable. Using a small accessory which is basically a audio amplifier, a defined sequence of tones can now be picked up at a distance of up to 30 or 40 centimetres from the cable. This enables the run of the cable under a false floor or behind a partition to be traced. Prices for cable testers are between £750 and £3,500.

Examples (alphabetically by manufacturer):

* LANcat 1500:   Datacom Technologies;
* FDDI Port: Hewlett-Packard;
* NEXT Scanner: Microtest.

5.4.3   Spectrum Analysers

In environments with high electromagnetic loads, for example production areas with electric motors, welding equipment or goods lifts, the use of copper cabling may give rise to sizeable problems caused by induced interference voltages. If no obvious sources of interference are located nearby, the only way of finding out the cause of the interference is to start by investigating the frequency spectrum of the interference.

This is done using spectrum analysers. These very expensive items of hardware are capable of showing voltage amplitudes over a wide range of frequencies (this will vary depending on the model), allowing the amplitudes, frequencies and harmonics of interference sources to be precisely determined. Spectrum analysers can be obtained from about £7,500 upwards.

5.4.4   Oscilloscopes

Pointers to the source of interference voltages can also be gained from the use of an oscilloscope. In general, an oscilloscope will provide much the same information as a spectrum analyser: both units show voltage against time. However, a spectrum analyser also sweeps (or 'wobbles') continuously over the selected spectrum of frequencies. When an oscilloscope is used, this has to be done by hand, and this is reflected in the price of digital oscilloscopes, which can be bought for as little as £2,000. Figure 5.1 shows the record of a collision on an Ethernet network provided by a digital oscilloscope. The superimposition of signals on the illegally high signal level of more than 3.5 volts can be clearly seen, along with the collision and the normal data traffic following.

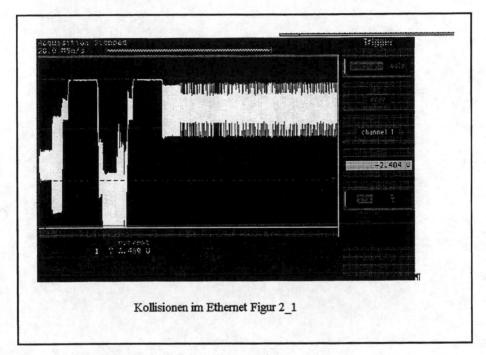

Kollisionen im Ethernet Figur 2_1

Figure 5.1   Collisions in an Ethernet network

6

Transfer media

Three principal types of transfer media are used in local networks:

- coaxial cable ('coax'),
- twisted-pair cable,
- optical fibre.

The great majority of cabling installed still consists of coaxial media, as the pie chart (Figure 6.1, statistics for 1991) shows.

However, twisted-pair and optical fibre are showing very high growth rates, and coaxial cable can be expected to lose its dominant position in the medium term. Each of the three types of cable has its own advantages and disadvantages, and we will now examine them with particular reference to the part they may play in faults and problems and their elimination.

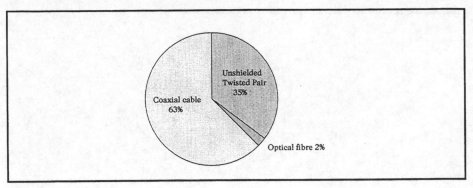

Figure 6.1

6.1   Coaxial cable

6.1.1   Structure and connection of coaxial cables

A widely used transfer medium, especially in the Ethernet environment, is 50-ohm coax cable. A coax cable consists of a copper wire core surrounded by an insulating layer. This insulating layer is in turn surrounded by a second conducting (shielding) layer, usually of braided wires. An outer layer of plastic protects the cable from external damage (Figure 6.2).

There are two ways in which network components can be connected to the cable. One of these consists of splitting the cable and inserting a T piece. The second possibility involves what is known as a vampire plug. For this, a hole of defined depth is drilled into the cable, so that it reaches into the copper core. A special plug is then screwed into this hole to make the electrical contact. The vampire plug method is mainly used for 10Base5 Ethernet cables (also called 'yellow cable' and 'thick LAN') – that is, thicker cables with lower attenuation (to a maximum of 8.5 dB in 500 metres). T pieces are widely used in 10Base2 Ethernet networks (also known as 'thin-LAN' or 'CheaperNet': maximum attenuation 8.5 dB in 185 metres). The advantage of the vampire plug method is that it does not require a break in network operation to install it, which may for instance be an important criterion in production networks. Against this, serious networking problems may be caused if the hole is drilled too deeply (the cable core may break) or not deeply enough (resulting in intermittent contact). As a rule, 10Base5 cables are fitted with Type N connectors and 10Base2 cables with BNC connectors. A 50-ohm terminating resistor must be connected at either end to prevent reflections of the signals carried by the cable.

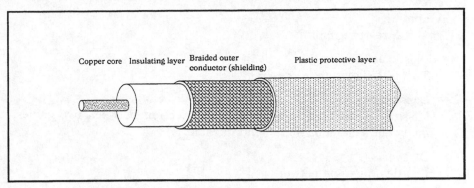

Figure 6.2   Coaxial cable

6.1.2   Coax cable problems and their causes

Problems occur ing in a coax cable take many forms:

- Symptom:
  Intermittent loss of connection.

  - Diagnosis:
    Poor connection or no connection to the network cable itself.

  - Cause:
    BNC connector loose, vampire plug not drilled deep enough.

- Symptom:
  Total failure of a segment.

  - Diagnosis:
    Short circuit somewhere in the cable.

  - Cause:
    Kink in cable, faulty cable, vampire plug drilled too deep. Short circuit caused by wire from braided shielding.

- Symptom:
  Unusually high number of collisions.

  - Diagnosis (1):
    Strong reflections in cable causing collisions.

  - Cause (1): Missing terminating resistor, faulty or incorrect terminating resistor, too many MAUs connected (100 in 10Base5, 30 in 10Base2).

  - Diagnosis (2):
    Earthing problems.

  - Cause (2):
    Multiple earthing of segment.

- Symptom:
  Total failure of segment.

  - Diagnosis (1):
    TDR test shows cable open.

  - Cause (1):
    Missing terminating resistor, poor connection between two cables, faulty cable, kink or sharp bend in cable.

  - Diagnosis (2):
    Illegal voltages on network.

  - Cause (2):
    Faulty MAUs, no earthing.

- Symptom:
  Irregular or frequent collisions and fragments.

  - Diagnosis:
    Interference voltages being induced.

  - Cause:
    Cable acting as aerial: electromagnetic interference close to cable inducing voltages.

- Symptom:
  Intermittent loss of connection or no link to new installation.

  - Diagnosis (1):
    Att/n too high

  - Cause (1):
    Losses in cable, variations in impedance between connectors or in patch panels.

  - Diagnosis (2):
    Interference.

  - Cause (2):
    Induction of signals via vampire plug acting as mini-aerial.

6.1.3 Isolation of fault sources

6.1.3.1 Voltage tests on coax cable

The simplest way of testing the voltage level of a network segment is by using a voltmeter on a free T piece or vampire plug. If the voltage is less than +/- 100 mV (+/- 200 mV at the end of the cable) it is most unlikely that there is any voltage problem. If the voltage measured is significantly above 100 mV, up to several volts, it may be that the power supply to a MAU unit or some other component directly connected to the network is being illegally fed to the network. The measured voltage up to 100 mV is the DC mean of the AC signals on the coax cable.

All MAUs should now be systematically removed, with the voltage being tested each time. As more than one unit could be faulty, deactivated units should not be reconnected to the network until the source of the fault has been isolated. If the voltage level is still too high after all the network components have been removed, it is probable that the cabling is earthed at more than one point, so that the potential difference of the two earthing points is being applied to the network. All the earthing connections except one should then be removed.

Quite a few network components no longer provide electrical isolation between the connected unit and the network medium when they are faulty, which means that a perfectly ordinary network card can often be the cause of a double-earthing nuisance.

6.1.3.2 Cable resistance tests

Before a cable resistance is measured, all the network components, without exception, must be taken out of circuit. The resistance can then be measured at the T piece or the vampire plug (Figure 6.3).

If the values are between 24.0 and 26.6 ohms (10Base5) or between 24.4 and 26.6 ohms (10Base2) there is no resistance problem.

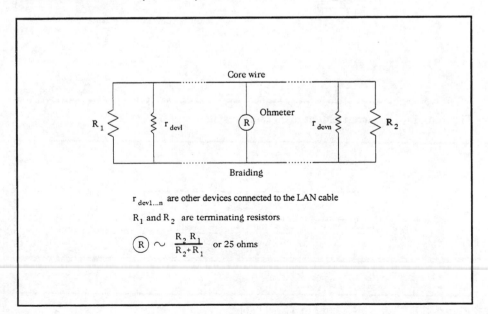

Figure 6.3

If a higher resistance, around 50 ohms or more, is measured, this indicates that the cable is open at some point. The cable must then be opened and tests carried out as shown in figures 6.4 and 6.5. From the point where 50 ohms is measured in these tests, the cable is good. (Because of the open cable, there will not be two 50-ohm resistances in parallel at any point.)

If a very low resistance is measured, this means that the cable is short-circuited. If you are the happy owner of a TDR (Time Domain Reflectometry) meter, the faulty location can be localised more quickly by means of a single test.

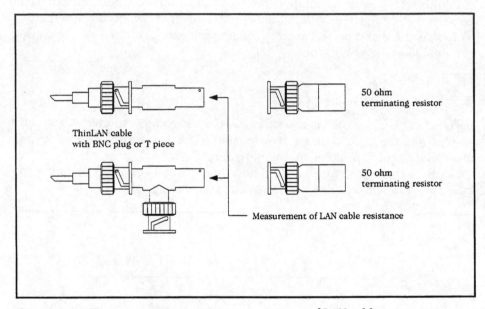

Figure 6.4   Test arrangement to measure resistance of LAN cable

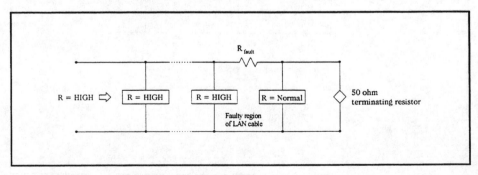

Figure 6.5   Locating a fault in a LAN cablee

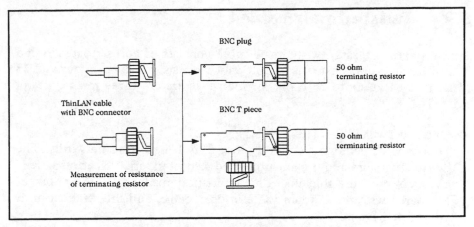

Figure 6.6   Test arrangement to measure resistance of terminating resistor

6.1.3.3 Testing the terminating resistor

If a terminating resistor is suspected of being faulty, bear in mind that the T piece and the terminating resistor are tested together. It may be that a perfectly good terminating resistor is connected to a faulty T piece (Figure 6.6).

6.1.3.4 Testing for electromagnetic interference

The frequency range of the interference can be found by taking noise measurements with a cable scanner or testing with a spectrum analyser. The interference voltage should be measured between the shielding and the core. Those lucky enough to have a spectrum analyser at their disposal can also probe to determine the frequency spectrum. Typical interference frequencies are:

* 40 kHz – 150 kHz: Strip lighting, electric motors.

* 16 MHz – 100 MHz: Radio, TV, computers.

6.1.3.5 Checking for reflections and short circuits

Reflections and short circuits can be measured using TDR meters. The test involves sending a signal and measuring the time taken for the reflected signal to arrive back. Any irregularity in a LAN will cause larger or smaller reflections, depending on the size of the impedance mismatch.

The TDR meter can now be set up to wait for the longest reflection, or a reflection measuring 30% of the original signal, and so on. This gives the distance to the source of each reflection. Removing the terminating resistor and triggering for the longest reflected signal will supply the length of the cable (unless the cable is broken at some point, in which case the test will show the distance to the fault).

6.2   Twisted-pair cable

As the name suggests, twisted-pair cable consists of cores twisted round each other in pairs. Most twisted-pair cables consist of between four and 25 pairs, twisted at six to 26 turns per metre. There are three main types of twisted pair:

- Shielded Twisted Pair (IBM Type 1):
  This type of cable is frequently found in Token Ring networks. The twisted pairs are additionally protected against external electromagnetic effects by metallic shielding. Characteristic impedance is 150 ohms, as compared with the 50-ohm value of coax cable, and the attenuation is around 45 dB/km.

- Data Grade Unshielded Twisted Pair (IBM Type 3):
  This 100-ohm cable consists of four pairs of cores and is used for 10Base-T networks among others (Figure 6.7).

- Distributed Inside Wire (DIW):
  This is the classic North American telephone cable, also known as AT&T Category 3 cable. It is difficult to determine precise values for attenuation or crosstalk.

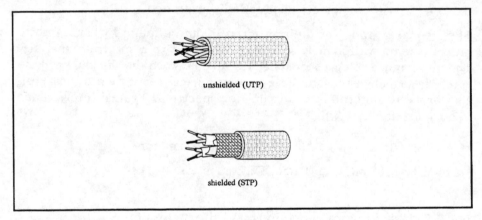

Figure 6.7   Twisted Pair Cable

The maximum permissible attenuation is 11.5 dB for the longest transmission route – which corresponds to about 100 m. However, this disadvantage as compared with coax or fibre optic cable is not severe, as an AT&T survey has shown that 95 per cent of all network nodes are located within a radius of 100 metres of a cable distributor.

The advantages of this type of cable lie in the low cabling cost and in the fact that the same medium can be used for both data and speech transmission.

Another distinct advantage is that the individual stations no longer need to be connected directly to the backbone cable, but can be linked indirectly via concentrators. This means that a fault will not affect data flow on the backbone itself.

When a problem occurs, this is usually detected by the concentrator, which interrupts access to the relevant network line (this applies for Ethernet). This means that other network users are not disturbed.

Modern concentrators can also be incorporated in network management platforms, allowing central monitoring of the activity of all stations.

6.2.1 Problems with Twisted-Pair Cables and their causes

- Symptom:
  Poor network performance, collisions, FCS errors, ring purges, beaconing.

  - Diagnosis:
    Crosstalk: when a signal is being carried by a cable pair, part of this signal may be induced in a neighbouring pair. This results in interference.

  - Cause:
    Pins have been wrongly assigned, so that the signal is being carried by a pair of wires that are not twisted round each other (e.g.: pin 1 is twisted with pin 2, and pin 3 with pin 4, but the station is using 1 + 3 and 2 + 4 as pairs: this will cause crosstalk). Another cause may be that the cable is simply not twisted enough, so that it is not suitable for high-frequency signals. In Token Rings, untwisted and unshielded sections inside the concentrator may also cause crosstalk.

- Symptom:
  Irregular or frequent collisions and fragments.

  - Diagnosis:
    Interference being induced.

  - Cause:
    Electromagnetic interference close to cable inducing voltages. UTP (Unshielded Twisted Pair) is particularly susceptible to this. The maximum permissible interference voltage is approx. 264 mV.

- Symptom:
  Intermittent loss of connection or no link to new installation.

  - Diagnosis :
    Att/n too high

- Cause:
  Losses in cable, cable too long, variations in impedance between connectors or in patch panels. Telephone lines are often wired via a number of patch fields and unsuited to the transfer of high-frequency signals (this applies in Germany).

- Symptom:
  No link to new installation.

  - Diagnosis:
    Test signals not reaching other station.

  - Cause:
    Reversed cores.

- Symptom:
  Total failure of one station.

  - Diagnosis:
    Cable is open.

  - Cause:
    Poor connection to cable, faulty cable, kink or sharp bend in cable.

6.3   Optical Fibre Cables

Optical fibre cables provide a high transfer bandwidth. They are immune to electromagnetic interference and can cover large distances (2000 metres and over). Fibre optics are therefore used as the transfer medium for backbone links when implementing Ethernet, Token Ring or FDDI networks. Of course, the high bandwidth, reliability and lack of electromagnetic sensitivity have their price: one metre of glass fibre cable will cost between £2 and £8 depending on the number of cores. Splicing a fibre will work out at around £40 to £60.

Optical fibre cables are usually classified as suitable for either internal or external use. External fibre optics cables usually have a sheath of UV-resistant and rodent-protected material. Internal cables are generally sheathed in PVC, with strain relief provided by aramid thread.

A minimum of two cores are required for a fibre optics link – one for each direction. (There are also techniques – using different wavelengths – enabling one core to be used for transmission in both directions, but these are rarely used.) Even where only one pair of cores is required, optical fibre cables with at least four core pairs should be laid, so that an alternative pair can be used in the event of breaks in a fibre. The length of an optical fibre route, or the permissible number of splices, depends on both the performance of the fibre-optics components used and the gauge of the fibre (62.5 or 50 µm).

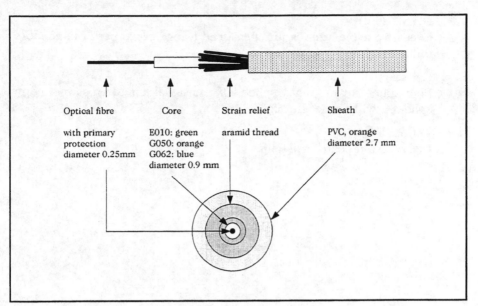

Figure 6.8   Structure of an optical fibre cable

As a rule of thumb, each splice attenuates the signal by 0.1 dB.

6.3.1   Problems with optical fibre and their causes

- Symptom:
  No connection.

  - Diagnosis:
    Test for a fibre break using either an optical TDR meter or a 'lighter test' (hold a cigarette lighter against the cross-section of the fibre at one end of the cable and test for light arriving at the other end using the naked eye – this will work for up to several hundred metres).

  - Cause:
    Fibre break due to external shock or bends at too tight a radius. (The bending radius should not be less than twenty times the cable diameter – that is, for a internal fibre-optic cable 3 mm in diameter the minimum bending radius is 6 cm.)

  - Action:
    Check bending radii and switch to pair of intact cores.

- Symptom:
  Intermittent problems with connection.

- Diagnosis:
  Excessive cable attenuation measured using optical performance loss unit.

- Cause:
  Poor splices or too many splices. If the signal has to cross too many splices it will not get through.

- Action:
  Inserting a repeater will help.

7

Network interface cards, MAUs and concentrators

There are two distinct varieties of network interface card : cards with integrated MAUs (these are connected directly to the network – via BNC plugs, twisted pair cable, RJ45 etc.) and cards with external MAUs (the connection to the network is then made using AUI interface cable and MAUs). The name MAU (Media Access Unit) derives from the 802.3 standard. In Ethernet, it is usually called a transceiver.

The different cards are configured using software supplied and/or by hardware switches (DIP switches or jumpers) on the card itself. Examples of configurable parameters are interrupts, active output (e.g. AUI or BNC), DMA addresses etc.

7.1   Network interface cards

7.1.1   Problems with Ethernet interface cards

7.1.1.1 Symptoms of faulty network interface cards

Symptoms such as incorrect frame check sequence and jabber packets (packets longer than 1518 bytes) frequently originate in faulty network interface cards. Most problems have the following causes:

- Symptom:
  Frequent collisions or jabber packets.

  - Cause:
    MAU module (carrier sensing) is faulty, the network card is sending without allowing for other stations.

- Symptom:
  Station not able to send at all.

  - Cause:
    Wrong configuration: wrong port active (coax instead of AUI or vice versa), interrupt used is already assigned.

- Symptom:
  No power supply to MAU (shown by LEDs on MAU).

  - Cause:
    Network card hardware faulty or fuse blown.

- Symptom:
  No connection, SQE LED lights up every time send attempted.

  - Cause:
    MAU sending heartbeat signal, but network card interpreting this (as specified in standards) as SQE = Signal Quality Error (collision, deformed signal). Heartbeat signal of MAU should be switched off.

- Symptom:
  No connection.

  - Cause (1):
    MAU sending no heartbeat signal, but network card waiting for read/write acknowledgement. Some older network cards (DEC cards) need an acknowledgement for every read/write operation (heartbeat) when running. This is carried by the lines of the AUI cable normally reserved for the SQE signal. In this case the MAU should be switched to 'heartbeat' mode.

  - Cause (2):

In 10Base2 networks: connecting cable between T piece and network card. The network card must be connected directly to the T piece on the backbone cable. The maximum permissible length of the connection between the T piece and the network interface card is 4 cm!!! (3 cm of this is taken up internally on the network card.)

7.1.1.2 Diagnosing faulty network interface cards

The first step in a diagnosis if an interface card with an AUI output is suspected of being faulty or wrongly configured should be to connect an AUI monitor plug. Once inserted between the network interface card and the MAU, this plug will show on its LEDs the send and receive lines, the SQE signal and the power supply.

If data is sent and the send LED does not light, the card is either configured wrongly or faulty. If no signal can be coaxed from the card after a thorough check of all configurable parameters and jumpers, it will have to be replaced. If the coaxial connection to a card needs testing, the simplest way is to connect one of the miniature networks described in section 7.2.4.2 and send some test loop-back packets.

If a station breaks down completely, a quick answer can be achieved by connecting a multi-protocol PC (*see* Section 5.2). If the PC connected in place of the problem station works without problem, the area of the fault has been narrowed down to the station that has been removed from the network (including the MAU and the AUI cable, if used). Otherwise, the fault is somewhere beyond the network connection.

If the network card is able to send and receive data packets (which can be seen via the AUI monitor plug) a conclusive pointer can be obtained from a list – produced by a protocol analyser – showing the stations sending the most faulty packets. If the faulty packets are so mutilated that this list cannot be produced due to the lack of any send or receive addresses, the activity of a number of stations will need to be measured over a period of time, along with the number of faulty packets sent.

If a correlation can be seen between the error curve and the activity curve of one of the stations monitored, this is in all probability the source of the fault.

7.1.2   Problems with Token Ring interface cards

7.1.2.1   Symptoms of faulty network interface cards

In Token Ring networks, faulty or wrongly configured network cards often cause beaconing. Most problems have the following causes:

- Symptom:
  Ring is beaconing.

  - Cause:
    Network card hardware faulty, holding concentrator port (relay) in closed position.

  - Action:
    Reset MAU port using MAU port plug. Replace the network interface cards (*see also* Section 10.3, 'Beaconing').

- Symptom:
  Station unable to log into ring.

  - Cause:
    Duplicate Token Ring address.

  - Action:
    Change Token Ring address.

- Symptom:
  Ring is beaconing.

  - Cause:
    Wrong ring speed configured.

  - Action:
    Configure correct ring speed.

7.1.3   Operating statistics for network interface cards

Most network interface cards store statistics for all the important operating parameters. These statistics are usually drawn up by the network software by reference to the card controller. If individual stations show performance problems, these statistics can therefore be a major help. Usually the following parameters are processed:

- Ethernet:
  - number of packets sent,
  - number of packets received,
  - packet wait times,
  - packets sent with one collision,
  - packets sent with more than one collision,
  - number of packets rejected due to buffer problems,

- number of packets with FCS error,
- misaligned data packets (packets where the length is not a multiple of 8 bits).

- Token Ring:
  - number of packets sent,
  - number of packets received,
  - number of packets rejected due to buffer problems,
  - number of packets with FCS error,
  - number of beaconing packets,
  - number of Claim Token packets,
  - number of error packets (E bit set).

7.2 MAUs (Media Access Units) and AUIs (Attachment Unit Interfaces) in Ethernet networks

A MAU in an Ethernet network makes the location of the network user independent of the network cable and standardises the connection between the network and its nodes. This is achieved by MAUs fitted directly to the network medium and connected to the station itself via an AUI interface cable. This means that, irrespective of the medium used (optical fibre, twisted pair, Thin LAN, Thick LAN etc.), all stations can be linked into the network using a standard AUI interface connector (a 15-pin 'D' plug). Multiport MAUs can even connect a number of stations to the network at the same time.

Thus, MAUs and AUI cables are the components which provide the actual connection between the network nodes and the network medium. This makes it vital that they operate faultlessly. Modern MAUs are suited to both Ethernet V 2.0 and IEEE 802.3 networks and are fitted with LEDs to indicate collisions, data transfer and SQE signals (Signal Quality Error: this signal is sent to the station by the MAU if non-standard signals are received, e.g. collisions or similar). Unfortunately, not all manufacturers comply with standards in their use of the SQE signal. Some MAUs send the network card an SQE signal (also known as a 'heartbeat') after every read or write operation. These heartbeat signals are required by some older network cards (e.g. early DEC cards).

7.2.1   Inserting and removing AUI cables and MAUs

If an MAU is plugged into an live network node, this may induce a current peak in the computer's power supply (plugging in the MAU creates a quasi-short-circuit for a fraction of a second, which is needed to build up the supply voltage for the MAU). This can result in damage to the data on the hard disk or to the hardware itself. The power supply should therefore always be switched off. As there are differences in the earthing of the network nodes and the LAN cable (e.g. AUI cables, LAN cables), network components and backbone cabling should not be touched at the same time.

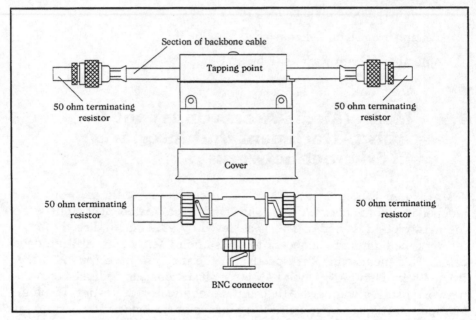

Figure 7.1   Miniature networks

7.2.2   Trouble-shooting equipment

The following components should be provided for fault-tracing in the MAU/AUI area:

a) Mini-network for the relevant network topology (Figure 7.1),

b) an MAU known for certain to be working correctly,

c) an AUI adapter with LED displays,

d) an AUI cable known for certain to be free of faults (and correct for 802.3/Ethernet V2.0),

e) a voltmeter.

7.2.3   Symptoms of faulty MAUs/AUIs

Faulty MAUs result in either a complete breakdown of the link between the network node and the rest of the network or an increased frequency of collisions and/or jabber packets. The causes of these faults are examined below.

7.2.3.1 IEEE 802.3 vs. Ethernet V2.0 AUI cables

Anyone connecting MAUs and network cards made to the Ethernet V2.0 standard to IEEE 802.3 cables is in for an unpleasant surprise. In IEEE cables, pins 14, 8, 4 and 11 are shielded; in Ethernet V 2.0 cables they are not. The results are earthing problems and spurious pulses on the line.

7.2.3.2 SQE problems

Not all MAUs send SQE signals only when non-standard signals such as collisions occur, in line with the standard. As some older network cards require an acknowledgement of every read or write operation (the 'heartbeat'), most MAUs allow for selection between Heartbeat and SQE modes. However, if an MAU outputting a heartbeat is connected to a conventional network card which conforms with the standard, the network card will be given an SQE signal on every read or write operation, and will understandably take this to indicate a collision – meaning that any attempt to send or receive will be abandoned. The same applies to repeaters, when not connected directly to the network: these must always be connected to a non-heartbeat MAU.

7.2.3.3 Failure to observe separation distance

Two MAUs must always be at least 2.5 metres apart in 10Base5 networks (0.5 metre in 10Base2), and wherever possible connected at the marks on the cable (this minimises any reflections that may arise). The AUI cable must not exceed 50 metres in length.

7.2.4   Diagnosing faulty MAUs

7.2.4.1 Loose connections

Checking every plug connection may be easy to extremely difficult, depending on the installation. If the AUI cable is not accessible, for example (if it has been routed in a false floor or above the ceiling), it will often be impossible to inspect the connections directly. In cases like this the only answer is a loop-back test. In all cases, however, terminating resistors and earth connections should be checked. It has happened more than once that the end of a cable has been connected directly to an MAU or a network card instead of a terminating resistor. In addition, MAU cable connectors should be given a special check in Thick LANs, where they are responsible for faults more often than in other topologies.

7.2.4.2 Loop-Back tests

Using the mini-networks described above, the source of a fault can be systematically narrowed down. To do this, the MAU is separated from the network cable and connected instead to the miniature network, which simulates a real network operating without problems. If it is possible to send test packets ('loop-back' packets) without error, the station, AUI cable and MAU are in order.

This means that the fault is located beyond the MAU and in the network itself; otherwise the MAU and AUI cable should be successively replaced with components known to be in perfect order until the fault is found. To make sure that the fault is in the MAU and not, for example, in the interface card, the supply voltage can also be measured between pins 13 and 6. According to specifications, it should be between 11.28 and 15.75 volts. Network cards are often provided with fuses to prevent excessive current drain. If this fuse is blown, the power supply for the MAU will be cut.

7.3   Concentrators in Token Ring networks

In Token Ring networks, the separate stations are linked into the network itself via concentrators, which have a number of MAU ports. Faultless operation of the concentrators is vital, as a breakdown almost invariably brings the entire network to a halt.

The connection between the concentrator and the network node consists of a shielded 150-ohm (+/- 15 ohms) twisted pair cable (Type 1) with one send and one receive pair. The send pair must carry a phantom voltage of 4.1 to 7 volts when logging in, and under 1 volt in by-pass mode (see also Section 11.3.10).

7.3.1 Trouble-shooting equipment

The following components should always be kept available for fault-tracing in the MAU/AUI area:

- a concentrator known for certain to be working correctly,
- a connecting cable between the MAU port and the station known for certain to be working correctly,
- an MAU port reset plug (to release jammed MAU ports),
- a miniature network (Figure 7.2)

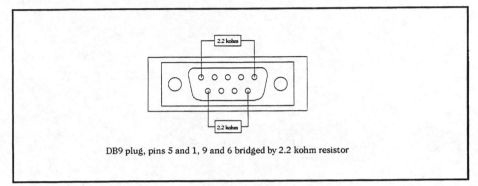

DB9 plug, pins 5 and 1, 9 and 6 bridged by 2.2 kohm resistor

Figure 7.2   Miniature network for Token Ring

7.3.2 Symptoms of concentrator problems

Problems in concentrators nearly always come to notice as a result of beaconing in the network. The cause can usually be traced to jammed relays or – indirectly – a faulty interface card keeping the relay permanently closed.

7.3.3 Diagnosing concentrator problems

To narrow down the area of the fault, the beaconing packet first needs to be analysed using a protocol analyser. Beaconing packets, containing the address of the next station upstream, are sent by any station no longer receiving tokens or data packets (at the end of the Claim Token process). The area of the fault is now known to comprise this neighbouring station, including all the cables and concentrators adjacent to it. To get the network back on stream as quickly as possible, the first step is to remove from the ring the concentrator which has been localised, along with all the stations connected to it, and replace it with a working unit. The precise source of the fault in the rump network can then be tracked down by connecting a miniature network and systematically replacing the components (MAU cables), network card etc. known to be functioning correctly.

Repeaters and hubs (star couplers)

8.1 Repeater problems

8.1.1 Repeaters in Ethernet

Repeaters are usually included to connect or extend parts of the network which would otherwise exceed the maximum permissible length of cabling or number of stations. Note that a maximum transceiver distance of 50 metres applies for repeaters too – that is, if the LAN segments that are being linked are more than 100 metres apart, half-repeaters will need to be used. Half-repeaters consist of a pair of repeaters connecting two sub-networks via fibre-optic links of up to 1000 metres. The units used are generally modular multi-port repeaters or star couplers rather than simple repeaters. These can link up a number of segments, irrespective of the type of cable used (twisted pair, optical fibre, type 1 etc.). Each of the segments separated by repeaters is limited in the number of stations it may contain. As well as this, repeaters must only be nested to a depth of four.

- 10Base5:
  - maximum distance between two repeaters: 500 m.
  - maximum number of stations per segment: 100
  - maximum distance between two stations: 5 segments or 3000 m (5 x 500 + 2 x 50 AUI + 4 x 50 AUI).
- 10Base2:
  - maximum distance between two repeaters: 185 m.
  - maximum number of stations per segment: 30
  - maximum distance between two stations: 5 segments or 1425 m (5 x 185 + 2 x 50 AUI + 8 x 50 AUI).
- FOIRL (Fibre Optic Inter-Repeater Link):
  - maximum length of optical fibre link between repeaters: 1000 m.
  - maximum of 2 FOIRLs per segment.

The reason for this is the maximum permitted slot time (the slot time equals twice the signal transit time between the two stations furthest apart), which is restricted to 51.2 µs.

Every repeater and every additional cable adds delays to the transit time and therefore increases the slot time. The greater the signal transit time between two stations, the greater is the risk of collisions and the lower the efficiency of the network (*see also* Chapter 12: Network Performance).

8.1.2   Repeater functions

Present-day repeaters are responsible for the following functions:

- regeneration of signal amplitude and removal of phase jitter on clock edges.
- buffering of one data packet (buffered repeater) to enable the signal to be sent on with correct timing.
- carrier sensing: checking the data line for activity before sending the signal on.
- generating the preamble: every Ethernet data packet begins with a sequence of 62 bits consisting of 1010 1010 1010 ... which is used to synchronise network users' receive chips. The receive chips currently in use require about 10 bit cycles to complete the synchronisation process; a few additional bits are absorbed by the send circuitry and the cabling.

It is therefore necessary for the repeater to fill the entire preamble, otherwise it would be 'used up' by no later than the second repeater.

- extending fragments to at least 96 bits using jam signals. This ensures that collisions will be properly detected throughout the network.

- detection of collisions.

- generation of jam signals: if a repeater detects a collision it sends a jam signal to all the segments connected, so as to act as soon as possible to prevent data being send to the rest of the segment. The jam signal may contain any arbitrary data pattern, but the first 62 bits must be set to 1010 1010 1010 ... – that is, the preamble sequence. The minimum jam signal length is 96 bits; and an important secondary condition is that a jam signal must not contain a correct checksum.

- self-test.

- errors at higher levels, such as incorrect frame check sequences (FCS), wrong packet sequence etc., are not detected.

8.1.3 Problems in Ethernet networks with repeaters

Valuable help in trouble-shooting is provided by noting whether, and if so how many and what types of repeater are installed in a network:

8.1.3.1 Localising collisions

Collisions are caused by two data packets arriving at the same time. The two signals are added together, resulting in a doubling of the signal voltage. In the worst case, a packet will take 51.2 µs to travel from one end of the cable to the other and back (if IEEE 802.3 specifications are adhered to) – that is, 512 bit cycles, or 64 bytes. In other words: a data packet can travel along the cable for a maximum of 25.51 µs before the last station detects it via its carrier sensing function, during which time it may send a packet of its own, thus causing a collision. After another 25.51 µs this collision will reach the original sending station. What this means is that any 'normal' collision has to happen within the first 64 bytes. (There are also collision packets which occur later than this and are known as 'late collisions'; however, these only occur in illegally long segments.)

Repeaters detect these collisions and send a jam signal to the connected segments. The collisions in one LAN segment thus produce 'runt' packets or 'remote collisions' (other names for these jam signals) in the other segments. On a purely physical level, these runt packets are valid signals with the correct voltage amplitude and a correct preamble but no meaningful data (hence, a jam signal). However, they are shorter than 64 bytes and do not have a correct frame check sequence. Remote collisions therefore differ from 'local collisions' in having the correct signal amplitude.

Runt frames – short packets – may also have other causes, such as incorrect protocol implementation or faulty interface cards. These runt frames, however, typically have a correct FCS and at least partially decodable data content, which allows them to be distinguished from jam runts or 'remote collisions'. If you encounter a large count of runt frames in one of your segments and the FCS in these runts is not a valid one, this suggests that your runt frames are nothing other than collisions or fragments of collisions 'imported' by a repeater. If a typical development of runt frames over time in the segment affected is recorded and this is compared with the corresponding record of collisions(!) in neighbouring segments (coupled via repeaters), the source of all the collisions can be systematically localised.

8.1.3.2 MAU jabber lock-up

Another major class of symptoms derives from the repeater's MAU jabber lock-up failsafe. If a repeater port is not connected to a segment and has not been fitted with a terminating resistor in its place, the repeater will send 5 ms of jam signals with 0.01 ms gaps. (This is to avoid triggering the network cards' jabber lock-up function – if a receive module encounters jabber frames longer than 5 ms it will send its own jam signals to silence the jabber station.) If an investigation with a network analyser shows evidence of jabber frames 5 ms long (= 6250 bytes) and 10 μs (100-byte) apart it can be concluded that there is an open repeater port or a connected segment with an open cable. In a case of this sort, more intelligent repeaters will carry out 'auto-partitioning': that is, they will automatically disconnect the affected segment from the remainder of the network.

8.1.3.3 Phantom addresses

When examining network user lists or statistics, readers of this book will certainly have encountered on more than one occasion source or destination addresses like those below:

The address 5555-5555 or AAAA-AAAA often appears as the send address of a potentially faulty packet. The same thing crops up in the decoding of a runt frame. At first glance, this may seem to be a mysterious bit error or transmission fault, but if we look at the corresponding binary the hex notation begins to make sense:

- 5555 5555 works out as
  0101 0101 0101 0101 0101 0101 0101 0101

and

- AAAA AAAA converts to binary as
  1010 1010 1010 1010 1010 1010 1010 1010.

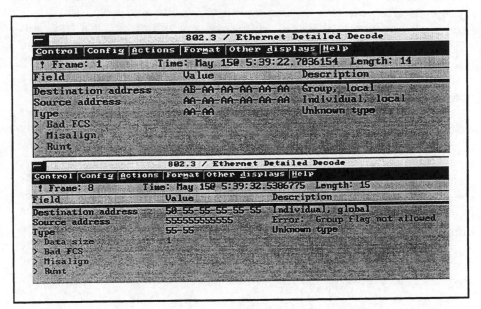

Figure 8.1

These 1010... sequences are the jam signals transmitted by the sending station as soon as a collision is detected. The content of the jam (interference) signal to be sent is not specified, but will usually be a 101010 sequence (in fact, for jam sequences sent by FOIRLS the first 62 bits ~must~ consist of zeroes and ones, with the first bit being 1). It therefore makes a good deal of sense to find out from the manufacturer how the jam sequences are implemented: this could be key evidence in finding out where the jam signals are coming from. The minimum length of jam signals is 96 bits, and the frame must not contain a correct FCS. In other words, these 'phantom addresses' are simply jam signals which have been identified as faulty packets with an attempt to display the send or receive address.

8.1.3.4 Missing packets

If a station does not keep to the required minimum inter-frame spacing gap of 9.6 µs between two data packets, most repeaters will be unable to repeat these packets. The packets will not be sent on and will be lost. This will only be noticed by higher protocol levels, which will react appropriately by requesting a fresh send of the packets. An inter-frame gap may be too short for a number of reasons. Some stations send a data packet very quickly immediately after a collision, but otherwise behave normally. Others always send right on the 9.6 μs limit or below.

Another cause is the frequent occurrence of packet fragments. Every repeater is given the task of padding out to 96 bits any packet fragments shorter than this minimum (including the preamble). So, if a fragment arrives with a length of 64 bits, for example (including the preamble), the repeater will add 32 bits of padding to the 64 it has received, thereby reducing the gap to the next data packet by 32 bits, or 3.2 μs. This can give rise to jabber packets in nested networks.

Later-model repeaters are therefore able to keep the inter-packet spacing constant. But performance problems at the protocol level can easily be rooted at repeater level. If a file transfer via a repeater takes noticeably longer than within the same segment, it is a good idea to check the inter-frame spacing and the sequence numbers of the individual packets (as specified by the respective protocol) before and after the repeater. For instance, if all the packets are present, with their correct sequence numbers, before a repeater in TCP/IP, but there are continual gaps in the sequence after the repeater, the repeater is the cause. As a result, file transfer will often go through at only 50 kbytes/sec instead of 300–600 kbytes/sec, as the lost packets have to be repeated.

8.1.3.5 Earthing problems

A network segment must only be earthed at one point. If an earthed repeater and an earthed terminating resistor form a current loop, and if there is an electrical potential difference between the earth for the terminating resistor and that for the repeater, there will be currents flowing along the network cable. These currents may result in sizeable interference, collisions and not infrequently in the total breakdown of the network.

8.1.3.6 Problems due to excessive nesting

If a data packet not only has to travel over a long length of cable, but also has to pass through a number of repeaters, the maximum permissible signal transit time of 51.2 μs can easily be exceeded (because every repeater adds its own delay component). The greater the maximum possible signal transit time, the less efficiently the CSMA/CD mechanism will work (*see also* Section 12.2). The result will be frequent collisions (most in the form of late collisions, that is, collisions longer than 64 bytes) and reduced network performance. It is therefore always best to keep careful track of the exact network topology and the lengths of cable used. As mentioned earlier, the nesting of repeaters is limited to a depth of four.

8.1.3.7 Hardware problems

If hardware problems are suspected, a check on the power supply, the plugs and the repeater self-test will provide answers.

8.1.4 Token Ring and FDDI

In Token Ring and FDDI, all active stations in the ring act as repeaters. Problems arise here principally when the maximum permissible distance between two stations is exceeded after a number of stations have logged out of the ring (in FDDI this affects DAS/Dual Attached Stations and SAS/Single Attached Stations with optical bypass switches).

- Maximum distance between two stations:

  - Token Ring, 4 Mbits/sec: 375 metres.

  - Token Ring, 16 Mbits/sec: 145 metres.

  - FDDI: 2000 metres.

These parameters must always be strictly observed when planning and operating ring networks.

8.2 Problems with star couplers (multi-port repeaters)

As far as the operating principle is concerned, star couplers (hubs) are simply multi-port repeaters, but in practice they usually offer a wider range of integrated functions integrated into them. As a rule they can connect up more segments than a conventional multi-port repeater, and work irrespective of the cable type (coax, IBM Type 1, optical fibre etc.). Optical star couplers allow considerably longer fibre optic routes between two hubs than between two standard repeaters (up to 2000 metres). However, there is no unified standard for these units.

8.2.1 Optical star couplers without repeater functions

Optical star couplers of the first generation do not have repeater functions and are mainly simple converters from coaxial or twisted-pair media to optical fibre. They hardly ever fulfill such repeater functions as:

- regeneration of the amplitudes and removal of phase jitter on clock edges.

- buffering of a number of data packets (retiming) to enable the signal to be sent on with correct timing.

- carrier sensing (checking the data line for activity before sending the signal on).

- preamble generation.

- extension of fragments to at least 96 bits.

- collision detection.

As all they do is convert a voltage to light output, these components do not add any appreciable delay and, according to the manufacturers' information, can be cascaded 'to any depth' (but follow this with care!). The restrictions for Ethernet accordingly apply only before and after the conversion of the signal. The components themselves are not made to any existing standard.

State-of-the-art optocouplers often have the following integrated control functions:

- collision detection,

- extension of fragments,

- auto-partitioning (automatic disconnection of problem segments),

- jabber control,

- adjustment of the optical send strength in stages,

- facility to set up redundant routes: if the hubs are connected in ring topology, an alternative signal path can automatically be selected if another one fails.

- retiming and amplitude regeneration is usually only possible by means of additional retiming boards.

8.2.2   Star couplers with repeater functions

Star couplers with repeater functions satisfy all the repeater functions defined in the Ethernet standard. When buying one of these, always check whether the component in question provides interfaces to network diagnosis and/or management systems.

8.2.3   Problems with star couplers in Ethernet networks

8.2.3.1 Problems with optical star couplers not conforming to repeater standards

If optical star couplers not conforming to repeater standards are used in extended cascades, serious problems often arise:

- runt packets,
- short inter[-]frame [spacing] gap,
- noisy signals (when using optocouplers without retiming boards, as the amplitude is not regenerated and phase jitter is not removed).

8.2.3.2 Light output problems

Most optocoupler modules in star couplers allow adjustment of the light strength at which the converted signal will be transmitted. If the light output is too low, there may be transmission problems, especially where a data packet has to be sent via a number of optical fibre links. Comparative measurements on the separate optical fibre links and a check on the adjustable parameters would then be useful. Symptoms of light output problems include a large number of runt packets and poor network performance.

8.2.3.3 Hardware problems

As with simple repeaters, if hardware problems are suspected, a check on the power supply, the plugs and the self-test will provide answers.

9

Bridges and routers

Bridges are network components connecting parts of the network with each other. This is carried out at OSI Layer 2 – in other words, they receive, store, filter and send all incoming data packets independently of protocols. As well as connecting networks of the same or different types, their main task is to prevent the spread of local data traffic onto the whole network.

9.1 Types of bridge

There are three basic types of bridge: local bridges, remote bridges and multi-port bridges. Local segments in networks are connected together directly. Links via remote bridges are made using long-distance links. Multi-port bridges are able to link together up to 8 sub networks. The structure and functions of bridges are very much more complex than with repeaters, and the scope for problems is correspondingly greater.

9.2   Linking networks of different types

When linking networks of different types, the following basic problem areas need to be considered:

1) All three topologies involved use different frame formats. Every transfer of a data packet from one network type to another therefore requires a reformatting operation and additional use of the CPU.

2) Ethernet, Token Ring and FDDI use different transfer rates. If an extensive sequence of data packets is being transferred from a 16 Mbits/sec Token Ring to a 10 Mbits/sec 802.3 CSMA/CD network, the connecting bridge will not be able to send the packets at the same speed as they are received. The packets need to be buffered, in the hope that the buffer does not overflow.

3) Another major problem which is often given too little attention involves timeouts in the higher layers. If a counter in a Layer 3 protocol runs out before a packet has arrived at the receiving station in the slower LAN, the sending station will start a fresh attempt to transmit the packet. After a number of failed attempts, it will conclude that the destination is not available. This behaviour creates extra network load.

4) One of the most serious problems concerns the different frame lengths used on the different networks. The maximum frame length laid down for 802.3 is 1518 bytes. For 802.5 there is only an indirect limitation: the standard value of 10 ms for the maximum token holding time. (For a 4 Mbits/sec ring, this implies a maximum frame length of 4,500 bytes, and for a 16 Mbits/sec ring 17,800 bytes!) If an overlong data packet arrives, there is no alternative but to reject it. At Level 2 there is no mechanism for splitting a packet into a number of parts and reassembling it.

9.3   Critical bridge parameters

The following critical bridge parameters may be the cause or source of transmission problems in bridges.

9.3.1   Throughput capacity and throughput rate

The throughput capacity is given in frames per second, with manufacturers usually taking the shortest possible frame length for the network topology in question. On the other hand, where throughput is given in bytes per second, the figures usually refer to the respective maximum possible frame length!

Throughput capacity and throughput rate should be checked, especially when dealing with older models of bridge. If the various frame lengths on which the specifications are based are taken into account, most manufacturers' figures for throughput capacity and throughput rate are precise enough and will not need to be double-checked by measurement. Current-model bridges have throughput capacities well in excess of the frame rate occurring in practice, which means that bottlenecks caused by limited throughput capacity now rarely occur.

9.3.2 Loss of data packets

There are a number of conditions under which a correctly functioning bridge will fail to transfer a data packet:

- Damaged or mutilated data packets such as runts, jabbers, collisions and fragments of collisions in Ethernet and line errors or burst errors in the Token Ring.

- Data packet lifetime over-range: Although a bridge does not examine the time stamp on a data packet (this is reserved to the higher protocol layers), it can place a limit on the delay time of a packet inside the bridge. If this delay time is exceeded, the packet is deleted. A faulty, overlong or short delay time can cause sizeable problems to network operation.

9.3.3 Buffering

The bridge's buffer is full and unable to accept any further packets.

9.3.4 Data packets too long

If the maximum permitted packet length for the destination sub-network is exceeded, the higher protocol layers are forced to send shorter packets. The maximum packet length that can be transferred by a bridge can also be set manually and is often a major cause of performance problems. For example, if we compare the boot procedure for a client in the same sub-network as the server with the same process where the two participating stations are on opposite sides of a bridge, the markedly longer time taken for the same process when a wrongly configured bridge is involved is apparent at a glance. Problems arise especially when time-critical applications like LAT are also involved.

9.3.5   Changes to packet sequence

As a rule, bridges transfer packets in the same order as they are received. However, if the bridge is using distributed load-sharing (DLS) – where the packets are sent over a number of redundant links or bridge ports, and do not arrive in exactly the same order as they are sent (a non-FIFO load-sharing process) – only those protocols which can tolerate changes to the packet sequence (TCP/IP, XNS, IPX ...) will be able to communicate successful across the bridge. For example, UDP (User Datagram Protocol) relies on finding the correct packet sequence. In an application set up using UDP, any irregularity in the transfer sequence will need to be corrected, which is often not done. For this reason, UDP applications will often work without trouble within a local segment but throw up sizeable problems when transmitted across bridges or routers.

9.3.6   Address tables

Most bridges have a self-learning function which enables them to set up and maintain a dynamic address base. All sender addresses on each side of the bridge can be collected and used as a basis for the transfer decision to be made for each data packet.

In addition, an 'ageing' algorithm ensures that the address table only includes stations which are currently active and that no confusion arises when addresses are moved or the topology is changed. (Addresses which have reached a certain 'age' since they were last required are simply deleted. The maximum achievable age can also usually be entered manually: 10–1,000,000 seconds.)

Alongside the dynamic address base described above, there usually exists a static address table which needs to be set up manually, and which may also contain broadcast or group addresses. Operation solely on the basis of the static address table is also known as 'protected mode'.

Faulty or incomplete address tables are among the most frequent causes of errors in local networks where bridges are involved. If it is impossible to set up a connection across a bridge, therefore, the address tables are the first thing to check. The same applies for any filter table which is included.

9.3.7   Filter table

If used correctly and in moderation, bridge filters are a useful way of excluding certain fault situations from the start and keeping the load down. Filters can be defined according to various criteria, such as send address, receive address, type field or an individual bit mask. As well as this, they can be logically combined with themselves or with other filters. The following potential sources of faults go hand in hand with the use of bridge filters: Over-complex filter structures, whose effect cannot be foreseen in every operational situation, may result in unwished-for filtering under certain operating conditions. Where multi-port bridges are used in redundant areas of the network, it must be remembered that, in back-up situations (fault conditions), data which normally have their own transmission path may also be carried by the back-up port. Filters therefore need to be checked to ensure that they do not hinder 'emergency operation' in back-up mode. Some types of bridge cause considerable losses of throughput when extensive filtering is used.

9.3.8   Spanning tree and source routing

If two sub-networks are available via more than one route within the network (redundant linking), there is a need for a procedure to determine the optimum route at any time between the sender and the receiver. In the Ethernet world, the most commonly used algorithm is 'spanning tree' and in token rings 'source routing'. Along with explicit route assignment for the data to be transferred, these algorithms also ensure that the network is free of packet loops.

If bridges which do not support any of these algorithms are implemented in a network which is not free of packet loops (that is, a network with redundant connections), the result will be 'rogue' packets permanently circling round loops in the network. This is because every bridge will be transferring every packet it receives via all its output ports (unless this is prevented by address tables or filter tables). This will cause multiple copies of packets.

Although one of these multiple packets will reach its intended destination, it will be at the potential cost of one or more of the copies of the data frame going round and round the network as a 'rogue', and adding measurably to the load on it. If the list of stations in a sub-network sending or receiving the most packets is sprinkled with sender or receiver addresses outside the segment, 'rogues' are the likely culprits. The network should then be checked for the presence of redundant connections, or, if the network is intentionally of redundant construction, the bridges installed should be checked to see that they have loop suppression mechanisms implemented.

In addition, spanning tree and source routing can markedly affect the throughput capacity of a network. The proper implementation and set-up of the algorithms used is important, and should especially be checked in LAN-LAN links with different transmission speeds and in LAN-WAN links. This is done in the Ethernet spanning tree algorithm by allocating a 'route cost' to each sub-network (1000 / transmission speed in Mbits/sec). The route with the least cost is then selected for data transfer. If this route cost is not defined with sufficient care, transfer bottlenecks may come about very quickly on some sections (e.g. WAN routes).

In the source routing system used in token rings, a 'Route Discovery Frame' is transmitted by the sending station. Every bridge passed by the route discovery frame enters its identification in the data packet (along with other data). On receiving this 'explorer' frame, the receiving station returns it to the sending station by the same route. One of these route discovery frames is sent by each possible route, and returned by the same route by the receiving station, so that in complex networks a number of these frames will be sent. The route of the RDF returning to the sender most quickly is usually considered the optimum transmission route (in some cases the specification may allow for further selection criteria besides time). However, this does mean that, as the network load increases, the overhead frames for route selection will also increase in number, which in itself adds to the load, just when the network is at its most critical.

When a combination of spanning tree and source routing algorithms is used, the two are kept completely separate and no 'mixed' spanning tree/source routing routes are allowed. The two systems stay in two separate worlds, with no communication between them. The only way of combining them is by using a source-routing-to-spanning-tree bridge.

Destination	Transparent bridge	Bridge with source routing
Orientation	Connection-dependent	Connection-oriented
Transparency	Fully transparent	Non-transparent
Configuration	Automatic	Manual
Routing	Non-optimised	Optimised
Tracing	Learning from experience	Search frame
Malfunctions	Handled by bridges	Handled by hosts
Complexity	In bridge	In hosts

Figure 9.1   Comparison of transparent bridge and bridge with source routing

9.3.9   Wrong mode: Ethernet V. 2.0 vs. IEEE 802.3

With network cards from a number of manufacturers, error behaviour can still be caused by a bridge set to the wrong mode, i.e. Ethernet V2.0 instead of IEEE 802.3 or vice versa. However, most of the products now on the market automatically detect which type of Ethernet packet they are handling, and behave appropriately.

9.3.10 No packet length limit

On the token ring or FDDI side of a token ring/FDDI-to-Ethernet link, packet length must be restricted to 1500 bytes, as packets longer than this will be rejected by the bridge.

9.3.11 Differences in protocol implementation

Communication problems across bridges otherwise working correctly can be caused not only by differences in the implementation of broadcast addresses, but also by incompatibilities at higher protocol layers (e.g. netware).

9.3.12 Problems with remote bridge cables

It often happens that the data medium by which two remote bridges communicate with each other is under-dimensioned or of poor quality. In both cases, this results in the need for packets to be re-sent (from timeouts during overload periods and through loss of packets if the line is bad). This problem can be solved by using data compression or switching to lines with a higher transfer bandwidth. Both cases recommend checking the loading and quality of the line with a protocol analyser.

9.3.13 Wrong ring speed (Token Ring)

If the ring speed has been set up incorrectly, this will cause beaconing and ring purges in some bridges.

9.4   Functions of the various types of network

Taking the three most common network topologies – Ethernet, token ring and FDDI – there are nine possible combinations that can result from coupling up sub-networks of these three network types. The following survey of the different bridges required in each case to link the two topologies summarises the functions and main problems of these special bridges.

9.4.1   Bridge from Ethernet to Ethernet

The only thing liable to cause problems in this arrangement is overloading of the destination LAN, preventing the linking bridge from sending on the packets it receives, so that the buffer overflows and packets are lost.
Function of bridge:

- buffering of packets received during heavy loading of destination segment.

9.4.2   Bridge from Token Ring to Token Ring

Unlike IEEE 802.3 bridges, token ring bridges are unlikely to be troubled by an overload on the target LAN, as the bridge picks up the token at regular intervals in the same way as every other station, enabling it to send on its data packets.
Functions of bridge:

- collecting sent packets from the ring,
- setting A and C bits (dummy)

9.4.3   Bridge from FDDI to FDDI

Exactly the same applies as for token-ring-to-token-ring bridges.
Functions of bridge:

- collecting sent packets from the ring,
- setting A and C bits (dummy)

9.4.4   Bridge from Ethernet to Token Ring

Apart from the requirement for the bridge to generate priority bits for the 802.3 packets it receives, there are generally no problems.

Functions of bridge:

- reformat frames,
- reverse bit sequence (address bits),
- calculate new checksum (FCS),
- generate dummy priority,
- compensate for differing transfer rates.

9.4.5   Bridge from Token Ring to Ethernet

In the 802.5 frame format, the 'A' and 'C' bits in the frame status byte are set to inform the sending station that the destination station has received the frame and copied it to its receive buffer. Automatic setting of these bits by the bridge will work – but only until such time as the destination station is not ready to receive. Then the problems will start!

Functions of bridge:

- reformat frames,
- reverse bit sequence (address bits),
- calculate new checksum (FCS),
- ignore priority,
- set A and C bits (dummy),
- compensate for differing transfer rates,
- reject data packets if too long.

9.4.6   Bridge from Ethernet to FDDI

As with bridges from Ethernet to token ring, the bridge has to generate priority bits.

Functions of bridge:

- reformat frames,
- reverse bit sequence (address bits),

- calculate new checksum (FCS),
- generate dummy priority,
- compensate for differing transfer rates.

9.4.7   Bridge from FDDI to Ethernet

In the FDDI frame format, as in token ring, the 'A' and 'C' bits in the frame status byte are set to inform the sending station that the destination station has received the frame and copied it to its receive buffer. Here again, if the bridge sets these bits automatically, this will work only as long as the destination station is ready to receive. The sender in the FDDI network will be told that the frame has arrived, even if the Ethernet station is not active at all.

Functions of bridge:

- reformat frames,
- reverse bit sequence (address bits),
- calculate new checksum (FCS),
- ignore priority,
- set A and C bits (dummy),
- compensate for differing transfer rates,
- reject data packets if too long.

9.4.8   Bridge from Token Ring to FDDI

Overloading of the destination LAN can never happen in token-ring-to-FDDI bridges, as the frame forwarding capacity of FDDI is several times greater than the data throughput. However, we still have the problem of the A and C bits in the frame status byte.

Functions of bridge:

- collect sent packets from the ring,
- set A and C bits (dummy)
- compensate for differing transfer rates.

9.4.9   Bridge from FDDI to Token Ring

Here again, the A and C bits in the frame status byte must somehow be set without this indicating actual confirmation of receipt.

Functions of bridge:

- collect sent packets from the ring,

- set A and C bits (dummy)

- compensate for differing transfer rates.

9.5   Routers

Routers are network components which link up parts of networks at OSI Layer 3 level. Whether a data packet is transferred, and if so, by which routes, depends on the higher protocol layers of the data packet. The higher layers of a protocol are usually able to determine more or less optimal routes and send their data by these routes.

Routes are determined using a number of algorithms. Two of the most common are Vector Distance (Bellman-Ford) routing and Link State or SPF (Shortest Path First) routing.

9.5.1   Vector Distance (Bellman-Ford) Routing

In vector distance routing, the distance between the separate gateways is given in 'hops', where a hop denotes each further gateway/router between the starting segment and the destination network.

Each gateway sets up a table of the possible routes and their availability, measured in 'hops', and sends it at periodic intervals to the adjacent gateways, which do the same in turn.

The drawbacks to this algorithm are that route changes only spread across the network slowly, and that the size of the route update data is proportional to the size of the network (because every routing update includes an entry for every possible route).

9.5.2   Link State or Shortest Path First Routing

In SPF routing, every gateway has two tasks: firstly, to test the status of directly available adjacent gateways, and secondly, to send routing tables of the link status of adjacent gateways, as a broadcast to all the gateways. On the one hand, this makes the size of the routing update packet independent of the size of the network, as it is only the directly adjacent gateways whose status is transmitted, and on the other, it means that every router has an updated routing table covering the whole of the network. As a result, the optimum routes are calculated only by the router concerned, and there is no dependence on the route distances calculated by the other routers (as in vector distance routing).

To prevent misrouted data packets ('rogues') circulating, 'time to live' counters are implemented in the higher routable protocols: once these run out, the next gateway will take the packet out of the data stream. Another important function concerns what is known as fragmentation.

Different protocols and different network components usually support data packets of different maximum lengths. To enable longer packets to be routed into environments only supporting shorter packet lengths, the packet needs to be split up, that is, fragmented. However, when dynamic route optimisation is employed it is quite possible that – as with individual, non-fragmented data packets – the separated fragments may arrive at the receiver in a different order from the one they were originally sent in. Most protocols can live with this, and will re-arrange the fragments into their original sequence. Other protocols, however, cannot do this (UDP), and therefore have limited routability.

The aim of this short section was merely to provide a brief introduction to problems which might be encountered with routers. For a more comprehensive examination of router problems, we would need to go into the various higher protocols in detail, which is beyond the scope of this book. The following examples are therefore restricted to the lower levels, and give a summary of the most common router problems at levels 1 and 2.

9.5.3   Problems with routers and their causes

- Symptom:
  No connection.

  - Cause (1):
    Router not active.

  - Action:
    Check router ports, self-test.

  - Cause (2):
    Protocol not active.

  - Action:
    Send echo packets for the protocol used through the router (ping, ARP), enable the protocol.

- Cause (3):
Selected filter settings blocking certain stations or segments.

- Action:
Check filter tables.

- Symptom:
Very long response times.

  - Cause (1):
Overloading of router buffer.

  - Action:
Monitor activity of stations using the router, check response times using echo packets.

  - Cause (2):
Problems with routing algorithm, re-routing, causing timeouts and retransmissions.

  - Action:
Check router protocol using protocol analyser, especially in token ring networks.

- Symptom:
Beaconing of destination ring whenever routing attempted.

  - Cause (1):
Wrong ring speed at router port (4/16 Mbits/sec).

  - Action:
Check repeater port and reconfigure.

10

Network problems: symptoms – causes – actions

This chapter is designed to be used for reference and lists a wide variety of symptoms and their possible causes, systematically organised according to the OSI layers model and by the different network topologies. The 'Action' heading offers tips on solving the problem. The symptoms/ causes/actions listed for the physical layer are covered in Chapter 6 in more detail. The tools frequently mentioned under the 'Action' heading, and how they are used, are discussed at length in Chapter 5.

10.1 Layer 1: the physical layer

10.1.1 Coaxial cable

- Symptom: Total failure of segment

- Diagnosis (1):
  Short circuit – the cable has shorted out at some point (cable test shows very low resistance).

- Cause (1):
  Kink in cable, faulty cable, vampire plug drilled too deep.

- Action:
  Check cable route, find location of short circuit using TDR meter.

- Diagnosis (2):
  Cable is open (cable test shows 50 ohms or very high resistance).

- Cause (2):
  Missing terminating resistor, poor connection between two cables, faulty cable, kink or sharp bend in cable.

- Action:
  Find location of short circuit using TDR meter (cable scanner).

- Diagnosis (3):
  Illegal voltages on network.

- Cause (3):
  Faulty MAUs, no earthing.

- Symptom:
  Intermittent loss of connection.

  - Diagnosis:
    Poor connection or no connection to the network cable itself.

  - Cause:
    BNC connector loose, vampire plug not drilled deep enough, AUI cable loose, wrong cable, wrong/faulty terminating resistor, earthing problems.

- Symptom:
  Unusually high number of collisions.

  - Diagnosis (1):
    Strong reflections in cable causing collisions.

  - Cause (1):
    Missing terminating resistor, faulty or incorrect terminating resistor, too many MAUs connected (100 in 10Base5, 30 in 10Base2).

  - Diagnosis (2):
    Earthing problems.

  - Cause (2):
    Multiple earthing of segment.

- Symptom:
Irregular or frequent collisions and fragments.

  - Diagnosis:
  Interference voltages being induced.

  - Cause:
  Cable acting as aerial: electromagnetic interference close to cable inducing voltages.

  - Action:
  Check for interference using multimeter or test noise level with cable tester. If interference detected, check cable routes for proximity to lifts/lift shafts, lighting ducts, electrical machinery, transformers etc. If this does not help, the frequency range of the interference can be found using an oscilloscope or spectrum analyser. This will supply pointers to the source of the trouble.

- Symptom:
Intermittent loss of connection or no link to new installation.

  - Diagnosis (1):
  Attenuation too high

  - Cause (1):
  Losses in cable, variations in impedance between connectors or in patch panels.

  - Diagnosis (2):
  Interference.

  - Cause (2):
  Induction of signals via vampire plug acting as mini-aerial.

10.1.2 Twisted pair cable

- Symptom:
Poor network performance, collisions, FCS errors, ring purges, beaconing.

  - Diagnosis:
  Crosstalk: when a signal is being carried by a cable pair, part of this signal may be induced in a neighbouring pair. This results in interference.

  - Cause:

Pins have been wrongly assigned, so that the signal is being carried by a pair of wires that are not twisted round each other (e.g.: pin 1 is twisted with pin 2, and pin 3 with pin 4, but the station is using 1 + 3 and 2 + 4 as pairs. This will cause crosstalk). Another cause may be that the cable is simply not twisted enough, so that it is not suitable for high-frequency signals.

- Symptom:
Irregular or frequent collisions and fragments.

  - Diagnosis:
  Interference being induced.

  - Cause:
  Electromagnetic interference close to cable inducing voltages. UTP (Unshielded Twisted Pair) is particularly susceptible to this.

  - Action:
  Measure interference voltage with multimeter or noise level using cable tester. If interference is detected, check cable routes for proximity to lifts/lift shafts, lighting ducts, electrical machinery, transformers etc. If this does not help, the frequency range of the interference can be found using an oscilloscope or spectrum analyser. This will provide pointers to the source of the trouble.

- Symptom:
Intermittent loss of connection or no link to new installation.

  - Diagnosis :
  Attenuation too high

  - Cause:
  Losses in cable, cable too long, variations in impedance between connectors or in patch panels. Telephone lines are often wired via a number of patch fields and unsuited to the transfer of high-frequency signals (this especially applies in Germany).

- Symptom:
No link to new installation.

  - Diagnosis:
  Test signals not reaching other station.

  - Cause:
  Reversed cores.

- Symptom:
Total failure of one station.

  - Diagnosis:
  Cable is open.

- Cause:
  Poor connection to cable, faulty cable.

- Action:
  Check with TDR meter and find location of fault.

10.1.3 Optical fibre links

- Symptom:
  No connection.

  - Diagnosis:
    A check for a fibre break can be carried out either using an OTDR (Optical Time Domain Reflectometer) or, over short distances, by a 'lighter test'. This involves holding a cigarette lighter against the cross-section of the fibre at one end of the cable and checking for light arriving at the other end using the naked eye. This will work for distances of up to several hundred metres.

  - Action:
    Check bending radii and switch to pair of intact cores.

- Symptom:
  Intermittent problems with connection.

  - Diagnosis:
    Excessive cable attenuation measured using optical performance loss unit.

  - Cause:
    Poor splices or too many splices. If the signal has to cross too many splices it will not get through.

  - Action:
    Inserting a repeater will provide a remedy.

10.2 Ethernet

- Symptom:
  Poor network performance.

  - Diagnosis (1):
    High count of FCS errors.

  - Cause (1):

Incorrect Frame Check Sequence errors – within limits – are a 'natural' side-effect of collisions (runts with bad FCS). So, if collisions are the source and the number of collisions is not too high, there is no reason to worry.

- Action:
Make a record of FCS errors and collisions against time using a protocol analyser, and compare the two graphs. FCS errors not caused by collisions will often trace back to faulty network interface cards.

- Diagnosis (2):
Signal noise and interference on the network.

- Cause (2):
The most common cause of noise is an unearthed or badly earthed section of the network.

- Action:
Check noise level using cable scanner or interference using multimeter. A network segment must only be earthed at one point, as otherwise electrical potential differences between two earthing points may manifest themselves as earth loop currents.

- Cause (3):
Electromagnetic interference affecting network cabling.

- Action:
Measure interference voltage with multimeter or noise level using cable tester. If interference is detected, check cable routes for proximity to lifts/lift shafts, lighting ducts, electrical machinery, transformers etc. If this does not help, the frequency range of the interference can be found using an oscilloscope or spectrum analyser. This will provide pointers to the source of the trouble. If none of this helps, there is nothing for it but to carry out a binary search.

- Cause (4):
Faulty network interface cards.

- Action:
If the network card is able to send and receive data packets (which can be seen via the AUI monitor plug) a conclusive pointer can often be obtained from a list – produced by a protocol analyser – showing the stations sending the most faulty packets. If the error packets are so mutilated that this list cannot be produced due to the lack of any send or receive addresses, the activity of a number of stations will need to be measured over a period of time, along with the number of faulty packets sent. If a correlation can be seen between the error

curve and the activity curve of one of the stations monitored, this is in all probability the source of the fault.

- Cause (5):
  Loose or faulty connectors.

- Action:
  Check connectors.

- Diagnosis (6):
  Collisions: to a certain extent, these are endemic to the system.

  - Cause (6):
    The usual causes of increased numbers of collisions are cable problems (cables too long), faulty network interface cards, too many repeaters or missing terminating resistors. To narrow down the root of the trouble, the first step is to find out whether the problem is 'late collisions' (runt frames) or ordinary 'early collisions'.

- Diagnosis (7):
  Late collisions are collisions occurring after the end of the 512-bit collisions window.

  - Cause (7):
    Cable too long: maximum segment lengths are 500 metres for 10Base5, 185 metres for 10Base2 and 100 metres for 10BaseT. There must be no more than 4 repeaters, each with a maximum cable length of 50 metres, between the two stations furthest apart (*see also* Chapter 6).

  - Action:
    Measure lengths with cable scanner.

  - Cause (8):
    Nesting of repeaters too deep. The longest possible communication route must have a maximum of 4 repeaters in it (may also result in jabber packets).

  - Action:
    Replace one of the repeaters with a bridge, or reconfigure the network.

  - Cause (9):
    Faulty MAU (carrier sensing problem).
  - Action (1): If a station is able to send and receive data packets (which can be seen via the AUI monitor plug) a conclusive pointer can often be obtained from a list – produced by a protocol analyser – showing the stations sending the most faulty packets. If the error packets are so mutilated that this list cannot be produced due to the lack of any send or receive addresses, the activity of a number of stations will need to be measured over a period of time, along with

the number of faulty packets sent. If a correlation can be seen between the error curve and the activity curve of one of the stations monitored, this is in all probability the source of the fault.

- Action (2):
  Binary search. If nothing else will provide an answer, connect a terminating resistor in the middle of the segment instead of a user. Using the protocol analyser, find out which half of the segment is producing collisions. Then sub-divide this half again; and so on, until the fault is located.

- Diagnosis (10):
  Early collisions: collisions occurring within the 512-bit collision window.

  - Cause (10):
    Faulty or missing terminating resistors.

  - Action (10):
    Check that all terminating resistors are present, and confirm the resistance with an ohmmeter: should be 48 ohms > R < 52 ohms.

  - Cause (11):
    Loose or faulty T connectors.

  - Action:
    Check connectors.

  - Cause (12):
    Too many connectors in one segment.

  - Action:
    Check the number of MAUs in each segment: maximum is 100 connectors (MAUs) in a 10Base5 segment, 30 in a 10Base2 segment.

  - Cause (13):
    Kink in a cable.

  - Action:
    Check for reflections using a cable tester to pin down the fault.

  - Cause (14):
    A cable not conforming to the 802.3 specification. Cables conforming to this specification are colour-marked every 2.5 metres (applies only for ThickLAN/10Base5). Connectors should only be inserted at these marks, to minimise reflections caused by a connection. Note: not all cables with BNC connections are 50-ohm cables. Although Ethernet will function over a few tens of metres using 75-ohm cables and the like, this will not work out in the long run. Always check the specifications of the cables used.

  - Action:

Check manufacturer's specifications (*see also* Chapter 6).

- Cause (15):
  Bridge or router buffer overloaded.

- Action:
  Check the statistics relating to the bridge (in particular, the number of rejected packets). Monitor network load. Find out which stations are producing most traffic for the bridge. Reconfigure the network so that the stations putting the most load on the bridge do not need to send via this bridge. Implement filters to prevent unnecessary forwarding of packets via the bridge.

- Symptom:
  Intermittent connection problems, network performance problems.

  - Diagnosis (1):
    Dribble bits: corrupted data packets with lengths which are not multiples of 8 bits, but with correct FCS.

  - Cause (1):
    Network interface cards sending a few extra bits after the FCS for the frame.

  - Action:
    Check the dribble frames using a protocol analyser. The cause, i.e. the faulty or unreliable network interface card, can be traced via the sender address.

  - Cause (2):
    Maximum permissible network length exceeded. The signal will or will not be adequate to travel the distance depending on which station is sending to which. This explains the intermittent nature of the problem.

  - Action:
    Check lengths using a cable tester and insert repeater or bridge as necessary. Check for occurrence of jabber packets using a protocol analyser.

  - Cause (3):
    Bridges and routers excessively cascaded, resulting in very long signal transit times and counters at protocol level constantly causing timeouts, so that packets need to be resent.

  - Action:
    Check response times (by sending pings or other echo packets and monitoring with protocol analyser). Check routing tables.

  - Diagnosis (4):

Runts, i.e. packets with a valid signal level but short of the minimum packet length of 64 bytes. By this definition, early collisions would also be counted as runts if the collision did not result in an illegally high signal level which allows them to be told apart. In small (short) networks based on coax cable, they should be practically non-existent, as the collisions will mostly occur within the preamble. They will be more common in longer coax-based networks and in 10BaseT networks: in 10BaseT networks the collisions occur inside the hubs. The resulting fragments are spread throughout the network. Over 99% of all runts come about through collisions spread to other parts of the segment via repeaters, star couplers etc. This is because, when a repeater detects a collision, it sends a 'jam' signal to the connected segments. The content of a jam signal is not specified (often 101010101), but is subject to the secondary condition that it must not contain a valid FCS. This means that collisions become visible beyond repeaters as runts with bad FCSs. The first distinction to be made is therefore between runts with valid FCSs and runts with bad FCSs.

- Diagnosis (5):
  Runts with bad FCSs derive from collisions in other parts of a segment, which are spread as jam signals.

- Action:
  Use a protocol analyser to record runts and collisions over time in all parts of the segment (in this context, 'part of a segment' means a part of the network separated from the rest of the segment by a repeater or star coupler). By comparing the number of runts and collisions in the various parts of the segment, a quick fix can be obtained on the section where the collisions appearing elsewhere as runts are occurring.

- Diagnosis (6):
  Runts with valid FCSs: usually the result of incorrect protocol implementation.

- Action:
  Where possible, decode the runt frames and identify the problem station from the send address. Some network components, such as bridges and routers, use runts to communicate with each other. If these runts are present on their network under normal conditions, there absence can cause problems.

- Diagnosis (7):
  Jabber frames – packets exceeding the maximum permissible length of 1518 bytes. In general, jabbers are related to serious network problems.

- Cause (7):

Duplicate earthing. If the network is earthed at more than one point, there may be DC currents on the network.

- Action:
Check earthing. The network must only be earthed at a single point.

- Diagnosis (8):
MAU jabber lock-up – jabber packets.

- Cause (8):
An important class of symptoms derives from the repeater's MAU jabber lock-up failsafe. If a repeater port is not connected to a segment and has not been fitted with a terminating resistor, it sends 5 ms of jam signals with 0.01 ms gaps (to avoid triggering the network cards' jabber lock-up function: if a receive chip encounters jabber frames longer than 5 ms it will send its own jam signals to silence the jabber station).

- Action:
Check using protocol analyser. If jabber frames 5 ms long (= 6250 bytes) and with 10 μs (100-bit) gaps are discovered, it can be concluded that there is an open repeater port or a connected segment with an open cable. In a case of this sort, more intelligent repeaters will carry out 'auto-partitioning': that is, they will automatically disconnect the affected segment from the remainder of the network.

- Cause (9):
Faulty network interface card/faulty MAU.

- Action:
Decode jabber frame and identify faulty network interface card by reference to address fields.

- Cause (10):
Inter-frame spacing gap too small. If a station does not keep to the required minimum inter-frame spacing gap of 9.6 μs between two data packets, most repeaters will be unable to duplicate the frame correctly. The packets will be passed on with short gaps and often mutate into jabber packets. This will only be noticed by the higher protocol levels, which will react accordingly by demanding a re-send of the packet.

- Action:
Check inter-frame spacing gaps using a protocol analyser. Check the stations sending with short gaps.

- Cause (11):
  Light output problems in optical fibre links. Most optocoupler modules in star couplers allow adjustment of the light strength at which the converted signal will be transmitted. If the light output is too low, there may be transmission problems, especially where a data packet has to be sent via a number of optical fibre links.

- Action:
  Comparative measurements on the separate optical fibre links and a check of the adjustable parameters.

- Symptom:
  A single network node has no connection.
  First, check whether the server is working and whether the station was still working until recently.

  - Cause (1):
    A sudden complete failure will usually be due to one of the following causes:
    - AUI plug not connected or loose,
    - break, short circuit or noise problem in connecting cable,
    - faulty network interface card.

  - Action:
    Check cable and connector, plus network interface card if necessary, and replace if appropriate. If a station known with certainty to be working correctly is available (multi-protocol PC: see Section 5.2), connect this in place of the faulty station to narrow down the location of the fault.

  - Cause (2):
    The ageing function in the bridge has been selected (the bridge deletes nodes from the forwarding table after a specified time with no sends), but the learn mode has not been set. As a result, the forwarding table will eventually lose all its entries, with no new network nodes being added.

  - Action:
    Print out forwarding table and set to learn mode.

  - Cause (3):
    Bridge port inactive or failed.

  - Action:
    Check bridge. Send echo packets through the bridge using a protocol analyser or a multi-protocol PC. Examine bridge statistics.

  - Cause (4):
    Filter in bridge set up in such a way that a specific station or group of stations is blocked.

- Action:
  Check bridge's filter tables.

- Cause (5):
  Connection between MAU and network cable or between network card and network faulty or loose.

- Action:
  Check connectors. Check that MAU is being supplied with power by the network card. Replace AUI cable with cable known with certainty to be functioning correctly.

- Cause (6):
  Duplicate Ethernet address (on DECNet).

- Action:
  Find duplicate address using protocol analyser: has a new station been installed recently? Change the Ethernet address.

- Cause (7):
  Duplicate network address (on TCP/IP).

- Action:
  Find duplicate address using protocol analyser and change the address.

- Cause (8):
  Wrong configuration of network card: wrong port active (coax port instead of AUI or vice versa) or selected interrupt already assigned.

- Action:
  Check configuration. It may help to replace the faulty station temporarily by one known with certainty to be functioning correctly (multi-protocol PC) to home in on the source of the fault and save the trouble of replacing hardware on spec.

- Cause (9):
  Network card hardware faulty or fuse blown.

- Action:
  Check whether the power supply to the MAU is intact. It may help to replace the faulty station temporarily by one known with certainty to be functioning correctly (multi-protocol PC) to home in on the source of the fault and save the trouble of replacing the network card on spec.

- Cause (10):
  MAU sending heartbeat signal, but network card interpreting this (as specified in standards) as SQE = Signal Quality Error (collision, deformed signal) and aborting transmission.

- Action:
  Monitor LEDs on MAU (if MAU does not have LEDs, AUI test connectors with LEDs can be inserted). If the SQE LED lights up every time a send is attempted, the MAU is configured for heartbeat, in which case the MAU's heartbeat signal should be switched off, or it will only support heartbeat operation.

- Cause (11):
  The opposite case: MAU sending no heartbeat signal, but network card waiting for read/write acknowledgement.

- Action:
  Switch MAU configuration to 'heartbeat' mode.

- Cause (12):
  A station is sending packets longer than the maximum packet length for which the bridge has been set up. Packets from this station are therefore rejected.

- Action:
  Monitor packet lengths occurring on the network and check against bridge configuration.

- Symptom:
  No connection between network segment or part of segment and remainder of network.

  - Cause (1):
    Repeater MAU in heartbeat mode, i.e. sending an acknowledgement signal to the repeater via the SQE line on every transmission from the repeater. Network card, however, interpreting this (as specified in standards) as SQE signal indicating collision or deformed signal. After a number of attempted transfers it will automatically disconnect the affected segment from the remainder of the network if it has this function integrated (auto-partitioning).

  - Action:
    Switch MAU from heartbeat mode to SQE operation. See also Section 4.2.

  - Cause (2):
    Bridge not active or bridge module not activated.

  - Action:
    Send echo packets (pings, etc.) into adjacent segment via the bridge. Check bridge settings. Self-test. Print out forwarding table for bridge. Check bridge statistics (number of rejected packets etc.). (See also Chapter 9.)

- Cause (3):
  The ageing function in the bridge has been selected (the bridge deletes nodes from the forwarding table after a specified time with no sends), but the learn mode has not been set. As a result, the forwarding table will eventually lose all its entries, with no new network nodes being added.

- Action:
  Print out forwarding table and set to learn mode.

- Cause (4):
  Filter in bridge set up in such a way that a specific station or group of stations is blocked.

- Action:
  Check bridge's filter settings.

- Symptom:
  Extremely high network load.

  - Cause:
    Routing or bridging problems.

  - Action:
    Use protocol analyser to identify most active stations and check network for routing or bridging problems. Are timeouts occurring? Systematic measurements of response times by means of echo packets will supply pointers to the source of the problems. Check tables of bridge and router statistics. How many packets have been rejected? Check bridges' forwarding tables and any filter settings.

- Symptom:
  Network slow, stations 'locking'.

  - Cause:
    The most common causes of poor network performance and stations 'locking' after logging in are large numbers of collisions (bursts) and above-average numbers of FCS errors.

  - Action:
    See: Collisions and FCS errors.

10.3 Token Ring

10.3.1 Faults endemic to the system

Like Ethernet, token ring networks have error conditions characteristic to the system which – provided a certain threshold value is not exceeded – are part of normal network operation. The following events will cause error messages:

- Station logs into ring

  - Active monitor:
    Ring Purge.

  - Station logging in:
    2 Duplicate Address Tests.

  - Downstream neighbour:
    1 Report NAUN Frame.

  - Station logging in:
    2–4 Request Initialization Frames.

  - Active monitor:
    Report Soft Error Frame (reports 1–4 lost tokens).

  - Downstream neighbour:
    Report Soft Error Frame (reports 2–4 burst errors).

  - Other stations:
    Report Soft Error Frame (reports around 1 lost frame).

- Station logs out of ring

  - Active monitor:
    Ring Purge.

  - Active monitor:
    1 Report Soft Error (reports 1–4 lost tokens).

  - Downstream neighbour:
    Report Soft Error Frame (reports 2–4 burst errors).

  - Other stations:
    Report Soft Error Frame (reports around 1 lost frame).

- Station on network switches off

  - Downstream neighbour and/or station with highest address:
    4 Claim Token Frames.

- New active monitor:
  Ring Purge.

- Downstream neighbour:
  Report Soft Error Frame (reports loss of old active monitor 1–4 burst errors).

- New active monitor:
  Report New Monitor Frame

- Downstream neighbour of old active monitor:
  Report NAUN Frame.

However, the following operating states should be given special attention:

- Ring purges not connected to stations logging in or out;

- Report Neighbour Notification Incomplete;

- Report Active Monitor Error;

- Active Monitor Changing;

- Beaconing/Streaming Beaconing.

Being a second-generation protocol, the token ring protocol also has a large number of integrated fault-diagnostic functions. These internal token ring messages are included in the following list of symptoms, as they can be tracked simply by monitoring the token ring protocol.

10.3.2 Token ring fault symptoms – causes – action

In alphabetical order by symptom:

- Symptom:
  Active Monitor Error or Active Monitor Change:
  indicates an error in the active monitor

  - Causes:
  a) The active monitor detects a 'Claim Token' frame, quits active monitor status and sends a 'Report Active Monitor Error' frame. This occurs if a standby monitor detects a fault in the active monitor. (Any active station in the ring which is not the active monitor is a standby monitor.)

  b) An active monitor detects an AMP frame (Active Monitor Present) which it did not originate. It sends a 'Report Active Monitor Error' frame with the sub-vector 2 (Duplicate Monitor).

c   A station in 'Monitor Contention Transit' mode detects a 'Claim Token' frame with its address as source address, but with a NAUN (Nearest Upstream Neighbour) address which does not match its NAUN address in memory. This station will now send a 'Report Monitor Error' frame with the sub-vector 3 (Duplicate Address during Monitor Contention). [The 'Monitor Contention' mode selects a new active monitor if the original active monitor fails or there is a hardware fault in the ring (*see also* Monitor Contention).]

* Symptom:
Address Recognized Error.

   * Cause:
   This error occurs if a station detects more than one AMP (Active Monitor Present) frame or else an SMP (Standby Monitor Present) frame not preceded by a corresponding AMP frame.

* Symptom:
Burst Errors
A Burst Error frame is sent if no signal is transmitted for 5 half-bits between the start and end delimiters of a frame.

   * Causes
   of this are hardware problems such as a faulty cable, network interface card/MAU or concentrator.

   * Action:
   Locate area of fault by decoding token ring messages: which is the error-reporting station, what stations are upstream from the error reporting station (by reference to list of active stations). Monitor the stations' traffic in the region of the fault. Check concentrator (self-test). Check cable using cable scanner.

* Symptom:
Beaconing.

   * Cause:
   Beaconing is the process by which the token ring attempts to regenerate itself after an electrical break in the signal route. The break will be noticed first by the station downstream from the fault. To pass on information about the fault, this station sends a 'Beaconing' frame to all other users, containing the address of the sending station plus the NAUN address. During beaconing no further stations can log into the ring. Each station forwards the Beaconing frame. If the NAUN of the station sending the Beaconing packet receives 8 beacon frames with its address, it assumes that it is faulty, logs out of the ring and carries out a self-test. If the result is positive, it logs back into the ring. After a specific time (usually 26 seconds), the station sending the Beaconing frames itself logs out, on the

assumption that it could itself be the source of the fault, and also carries out a self-test. At this point, if the cause of the fault has still not been corrected, the ring goes into 'Streaming Beacon State', indicating that the fault is of such a nature that the ring itself cannot correct it.

- Action:
  Analyse the Beaconing frames and trace the area of the fault from the addresses it provides for the sending station and its NAUN: the area of the fault comprises the station sending the Beaconing frame, its receive line, the sending station's NAUN and its send line and the concentrator(s)/MAU(s) between the two stations. All components within this fault area (network interface cards, concentrators, cables, connectors etc.) should now be inspected. The crucial step is correct determination of the fault area itself. It is therefore important to possess a diagnostic tool which can log into the token ring and analyse the beacon frames whatever its status (including beaconing).

- Symptom:
  Failed Insertion.

  - Cause:
    'Failed Insertion' indicates that a station has been unable to log into the ring. This may have the following causes:
    - Duplicate address: during its Duplicate Address Check (part of the logging-in process), the station logging in has detected a station in the ring with its own address.
    - The station has been unable to complete the 'Neighbour Notification Process'.
    - Station parameters not initialised or incorrectly initialised.

- Symptom:
  Frame Copied Error.

  - Cause:
    A 'Frame Copied' error occurs if a station in receive or repeat mode (meaning it should be either receiving the frame or copying it and forwarding it) detects that the Address Recognized bits are not zero, indicating that the frame has already been copied.

  - Possible cause:
    Duplicate MAC address.

  - Action:
    Check for Failed Insertion frames using protocol analyser.

- Symptom:
  Frequency Error.

  - Cause:
    Frequency errors occur if the ring clock and the quartz clock in the network card differ significantly from each other. Frequency errors are 'non-isolated errors', that is, they cannot be assigned to any particular station via the token ring protocol.

- Symptom:
  Intermittent faults and losses of connection.

  - Cause (1):
    Intermittent faults can have a wide variety of causes. The first questions to ask are: What changes have recently been made to the network topology? Do the faults occur periodically or at specific times?

  - Action:
    Record the main parameters, such as ring purges, load, token errors etc. against time using a protocol analyser.

  - Cause (2):
    A common cause of intermittent faults in relatively large rings is a situation where the distance to be covered by the token between two stations exceeds the permissible maximum. When a user logs out, this may result in the distance between the remaining stations exceeding the maximum permitted cable length, causing considerable problems (non-isolating errors, token errors etc.). In addition, the maximum distance between two stations is different for 4-Mbits/sec rings and 16-Mbits/sec rings.

  - Action:
    Check maximum possible distance between two stations:
    - Maximum distance for 4 Mbits/sec: 375 metres.
    - Maximum distance for 16 Mbits/sec: 145 metres.
    If a ring works satisfactorily at 4 Mbits/sec, there may still be serious problems for the same ring at 16 Mbits/sec.

- Symptom:
  Internal Error.

  - Cause:
    An 'Internal Error' frame is sent if a station detects an internal error which it can regenerate on its own. Internal errors are isolating errors, i.e. they can be assigned to particular stations.

  - Action:
    Decode error frames: localise and observe station.

- Symptom:
Isolating RSE Error.

  - Diagnosis:
Isolating RSE (Report Soft Error) errors are errors which can be narrowed down by the token ring protocol to a specific fault area: either a receiving station, a sending station, a concentrator or the cabling between two stations. Isolating errors are: line errors, burst errors, Address Recognized errors, Frame Copied errors, internal errors, Abort Delimiters. Symptoms are:
    - poor network performance,
    - stations 'locking'.

  - Causes
are usually line errors or burst errors, caused by:
    - short circuit in cable,
    - signal noise or crosstalk,
    - excessive token transfer time,
    - faulty adaptor card.

  - Action:
Decode the various RSE frames using a protocol analyser and trace the area of the fault. Inspect components affected within fault areas and replace if necessary. See also Beaconing, Line errors, Burst errors.

- Symptom:
No connection to server.
First check that the server is working and that the station has recently been functional.

  - Cause (1):
If the connection fails suddenly, the following causes are the most likely:
    - DB9 connector is loose or not connected,
    - break, short-circuit or noise problem in connecting cable,
    - faulty network interface card.

  - Action:
Check cable, connector and network interface card and replace if necessary. If a station known with certainty to be working correctly is available (multi-protocol PC), connect this in place of the faulty station to pin down the location of the fault.

  - Cause (2):
The ageing function in the bridge has been selected (the bridge deletes nodes from the forwarding table after a specified time with no sends), but the learn mode has not been set. As a result, the

forwarding table will eventually lose all its entries, with no new network nodes being added.

- Action:
Print out forwarding table and set to learn mode.

- Cause (3):
Bridge port inactive or failed.

- Action:
Check bridge. Send echo packets through the bridge using a protocol analyser or a multi-protocol PC. Examine bridge statistics.

- Cause (4):
Filter in bridge set up in such a way that a specific station or group of stations is blocked.

- Action:
Check filter tables for bridge.

- Symptom:
Intermittent loss of connection.

- Cause:
Duplicate MAC address: if a station with an address already active in the ring attempts to log in, it will receive a 'Request to Remove' frame.

- Action:
Filter 'Request to Remove' packets using protocol analyser. Analyse sender addresses.

- Symptom:
Extremely high load on network.

- Cause:
Routing or bridging problems.

- Action:
Use protocol analyser to identify most active stations and check network for routing or bridging problems. Are timeouts occurring? Systematic measurements of response times by means of echo packets will supply pointers to the source of the problems. Check tables of bridge and router statistics. How many packets have been rejected? Check bridges' forwarding tables and any filter settings.

- Symptom:
Network slow, stations 'locking'.

- Cause:
The most common causes of poor network performance and stations 'locking' after logging in are line errors or burst errors; also FCS

errors and unnecessary ring purges. The cause of these burst errors is usually a faulty receive cable for the error reporting station, a faulty send cable at the NAUN for this station or a faulty patch cable.

- Action:
Inspect network for line errors and burst errors. Where are line errors and burst error packets being sent from? Check concentrators and cabling upstream from error-reporting stations.

- Symptom:
Line Error.

  - Cause:
  A Line Error frame is sent if a station detects
    - an illegal code between the start and end delimiters of a frame,
    - an illegal code in the token,
    - in incorrect FCS (Frame Check Sequence).

  - Causes of this are hardware problems such as:
    - faulty cable,
    - faulty network interface card/MAU,
    - faulty concentrator.

  - Action:
  Locate area of fault by decoding token ring messages: which is the error-reporting station, what stations are upstream from the error reporting station (by reference to list of active stations).
    - Monitor traffic by stations in the region of the fault.
    - Check concentrator (self-test).
    - Check cable using cable scanner.

- Symptom:
Lost Frame Error.

  - Cause:
  A 'Lost Frame' error occurs if a station is in transfer mode and fails to receive a frame. This can happen, for example, when stations are logging in or out. This error is non-isolating and cannot be assigned to any particular area of faults.

  - Action:
  See Non-Isolating Errors.

- Symptom:
Monitor Contention.

  - Cause:
  Monitor Contention mode is the phase in which a new active monitor is selected after the original active monitor has failed or a hardware error has occurred somewhere in the ring. There may be one of the following *reasons* for this:

- The active monitor detects loss of signal.
- The AMP frame (Active Monitor Present) has not circulated round the full ring.
- The active monitor is not receiving enough of its own Ring Purge frames.
- The active monitor has not received a valid token before the Good Token timer runs out (= 2.6 seconds).
- The active monitor detects a Neighbour Notification Process.
- A station logs into the ring and cannot detect an active monitor.

The station which has detected one of the states listed above switches to Monitor Contention Transmit mode and sends Claim Token frames. It then starts a timer (the Monitor Contention Timer), which specifies how long the ring is permitted to stay in Monitor Contention mode. If this timer runs out, the station goes into beaconing. Each active station not yet in Monitor Contention mode compares its address with the Claim Token frame's source address. If this address is higher than its own, it repeats the Claim Token frame. If it is lower, it sends its own Claim Token frame. If a station receives three of its own Claim Token frames, it is the new active monitor. The ring is now back in Monitor Contention mode, and the new active monitor executes a ring purge, sets up a new token and sends a Report New Active Monitor frame to the configuration report server.

- Symptom:
Neighbour Notification Error.

  - Cause:
  The Neighbour Notification process could not be successfully terminated. This process is initiated every 7 seconds by the active monitor sending an AMP frame (Active Monitor Present). Any station detecting an AMP frame starts by comparing the Address Recognized bits and the Frame Copied bits in the AMP frame. If the frame has not yet been copied by any other station, the receiving station compares the source address of the AMP frame with its own NAUN address. If the addresses are different, the AMP frame's source address is stored as the new NAUN address and a Report NAUN Change frame is sent to the configuration report server. If the active monitor does not receive back the AMP frame it sends before the Neighbour Notification timer runs out, it sends a Neighbour Notification Process Incomplete frame to the ring error monitor and initiates a new AMP frame.

- Symptom:
Network performance poor all round.

  - Cause:

Loss of network performance can have a number of causes. The first question to ask is: What changes have recently been made to the network topology?

- Action:
Monitor the main parameters, such as ring purges, frames per second, load, token errors, beaconing frames, soft errors etc. using a protocol analyser. Record the main parameters affecting network performance against time, along with the number of stations, and compare the traces. Analyse the token ring messages. Are there messages such as Receiver Congestion?

- Symptom:
Network slow despite low load.

  - Cause (1):
  The load on a network (in %) is not the only factor determining the network's performance. Other important factors include packet size and packet type. Logical Link Control (LLC) data packets, for example, carry no user data but serve only to set up and maintain the connection. A large number of short LLC and MAC packets indicates an inefficient protocol. In the NetBIOS/SMB protocol, for example, the ratio of LLC packets to user data packets is 1:1! The reason for this remarkably poor figure is that NetBIOS/SMB uses a connection-oriented protocol at LLC level. NetWare IPX, on the other hand, uses a connectionless service, in which user data are transferred without waiting for acknowledgement of receipt. Connection-oriented protocols are often unnecessary and usually generate a vast number of management packets. In IPX, therefore, you will rarely see LLC packets.

  - Action:
  Statistical analysis: type and size of data packets. Change from connection-oriented protocols (e.g. NetBIOS/SMB) to connectionless protocols (e.g. NetWare).

  - Cause (2):
  However, a small packet size can also be due to other causes. The data packet size that can be handled by a network adapter card depends on its main memory. In a 4-Mbits/sec ring the maximum packet size is 4500 bytes, and in a 16-Mbits/sec ring 17800 bytes. Adapter cards with 8 kb of RAM will only process data packets up to a maximum of 1000 bytes in length. Older cards, with 1 kb of RAM, can handle packets up to 2000 bytes long. IBM's 16/4 adapter cards (64 kb of RAM full-slot or 16 kb half-slot) support the maximum packet lengths of 4500 and 17800 bytes.

  - Action:
  Check the maximum packet processing size for the adapter cards.

When a connection is set up, the stations negotiate a packet length, which will be the maximum length supported by the weaker station. A memory upgrade of the individual network adapter cards can thus result in a sizeable increase in throughput. As well as this, some network operating systems restrict the maximum packet length: the maximum packet size supported in NetWare 3.11 is 4000 bytes, irrespective of whether the ring is capable of 4 or 16 Mbits per second.

- Cause (3):
  Undesirable restrictions on packet size can also result from badly configured bridges and routers.

- Action:
  Check all bridge and router parameters. In general, throughput in 4-Mbits/sec rings falls off significantly at packet sizes below 256 bytes. The same applies in 16 Mbits/sec rings for packets between 512 and 1000 bytes.

- Symptom:
  Non-Isolating Error.
  Non-isolating RSE (Report Soft Error) faults are errors which cannot be assigned to any particular area of faults. Non-isolating errors are: Lost Frame Error, Frame Copied Error, Receiver Congested Error, Token Error and Frequency Error.
  Symptoms are:

- permanent ring purges,

- stations 'locking',

- problems logging on to a server,

- problems logging into the ring.

- Cause:
  - Token either corrupted or lost.
  - Token no longer able to complete a circuit of the ring within the token ring time limit.
  - Receiving station overloaded.

The problems which may bring one of these situations about, in order of likelihood of their occurrence, are:

- A station logging into/out of the ring;

In the context of an adapter:

- short-circuited cable,

- signal noise,

- excessive token transit time,

- faulty adapter card,
- performance problems with servers/bridges/routers,
- extremely high number of broadcasts.
- Action:
  - Inspect ring for presence of 'Isolating RSEs' to narrow down the fault area.
  - check data for presence of unusual broadcasts,
  - replace adapter card,
  - add extra memory for network nodes,
  - faster PCs.

- Symptom:
  Request Station Removed.

  - Cause:
    Configuration report server requesting station to log out of the ring. The most common reason for this is a duplicate token ring MAC address.

  - Action:
    Filter for 'Request to Remove' data packets using the protocol analyser and inspect send addresses.

- Symptom:
  Ring purges.

  - Cause:
    Ring purges are initiated by the active monitor, the purpose being to delete all signals in the ring in preparation for setting up a new token. They occur every time a station logs into or out of the ring, at which point the active station sets up a new token. If ring purges occur without an associated logging in or out, this is an indication of hardware problems in the ring.

  - Possible *causes*, listed by frequency of occurrence:
    - short-circuited cable,
    - signal noise or crosstalk,
    - token transit time too long (375 m for 4 Mbits/sec, 145 m for 16 Mbits/sec),
    - faulty token ring adapter card.

  - Action:
    Search for other Report Soft Error frames using a protocol analyser. Note the first occurrence of the RSE frames (the same error is often reported by a number of stations). Locate area of fault by reference to the RSE frames. The source of the error is always upstream from the station reporting the error. Check connecting cables in the area

of the fault and replace if necessary. Check ring adapter cards and replace if necessary.

- Symptom:
  Ring Resetting.

  - Cause:
    Ring resetting indicates that 10 Claim Token frames have been sent in succession, so that the ring can only be regenerated by beaconing.

- Symptom:
  Report Neighbour Incomplete.

  - Cause:
    The Neighbour Notification process – also known as 'ring polling' – informs each station of the identity of its upstream neighbour. All ring stations must take part in this polling process. The reason for an incomplete Neighbour Notification process is often a duplicated token ring MAC address.

  - Action:
    Search for 'Request to Remove' data packets using a protocol analyser and analyse the packet data.

- Symptom:
  Receiver Congested.

  - Cause:
    This error message is generated if a receiving station in Repeat mode (meaning that it should copy and forward a packet) detects a packet addressed to itself but does not have enough spare buffer memory to copy the frame.

  - Action:
    Increase buffer capacity of stations on network.

- Symptom:
  Streaming Beacon.

  - Cause:
    If a ring is unable to regenerate itself via the beaconing process, it goes over to Streaming Beacon state.

  - Three typical problems can be the *cause* of Streaming Beaconing:
    - faulty send cable,
    - faulty receive cable,
    - faulty MAU port (concentrator port).

- Action:
Analyse the Beaconing frames and trace the area of the fault from the addresses it provides for the sending station and its NAUN: the area of the fault comprises the station sending the beacon frame, its receive line, the sending station's NAUN and its send line, plus the concentrator(s)/MAU(s) between the two stations. All components within this fault area (network interface cards, concentrators, cables, connectors etc.) should now be inspected. The crucial step is correct determination of the fault area itself. It is therefore important to possess a diagnostic tool which can log into the token ring and analyse the beacon frames whatever its status (including beaconing). Check send/receive cables and concentrators within the fault area and replace if necessary.

- Symptom:
Token Error.

  - Cause:
  Token errors occur:
    - if a token with a priority not equal to zero and a monitor count of 1 is detected beyond the active monitor (that is, it is already on its second circuit),
    - if a frame with a monitor count of 1 occurs (the frame is already on its second circuit),
    - if no token or frame is encountered before the Good Token Timer runs out (10 ms),
    - if an illegal code is detected.

  - Token errors are non-isolating errors and cannot be assigned to any particular area of faults.

  - Action:
  See Non-Isolating Errors.

- Symptom:
Token direction reversed.

  - Cause:
  The direction in which the token is circulating can be found by inspecting the monitor bit in the data packets. If this bit is set to 1, the frame has already passed the active monitor (AM) once. If the monitor bit is still set to zero, the packet is still travelling towards the AM. If a protocol analyser is now used to examine the data packets from the (physically) immediate neighbour station (neither the analyser itself nor the neighbour station should be the AM), the direction of the token can be found very quickly:

  - Monitor bit = 1:
  Token travelling from analyser to neighbour station.

- Monitor bit = 0:
  Token travelling from neighbour station to analyser.

If the token has changed direction, this confirms that the ring has been regenerated at least once in the meantime.

10.4   Fault symptoms in FDDI networks – causes – action

- Symptom:
  Light output too low, high bit error rate, poor throughput.
  The maximum attenuation between two stations in FDDI is set at 11 dB and the maximum distance between stations at 2000 metres. The first step in fault-tracing is to test the average light strength reaching the problem station, using a power meter. If it is below -31.0 dBm, either the attenuation on the line is too great or the sending signal is too weak. Measuring the signal strength at the sending station will provide the answer. The average signal strength measured during continuous sending of a HALT signal current must be at least -20 dBm.

  - Cause (1):
    Connector loose, fibre contaminated by dust or fingerprints, causing high bit error rate.

  - Action:
    Check connection, clean the connector.

  - Cause (2):
    Low light output can also be caused by the deactivation of a Dual Attached Station (DAS) or a concentrator, if this causes the maximum distance between two stations to be exceeded. In high-redundancy networks, therefore, network nodes should be no more than 400 metres apart, to ensure that even if up to four (adjacent) stations drop out the system will still be fully available.

  - Action:
    Reconfigure the FDDI ring so that no two stations are more than 400 metres apart (or 500 metres, according to redundancy requirements). The maximum permissible distance between two stations will then only be exceeded once more than 4 (3) adjacent stations have dropped out.

  - Cause (3):
    Activated by-pass switches are also a frequent cause of heavy loss in light output. By-pass switches prevent the FDDI ring breaking up into two separate rings if more than one station drops out. However, by-

pass switches in by-pass mode cause a light output loss of up to 2 dB. At the maximum permissible loss between two stations of 11 dB, the activation of one or more by-pass switches can very quickly lead to excessive attenuation, giving rise to high error rates, resulting in turn in extra claim and beaconing frames.

- Action:
An analysis of the ring's SRF (Status Report Frame: see Section 11.4.14) will usually provide a clear pointer to the source of the trouble. All noteworthy changes to station status will be automatically recorded in the frame by the station itself.
Once a station with high error rates has been located, the identity of the station's actual neighbour can be found by examining the NIF packets (Neighbour Information Frames: see Section 11.4.14). If the upstream neighbour is not the next station in the ring, but the next but one, the by-pass switch for the intermediate station has been activated.
A test on the light strength arriving from upstream (with the by-pass activated) will then firmly identify the cause of the fault. If the light strength is too low, the activated by-pass is simply adding too much attenuation for fault-free operation of the FDDI ring to be guaranteed. This means that the ring will have to be reconfigured so that the light strength reaching the active stations is still high enough whether or not one or more by-pass switches are activated.

- Symptom:
System goes into Noise Line State (NLS).
If NLS is detected, this indicates that the incoming signals are noisy and – if the situation persists – that the physical connection concerned is faulty. (On most FDDI test equipment, the current line state is shown by LEDs; changes to the line state are reported by the stations, using Status Report Frames (SRFs): see Section 11.4.14.) In addition, the following events may be reported as noise indicators:

a) elasticity buffer error on receipt of signal;

b) decoding of a mixed signal pair (control indicator plus data).

- Cause:
See 'Symptom: Light output too low, high bit error rate, poor throughput'.

- Action:
See 'Symptom: Light output too low, high bit error rate, poor throughput'.

- Symptom:
Large number of Status Report Frames (SRFs).

- Cause:

Status Report Frames are used by the stations to report changes in their configuration or status (e.g. MAC Neighbour Change, bit error rate at a port etc.) to ring management. A large number of SRF packets can therefore be an indicator of problems in the ring.

- Action:
Collect and analyse available SRF packets using ring management or a protocol analysis system. If the SRF packets do not contain any unusual parameters, all stations can be polled for their status via an SIF request packet (Station Information Frame: see Section 11.4.14). However, one point must be remembered when examining the error counter for an individual station. Every station maintains counters at MAC level to record all frames received as well as frames with one or more errors. However, only those frames ending in a Frame Ending Delimiter (a T character) are counted. Data packets ending in idle characters or invalid characters are not included in the count, and these can only be observed and inspected by using a protocol analysis system.

Frame_Ct
This counter records all frames received.

Error_Ct
This counter keeps a count of all error frames identified as such by the station itself (that is, all the frames in which the station itself has set the Frame Status Error Field E to S). Frames arriving with E=S are not counted.

Lost_Ct
This counter maintains a total of frames or tokens already in process of receipt via the MAC layer when an error occurs.
The MAC layer then augments Lost_Ct and sends idle characters to the ring in place of the remainder of the frame. The next station will not add this frame to its Lost_Ct, as it now ends in an idle character.

- Symptom:
FDDI ring overloaded.

  - Cause:
  Too many stations with heavy load.

  - Action:
  Setting a low T_Pri for low priorities can relieve a heavily loaded ring.

- Symptom:
Large number of Claim frames.

  - Cause (1):

There are three causes – apart from stations logging in or out – of Claim frames:

a) A station's Valid Transmission Timer (TVX) has run out because no frame or token has been received.

b) The Token Rotation Timer (TRT) has run out.

c) A high bit error rate has been detected at the primary or secondary link port.

- Action:
Record all Claim frames. Find out which station initiated the claiming process (by reference to the source address in the first recorded Claim frame). The simplest approach after this is to send a few SIF Operation Request Packets (Station Information Frame: see Section 11.4.14) to this station and decode its SMT response packets to inspect the most important SMT counters (LEM counter, LEM rejects etc.). Measure light strength at this station. If the station's link error rate is high, this is the cause of continuing Claim frames. The connecting cable should be checked and the connector cleaned (dust, fingerprints).

- Cause (2):
Problems due to TTRT timers (Target Token Rotation Time) set to different values.

- Action:
Using protocol analyser, send SIF Operation Request Packets (Station Information Frame: see Section 11.4.14) to all stations and record their SMT response packets. The T_Neg (Negotiated Token Rotation Time), TTRT (Target Token Rotation Time) etc. in these packets can then be inspected.
If T_Neg is 10 ms and the ring stations have a TTRT of 14 ms, this indicates that at least one station is configured to a lower TTRT. This means that whenever this station takes part in the claiming process it will always beat the other stations and block them. Stations which all send with much the same frequency should therefore all be configured with the same TTRT.

- Symptom:
Large number of Claim and Beaconing frames.
Claim and beaconing frames are normal for logging-in and logging-out operations. If there are no stations on the FDDI backbone ring, but only servers, routers and concentrators, no claim or beacon frames should be observed at any time. If this does happen, it indicates a Layer 1 problem, possibly a high error rate or excessive signal strength loss.

- Cause:
See 'Symptom: Light output too low, high bit error rate, poor throughput'.

- Action:
  See 'Symptom: Light output too low, high bit error rate, poor throughput'.

- Symptom:
  Problems with FDDI bridges.

  - Cause:
    A number of problems will arise when using FDDI-to-non-FDDI bridges (*see* Section 9.4). A major problem where local Ethernet systems interface with FDDI rings lies in the different maximum frame lengths. FDDI permits a maximum packet length of 4500 bytes, while Ethernet is restricted to 1518 bytes. (Token ring allows 4500 bytes in a 4-Mbits/sec ring or 17800 bytes in a 16-Mbits/sec ring.) Overlength packets sent to the Ethernet system from the FDDI ring have to be rejected or can in the case of TCP/IP be fragmented (if the bridge supports this). The heaviest load on the bridge will then derive from forwarding very long data packets rather than, as otherwise, from short packets. This means that if a large number of long packets (> 1518 bytes) are sent by the FDDI ring to the Ethernet segment the bridge may become overloaded, or may break off the connection if it does not support fragmentation.

  - Action:
    Use a protocol analyser to send 'pings' (TCP/IP Echo Request) with lengths of 500 bytes and 4000 bytes. If the shorter packets achieve an answer but not the longer ones, the bridge does not support fragmentation.

11

The standards

The following section contains a detailed description of the standards for the various network topologies: IEEE 802.2/ISO 8802-2 LLC, IEEE 802.3/ISO 8802-3 CSMA/CD, IEEE 802.5/ISO 8802-5 Token Ring and ANSI ASC X329.5/ISO 9314 FDDI. The description follows the original text very closely, both to avoid misunderstandings and to serve as a useful reference. With the exception of electrical specifications and state diagrams, which are primarily of interest to developers of network components, all the important passages in the standards have been included, with comments and analysis regarding potential faults that may be encountered. Experience has shown that many of the problems encountered in networks can be attributed to a failure to keep to the relevant standards. The appendix shows the main parameters for each standard in tabular form.

- All the IEEE standards can also be obtained on CD-ROM from IEEE themselves.

  CD-ROM publications from IEEE
  UMI
  300 North Zeeb Road
  Ann Arbor, MI 48106
  USA
  Phone: +1-313-761-4700
  Fax: +1-313-665-7075

- Hard copy issues of the standards, as well as a number of monthly IEEE magazines, can be ordered directly from IEEE:

  IEEE Customer Service
  445 Hoes Lane, P. O. Box 1331
  Poscataway, NJ 08855-1331
  USA
  Phone: +1-908-981-0060
  Fax: +1-908-981-9667

- The ISO standards are obtainable from ISO:

  International Organization for Standardization
  Case postale 56
  CH-1211 Geneva 20
  Switzerland

- In Germany, ISO standards will be supplied within about a week by Beuth Verlag:

  Beuth Verlag GmbH
  Abt. Auslieferung
  Burggrafenstr. 6
  1000 Berlin 30
  Germany
  Phone: +4930 26010
  Fax: +4930 2601 1231

- Product adherence to the various standards is tested by the following organisations:

  - FDDI:
    EANTC (European Advanced Networking Test Centre)
    Techn. Universität Berlin
    Sekretariat MA 073
    Straße des 17. Juni 136
    1000 Berlin

Germany
- Ethernet, Token Ring:
  GCO Communications
  London

11.1   ANSI/IEEE 802.2 /ISO 8802-2 Logical Link Control

Design and function

The IEEE 802.2/ISO 8802-2 standard describes the functions made available to the Network Layer (Layer 3) or the MAC sub-layer of the Data Link Layer by the LLC sub-layer of the Data Link Layer. The functions described are independent of the type of access protocol used (Figure 11.1). To enable the broadest possible range of applications to be covered, two classes of LLC modes are defined:

- Class 1:
  Exclusively non-connection-oriented data transfer.

- Class 2:
  Optional connection-oriented (e.g. HDLC) and non-connection-oriented data transfer.

11.1.1 The LLC data format

All LLC packets have the structure shown in Figure 11.2.
  Key:
  – DSAP:
  Destination Service Address Point address field.
  – SSAP:
  Source Service Address Point address field.
  – Control field:
  Length: 16 bits with sequencing numbers, 8 bits without
  – Information field:
  Length: a natural multiple of 8 bits.

Address fields

Every data packet includes two address fields: the DSAP (Destination Service Address Point) and the SSAP (Source Service Address Point). The DSAP defines one or more SAP addresses to which the transmitted information is sent, and consists of 7 address bits plus a bit (the I/G bit) specifying the address as an individual address (0) or a group address (1). Seven bits of the SSAP address field are also used as address bits, with the first bit (the C/R bit) indicating whether the data packet contains a command (0) or a response.

A DSAP address consisting entirely of ones is known as a global DSAP, and is sent to all SAP addresses. A DSAP address consisting entirely of zeroes is known as a null address and is not directed to any SAP address.

The control field

The control field consists of one or two octets and contains command or response functions which will be dealt with in more detail in the following section.

The information field

The information field can consist of any whole-number multiple (including 0) of 8 bits.

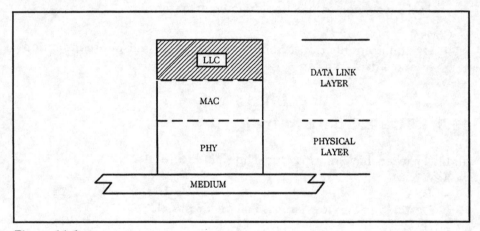

Figure 11.1

Bit sequence

Addresses, commands and responses are transmitted with the Least Significant Bit (LSB) first. The contents of information fields are sent in the same bit order as they are received.

Invalid LLC data packets

An LLC data packet is invalid if one of the following conditions is met:

DSAP address	SSAP address	Control field	Information field
8 bits	8 bits	y bits	8*M*bits

Figure 11.2   LLC-PDU 802.2

1) It is identified as invalid by Layer 1 or the MAC layer.

2) It does not consist of a natural multiple of 8 bits.

3) It does not contain two address fields, one control field and – optionally – an information field in the correct sequence and is correctly formatted.

4) It is shorter than 3 octets (for a 1-byte control field) or 4 octets (for a 2-byte control field).

Invalid LLC data packets are ignored.

LLC modes

LLC recognises two different modes:

1) *Non-connection-oriented data transfer (LLC Class 1)*:
Data packets are transmitted without any acknowledgement or error recognition algorithm. The Class 1 command set consists of the commands UI, XID, TEST and the responses XID and TEST.

2) *Connection-oriented data transfer (LLC Class 2)*:
The receipt of each data packet is confirmed by means of a numbering scheme (modulo 128), in which the receiving station informs the sender of the next expected transfer sequencing number. This may be done via a separate data packet or using the control field of a data packet containing information. Data transfer of this type is known as a logical point-to-point connection. The Class 2 command set consists of the following commands and responses:
– Commands:
UI, XID, TEST, I, RR, RNR, REJ, SABME, DISC.
– Responses:
XID, TEST, I, RR, RNR, REJ, UA, DM, FRMR.

11.1.2 The LLC protocol

The control field

The control field format specifies the different data packet types:

– numbered information packets,

– numbered supervisor packets,

– unnumbered control packets and

– unnumbered information packets

Key to Figure 11.4:

– N(S):
  Send sequencing number;

– N(R):
  Receive sequencing number;

– S:
  Supervisory function bit;

– M:
  Modification bit (encoding for the different commands or responses);

– X:
  reserved and set to zero;

– P/F:
  Poll/Final bit: read as a poll bit in a command packet and as a final bit in a response packet.

  Data packets with 'I' format control fields ('I' packets) are used for the transfer of information. 'S' format data packets ('S' packets) are used for supervisory functions, to confirm 'I' format packets and to request repeat transmissions. 'U' format data packets ('U' packets) are used for other control functions or for unnumbered data transfers.

Control field parameters

LLC Class 1 parameters
The only Class 1 parameter is the Poll/Final Bit. In a command packet, the poll bit is set to 1 if a response packet is required from the receiving station. In the corresponding response packet, the same bit – now referred to as the Final Bit – is set to 1 to indicate that the packet is in reply to a command packet with its poll bit = 1.

LLC Class 2 parameters
Numbering
Every 'I' data packet is numbered cyclically from 0 to 127. Every numbered packet received is acknowledged by the receiving station sending the next expected sequencing number. The maximum number of packets awaiting acknowledgement is likewise 127. Every station maintains the following variables for numbering management:

– *Send Status Variable V(S)*:

Contains the send sequencing number N(S) of the next data packet to be sent.

– *Receive Status Variable V(R)*:

Contains the receive sequencing number N(R) of the next data packet to be received.

The Poll/Final Bit
In a command packet, the poll bit is set to 1 if a response packet is required from the receiving station. In the corresponding response packet, the same bit – now referred to as the Final Bit – is set to 1 to indicate that the packet is to be taken as a reply to a previously received command packet with its poll bit = 1. Only one data packet with its poll bit = 1 may be awaiting acknowledgement at any time. If the poll bit timer runs out before an acknowledgement (a response packet with its final bit = 1) has been received, the packet is re-sent.

Command Transactions under LLC Class 1

The control fields of Class 1 command packets have the content shown above.

The UI command
No reply is expected to a UI command. It is not numbered or acknowledged by the receiving station; so it may be lost when there are transmission problems (line errors, receiving station not active).

The XID command
The task of an XID command is to negotiate the LLC mode (Class 1 or Class 2) and the receive window size – that is, the number by which V(S) is allowed to exceed V(R), or the maximum number of packets awaiting an acknowledgement. The parameters for this are set in the XID information field (see Figure 11.5). The receiving station must reply to an XID command with an XID response.

The TEST command
If a station receives a TEST command it must reply with a TEST response. An information field may be sent as an option.

The XID response
On receipt of an XID command, the station must reply with an XID response as soon as possible. For identification purposes, an information field with the same structure as in the XID command packet is used. The

final bit in the XID response should be set to the same value as the poll bit in the XID command.

The TEST response

On receipt of a TEST command (with an optional information field), a TEST response is sent (with an information field, if one was received). The final bit in the TEST response should be set to the same value as the poll bit in the TEST command.

Command Transactions under LLC Class 2

The 'I' Command and 'I' Response

The 'I' command and 'I' response are used to send numbered data packets with information fields via a connection-oriented link (Figure 11.6).

The 'S' Command and 'S' Response

The 'S' command and 'S' response do not contain an information field and do not therefore cause the send status variable V(S) or receive status variable V(R) to be augmented.

Figure 11.7 shows the structure of the control field in 'S' format.

Key:

– Receive Ready (RR)

Command and response. An LLC sends RR to indicate that it is ready to receive a (another) data packet.

– The N(R) in the RR packet confirms to the receiving station that all 'I' data packets with the sequence number N(R)-1 have been received.

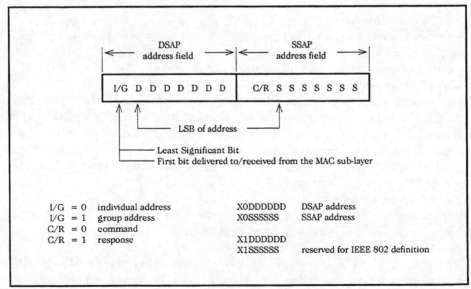

Figure 11.3

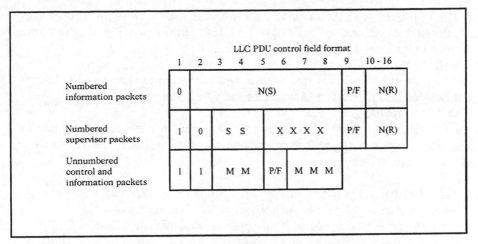

Figure 11.4 LLC PDU control field format

– Reject (REJ):
    Command and response: A REJ command requests a repeat send of all 'I' data packets with a sequence number beginning with N(R). Only one REJ packet at a time can request repeat sends.

– Receive Not Ready (RNR):
    Command and response: AN RNR command from an LLC indicates temporary inability to receive.

– The N(R) in the RNR packet confirms to the receiving station that all 'I' data packets with the sequence number N(R)-1 have been received.

Unnumbered ('U' format) Commands and Responses
'U' data packets are used for additional connection control functions. 'U' format packets do not augment the send status variable V(S) or receive status variable V(R). Figure 11.8 illustrates the structure of 'U' packets.

The SABME Command
The SABME (Set Asynchronous Balanced Mode Extended) command is used to set up an ABM (Asynchronous Balanced Mode) connection between two LLCs. The receive station responds with an UA (Unnumbered Acknowledgement) and sets its receive and send status variables V(S) and V(R) to 0. The send station follows suit on receipt of the UA. Any data packets awaiting acknowledgement remain unacknowledged.

The DISC Command
The DISC (Disconnect) command is used to terminate a connection set up using SABME. Before actual termination, the sending station must wait for a UA response from the receiving station. Any data packets awaiting acknowledgement at this point remain unacknowledged.

The UA Response

A UA (Unnumbered Acknowledgement) response is sent by the LLC to acknowledge and accept a SABME or DISC command. These commands cannot be executed without a UA response.

The DM Response

A DM (Disconnect Mode) response is sent to indicate that an LLC has no connection and is in ADM (Asynchronous Disconnected Mode).

The FRMR Response

An LLC sends an FRMR response to report that a data packet cannot be accepted for one of the following reasons specified in the FRMR response in the information field:

1) The data packet contains an invalid command or response, e.g.
   @ 'S' packet or 'U' packet with information field (not available).
   @ Final bit = 1 received without prior sending of poll bit = 1.
   @ Unmotivated UA response received.

2) 'I' packet length exceeds receiving station's capacity.

3) Receive sequencing number N(R) invalid (either already acknowledged or acknowledged without having been sent).

4) Send sequencing number N(S) invalid (if N(S) greater than N(S)+k, where k is the number of data packets awaiting acknowledgement).

The receiver of an FRMR response is now responsible for remedying the cause of the fault (e.g. by SABME or DISC). Figure 11.9 shows the structure of the information field in an FRMR response packet.

− V(S)

    is the value of the send status variable V(S) at the time the FRMR is sent.

− C/R = 1:

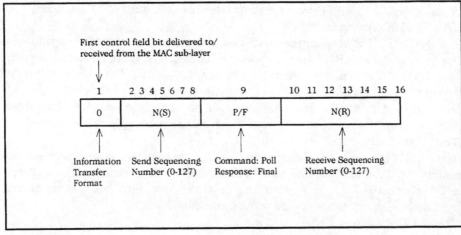

Figure 11.6

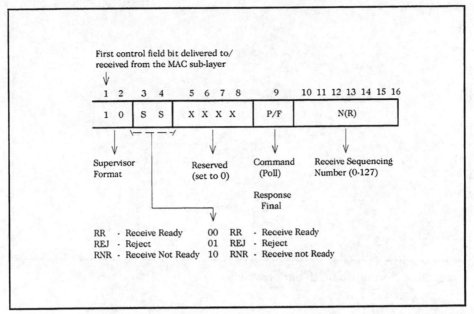

Figure 11.7 IEEE 802.2'S' format

The packet triggering the FRMR response was a response packet.

– C/R = 0:

The packet triggering the FRMR response was a command packet.

– V(R)

is the value of the receive status variable V(R) at the time the FRMR is sent.

– W = 1:

The data packet received was invalid.

– X = 1:

The data packet received was invalid because it contained an information field, contrary to specification (in this case W must also be set to 1).

– Y = 1:

The information field sent was too long for the receiving station to be able to process it.

– Z = 1:

The V(R) in the control field contained an invalid value.

– V = 1:

The V(S) in the control field contained an invalid value.

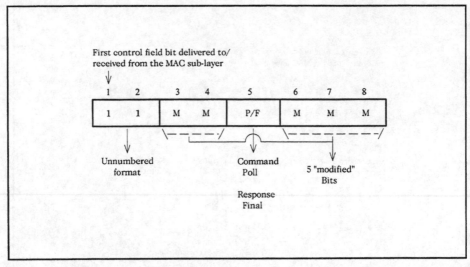

Figure 11.8 Structure of 'U' data packets

11.1.3 Timers

The following timers can be implemented:

– Acknowledgement Timer
The time within which an expected UA must be received.

– Poll Bit Timer
The time after sending a data packet with the poll bit = 1 within which a packet with the final bit = 1 must be received.

– Reject Timer
The time within which a response to a REJ-format packet UA must be received.

– Busy State Timer
Time for which an LLC waits for termination of Busy status at the the destination station.

– N2, maximum number of attempts at transmission
The maximum number of attempted sends after the acknowledgement timer, the poll bit timer or the reject timer has run out.

– Maximum number of octets in an 'I' format packet
Not specified. However, every MAC layer must be able to process information fields 128 octets in length.

– Minimum number of octets in a data packet
3 or 4, depending on whether the packet is in 'U' format, 'I' format or 'S' format.

Figure 11.10 shows an 802.2 data packet, decoded using a protocol analyser.

11.2 The IEEE 802.3/ISO 8802-3 standard for local networks

The following section takes as its basis the IEEE/802.3, 1992/ISO 8802-3, 1992 standard. This standard describes 10Base5, 10Base2, FIORL (Fibre Optic Repeater Link), 10Broad6 and 1Base5 networks. 10Broad6 and 1Base5 networks are not covered here, as there are very few installations in existence.

11.2.1 Design and Function

CSMA/CD is a method of data transmission in which two or more stations access a shared bus transfer medium. To transfer data, a station waits for a break in transmission (that is, a time when no other station is sending) and transmits the message in bit-serial form.

If the message being sent collides with one from another station after transmission has begun, each of the sending stations sends a few additional bytes to ensure that the collision is spread across the entire network (a 'jam signal'). Before making any further attempts at sending, both stations 'back off' for a randomly selected time – that is, they refrain from all sending activity.

Within the physical layer (OSI Layer 1), two standard interfaces are defined:

– *MDI: Medium-Dependent Interface*

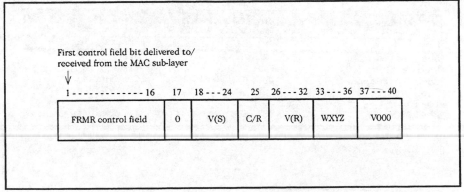

Figure 11.9   Information field in an FRMR response packet.

To guarantee compatibility, all stations must comply with the precise specification of this standard interface.

– AUI: Attachment Unit Interface

Many stations are located at some distance from the actual point of attachment to the transfer medium. In such a case, some of the electronic circuits will be directly adjacent to the transfer medium (MAU: Medium Attachment Unit), while most of the electronics and all of the software will be at the station itself (connected via the AUI cable).

11.2.2 Structure of MAC Frames

The Preamble Field

The Preamble Field is 7 octets long and enables the receive circuitry of the network cards to synchronise with the incoming data packet.

The bit pattern for the preamble is defined as follows:

10101010 10101010 10101010 10101010 10101010 10101010 10101010

The Start Frame Delimiter

The start frame delimiter field consists of the bit sequence 10101011. It immediately follows the preamble and indicates the start of the frame.

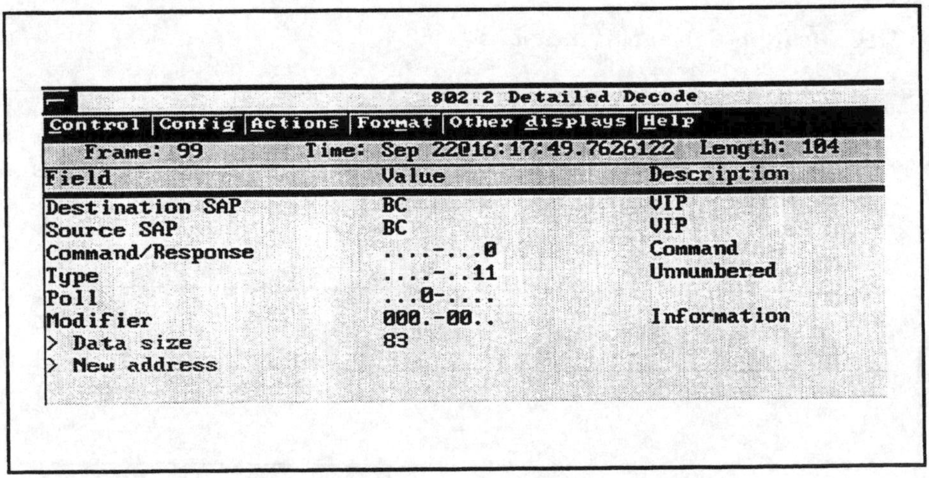

```
┌─                          802.2 Detailed Decode
 Control │Config │Actions │Format │Other displays │Help
    Frame: 99          Time: Sep 22 16:17:49.7626122  Length: 104
 Field                      Value                   Description
 Destination SAP            BC                      VIP
 Source SAP                 BC                      VIP
 Command/Response           ....-...0               Command
 Type                       ....-..11               Unnumbered
 Poll                       ...0-....
 Modifier                   000.-00..               Information
 > Data size                83
 > New address
```

Figure 11.10   802.2 data packet

The Address Fields

Every MAC frame contains two address fields: the destination address and the source address. Each address field consists of either 16 or 48 bits; but the length of the address fields must be the same for all stations in a network. The first bit in the destination address field (Least Significant Bit: LSB) is used to define the address as an individual address (LSB=0) or a group address (LSB=1). In the source address field the function of the first bit is reserved, and it is set to 0 by default.

In 48-bit addresses the second bit is used to distinguish between addresses used locally (bit 2 = 1) and global addresses with universal application (bit 2 = 0). This bit is also set to 1 for broadcast addresses. Each octet in the address field is transferred starting with the LSB. The addresses used in practice are almost universally 48 bits.

Address Types

There are two types of address:

a) *Multicast Group Addresses:*
   These are addresses allocated to a group of logically connected stations on the basis of a convention specified in the higher layers.

b) *Broadcast Addresses:*
   A predefined group address comprising all stations within a local network. This broadcast address consists entirely of ones for both 16-bit and 48-bit address fields. All the other stations in the network must be able to recognise this address.

The Length Field

The length field consists of two octets with a value giving the number of LLC data octets in the data field. Packets with a value in their length field exceeding the maximum permissible frame length will be ignored. If the value is smaller than the minimum necessary frame length, a pad field (a sequence of octets) will be inserted at the end of the data field (but before the FCS field).

The Data and Pad fields

The data field contains a sequence of n octets. A minimum of 46 octets is required for the CSMA/CD algorithm to work properly.

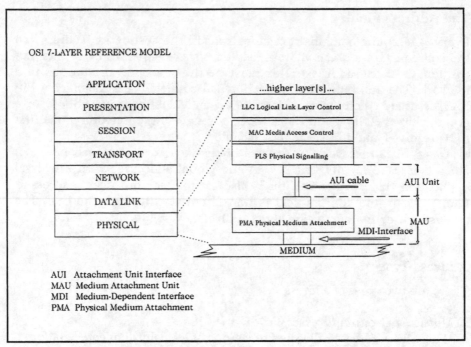

Figure 11.11   Relationship of the AN standard to the OSI 7-layer model

The maximum permitted number of data octets is 1500. If the number of octets falls short of the minimum, the data field is padded out with random pad bytes.

The Frame Check Sequence

The send and receive algorithms generate checksums for the packets transferred using a Cyclic Redundancy Check (CRC), to ensure fault-free transfer of data.

The checksums are entered in the FCS field, which is 4 octets long. The checksum is a function of all the fields in each frame except for the preamble, the start frame delimiter and the FCS itself. It is generated according to the following algorithm:

1) The complement of the first 32 bits of the frame is formed.

2) A polynomial M(x) to the degree n-1 is formed from the n bits of the frame (for example, the bit sequence 110001 has six bits and is interpreted as a polynomial with the coefficients 1,1,0,0,0,1, i.e. $X^5+X^4+X^0$).

3) M(x) is multiplied by the coefficient x^{32} and divided by the generator polynomial G(x), where

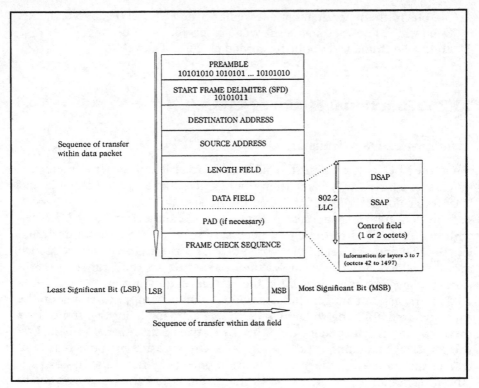

Figure 11.12   MAC Frame Structure

$G(x) = \backslash\backslash\backslash\backslash$.

The result is a 32-bit sequence, and the complement of this is taken as the checksum (CRC), which is entered in the FCS field – but with the most significant bit first (bit 1 = $x^{\wedge}311$, bit 2 = $x^{\wedge}30$ etc.). (All other fields are transferred LSB first.)

Although the checksum calculation looks complicated, it is in fact easy to implement by hardware using a simple shift register circuit.

A 32-bit CRC like the one shown here will detect all single and double errors, all errors due to an odd number of bits, all error sequences 32 bits in length or less, and with a probability of 99.99999998% all error sequences over 32 bits in length.

Invalid frames

An invalid frame is one which satisfies at least one of the following conditions:

1) The frame length does not match the content of the length field.

2) The number of octets in a frame is invalid (too high or too low).

3) The bits in the incoming frame (excluding the FCS field) generate a CRC value which does not match the value received.

An invalid frame will not be forwarded to the LLC level.

11.2.3 Functional Model of CSMA/CD

Incident-free Data Transfer

When the LLC level requests the MAC level under it to transfer a frame, the MAC level constructs a frame from the LLC data, adding the preamble and start frame delimiter (SFD) at the beginning.

The data field is generated according to the data from the LLC level, with pad bits added to the end if necessary to satisfy the minimum frame length. The address fields, the length field and the frame check sequence are also added on. The frame is then passed on to the Transmit Media Access Management component at the MAC level for transfer.

This transfer management component now attempts to transmit the frame without colliding with any other frames already being transmitted via the medium. This is taken care of by the Carrier Sense Signal provided by the Physical Signalling (PLS) Interface. If the transfer medium is free of traffic, the transfer of the frame is started once sufficient time has elapsed (the inter-frame gap, which enables the medium and the other stations to be regenerated). The MAC level then supplies the PLS interface with a serial bit stream for transfer. On completion of the transfer, the MAC level reports successful transfer to the LLC level and waits for the next transfer request.

Incident-free Receipt of Data

At each receiving station, an incoming frame is first detected by the PLS circuit, which synchronises with the incoming preamble and enables the carrier sense signal. The encoded data are converted back into binary data and passed through to the MAC layer (without the preamble and start frame delimiter). The Receive Media Access Management component of the MAC layer processes the bit stream from the PLS interface as long as the carrier sense signal is active. As soon as this signal is deactivated, the frame is truncated (if necessary) at an octet boundary and forwarded to the Receive Data Decapsulation component, which first checks the source address to determine whether the frame should be transferred to the station or not. If the frame is accepted for transfer, the destination address, source address and data field are passed through to the LLC level. The frame check sequence is checked at the same time.

Access and Regeneration Problems

If a number of stations are attempting to send frames at the same time, collisions may result despite carrier sensing. If the data transferred by two stations are superimposed, the outcome is what is called a collision. It is possible for a sending station to experience a collision during the start of transmission, that is, the period when the signal has yet to reach all the stations connected to the medium (the collision window), since at this stage carrier sensing will not be operating for the network stations which the signal has not reached. Once the end of the collision window has been passed without any collisions occurring, the sending station has the right to send.

No further collisions are now possible, as it can be assumed that all the other stations have observed the signal and halted transmission. The time taken to acquire the right to send on a medium is thus equal to the signal propagation time over the entire transfer medium and back (including the PLS interface).

When a collision occurs, it is detected by the sending station. The Transmit Media Access Management in the MAC component first intensifies the collision by sending a jam sequence. (The content of the jam sequence is not specified in detail: it can contain any bit pattern, except for the 32-bit checksum for the frame or fragment preceding the collision.) This ensures that the collision is clear enough to be detected by all stations. At the end of the jam sequence the station's transmit management halts all sending. After a randomly selected time interval, a fresh transmission attempt is begun. In the event of a further collision, a fresh transmission attempt is again begun after a further break in sending.

As repeated collisions are a sign of a heavily overloaded transfer medium, the algorithm selecting the break in sending between transfer attempts is constructed in such a way that the load on the network is successively reduced. This is achieved by increasing the break in transmission each time an attempt to send is unsuccessful (which means that stations sending large amounts of data and thus causing a lot of collisions have to wait longer than stations sending relatively little). The bits resulting from a collision are decoded by the receiving stations as if they were valid frames. However, the receive management component prevents these invalid bit sequences from being passed to the LLC layer.

The dynamic behaviour of collision handling is largely determined by a single parameter: the slot time. The slot time affects the three central aspects of collisions in the network:

- The slot time supplies an upper limit for the acquisition time (that is, the time taken before the right to send is acquired).

- The slot time determines the maximum length for a collision fragment.

– The slot time is the unit used in calculating the transmission break after an unsuccessful send attempt.

To fulfil these three functions, the slot time must be greater than twice the propagation time on the medium plus the maximum jam time.

Break in transmission after unsuccessful send and repeat send

If an attempt to send is broken off after being unsuccessful, it is repeated until it is successful or until the maximum permitted number of repeat send attempts is reached. The time at which a repeat send is allowed after an unsuccessful attempt is controlled by an algorithm known as 'truncated binary exponential backoff'.

This specifies that, after the tenth unsuccessful send attempt, a station must wait 2^{10}, that is, 1024 times the slot time before beginning a final attempt to send. With a slot time of 512 bits or 51.2 µs (in 10Base5), this makes the maximum possible waiting time 52.43 ms! The protocol may also be implemented so as to make these waiting times between attempts longer; but in no case may they be shorter than those given here.

Collision Detection

The minimum frame size equals the slot time expressed in bits (e.g. 51.2 µs corresponds to 512 bits or 64 bytes). All frames shorter than this are regarded as collision fragments.

Figure 11.14 shows how an 802.3 data packet looks when decoded. The upper half shows the decoding for the packet, which is interpreted in hexadecimal in the lower half.

11.2.4 Physical Signalling (PLS) and AUI Specifications

An AUI (Attachment Unit Interface) is required if the send station (DTE) is physically separated from the MAU. This makes it possible

1) to attach the sending stations to the MAU via one and the same AUI interface irrespective of the transfer medium actually used (coax cable, fibre optics, twisted pair).

2) to implement a physical separation of the DTEs by up to 50 m from the actual network cabling.

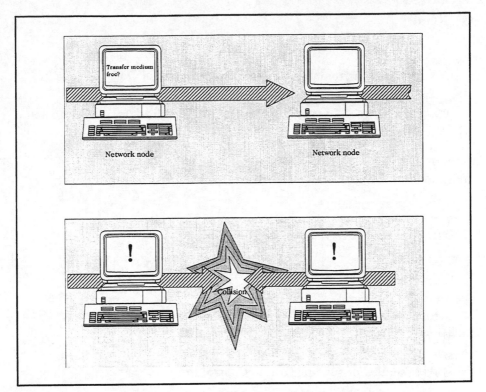

Figure 11.13

DTE-MAU Interface Protocol

The DTE and MAU communicate with each other using a simple protocol. This requires two pairs of cores for each direction: one pair for data and one for control signals.

Signals from DTE (PLS) to MAU

– *output:*
   Data output (data in CD 0 or CD 1 form)

– *output_idle:*
   No data (IDL to Data Out)

- *normal:*
   After Reset-and Identify message

Optional:

– isolate:
Isolates the MAU from the medium (CS 0 to Control Out)

– mau_request:
When the MAU sends 'MAU not available' and the DTE wishes to send (CS 1 to Control Out)

Signals from MAU to DTE (PLS):

– input:
Data received (data in CD 0 or CD 1 form)

– input_idle:
No data received (IDL to Data In)

– signal_quality error:
Error detected by the MAU (is sent if non-standard signals are received: collisions and output_idle signal) (CS 0 to Control In)

– mau_available:
MAU available for sending (IDL to Control In)

– mau_not_available:
MAU not available for sending (CS 1 to Control In)

Data Encoding

The code used for data transfer at an AUI interface is the Manchester Code (as distinct from the Differential Manchester Code in 802.5 Token Ring networks and 4B/5B in FDDI). This divides each bit symbol into two halves, with the second half representing the contents of the first half, inverted.

The first half of the signal then sends the logical complement of the unit of information to be transferred, which is contained in inverted form in the second half.

Although this means that clock information is implicitly being transmitted along with the data, it also enables the transfer to take place at a clock speed of 20 MHz. This means that all network components must be set up for a 20 MHz clock. (Similar conditions apply to 802.5 token ring networks: effective transfer rates of 4 and 16 Mbits/sec correspond to clock speeds of 8 and 32 MHz respectively. In FDDI, this doubling of the clock speed is avoided by the use of 4B/5B encoding. This gives a clock speed of 125 MHz at an effective data rate of 100 Mbits/sec.)

The result is that CD 0 (coded 0) is implemented as a bit character beginning with HI and ending in LO. CD 1 (coded 1) starts in LO and ends

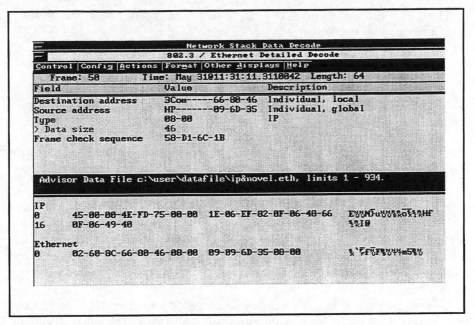

Figure 11.14   An 802.3 data packet

in HI. The idle signal IDL is also sent in encoded form: it always begins in HI and must be at least 2 bits long.

Encoding of Control Signals

Control signals are encoded for the AUI interface as follows:

– *CO 0:*
  Signal stream at current bit rate (BR) (10 Mbits/sec for 10Base5).

– *CS 1:*
  Signal stream at half the bit rate (BR/2 – 5 Mbits/sec for 10Base5).

– *IDL:*
  Definition as for data encoding.

Characteristics of AUI Cabling

The AUI Cabling consists of shielded twisted-pair cables. The attenuation between two cable pairs must be at least 10 dB. Attenuation on the cable at frequencies between BR and BR/2 (5 MHz to 10 MHz for 10Base5) must not exceed 3 dB. Transfer delays between the DTE driver and the MAU must not exceed 257 ns for each cable pair. Propagation speed on the AUI cable must be at least 0.65 c.

The Data-Out and Control-Out cable pairs are fed by the DTE, Data-In and Control-In by the MAU.

11.2.5 Specifications for MAUs, repeaters and cables

11.2.5.1Media Access Units

The task of the MAU is to attach the PLS (Physical Signalling) unit to the transfer medium itself via the AUI interface.

10Base5 MAU

A 10Base5 MAU must be able to transfer signals between the minimum (2.5 m) and the maximum (500 m) permitted segment lengths . In addition, the following functions must be available:
Jabber control:
There must be a hardware unit implemented in every MAU to ensure that a time window of 20 ms minimum and 150 ms maximum is available for data transfer. If 150 ms is exceeded, the MAU must disconnect the sending station from the transfer medium to prevent the transmission of illegally long packets (jabbers, packets > 1518 bytes).
Collision detection:
Every MAU must detect simultaneous sending by two stations and report this to the DTE within 9 bits. A maximum of 100 MAUs may be installed per segment (10Base5). MAUs must be installed at the marked points on the cable 2.5 m apart. This guarantees that the distance between two MAUs is kept to at least 2.5 metres and minimises resulting reflections.

In addition, a MAU must be constructed such that in the event of its failing the likelihood of other stations being affected is minimal. (If a fault causes a MAU to draw more than 2 mA of current, other stations will also suffer.)

10Base2 MAU

The same applies for a 10Base2 MAU as for a 10Base5 MAU, except for the following parameters:

– Signal transfer from 0.5 m to 185 m.

– maximum of 30 MAUs per segment.

– MTBF 100,000 hours.

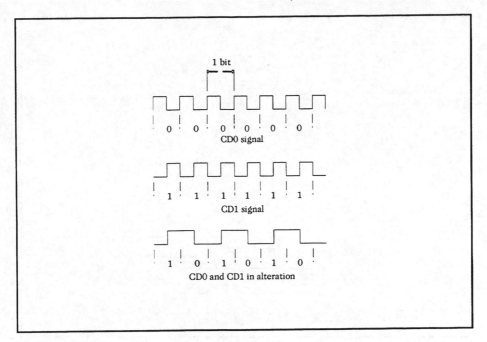

Figure 11.15   Examples of Manchester coding

11.2.5.2 Repeaters

The task of a repeater unit is to extend the physical topology of a network by connecting two or more segments. (A segment constitutes 500 m and 100 stations in 10Base5 or 185 m and 30 stations in 10Base2.)

A number of repeaters may be used at the same time so as to extend the network to a maximum of 2.5 km (between two MAUs). Repeaters may connect two segments either directly or – if Inter Repeater Links (IRLs) are used – via an optical fibre link and two repeaters.

Repeater units must satisfy the following functions:

Signal Regeneration

Signal amplification:
  The repeater unit must restore the amplitude characteristic of the signal.
Symmetry:
  The repeater unit must restore the symmetry of the signal.
Signal Retiming:
  The repeater unit must ensure that data output is within the jitter tolerance of the stations involved in the transfer.

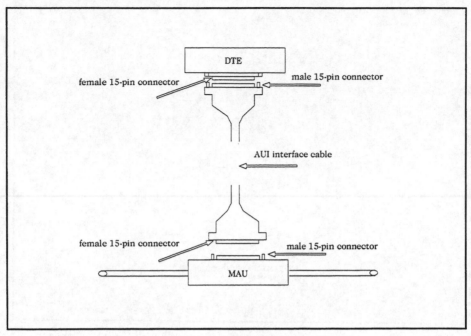

Figure 11.16   AUI cable connector (MIL-C-24308-1972)

Pin	Signal	Pin	Signal
3	Data out A	8	Control out Earth
10	Data out B	2	Control in A
11	Data out Earth	9	Control in B
5	Data in A	1	Control in Earth
12	Data in B	6	Minus Terminal
4	Data in Earth	13	+12V
7	Control out A	14	Earth
15	Control out B	Sheath	to Earth

Figure   Pin Assignments for AUI Connector

Carrier Sensing and Repeating

The Carrier Sensing function must be implemented. The repeater should output the data received or wait for a free line depending on whether data are already being carried on the medium.

Preamble Regeneration

The data output by the repeater must contain a preamble of at least 56 bits followed by a start frame delimiter.

Data transit times

The delay between first bit at input to first bit at output must not exceed a maximum of 7.5 bit cycles. The delay between last bit 'in' and last bit 'out' must not exceed a maximum of 9 bit cycles.

Fragment Padding

If the signal for transfer is shorter than 96 bits (including the preamble), the repeater will pad out the data fragment (with random data) so that the total number of bits output by the repeater is 96.

Collision Detection and Jam Generation

If the repeater detects a collision, it sends a jam signal to the connected unit on either side. The delay between SQE (Signal Quality Error) activation and the output of the first jam bit must not exceed 6.5 bits.

IRL (Inter-Repeater Link)

The implementation of an IRL can either be specific to the manufacturer or conform to the following FOIRL (Fibre Optic Inter-Repeater Link) specification. However, manufacturers' implementations must in any case conform to a maximum signal delay ensuring that the overall network transit time does not exceed the limits required in the standard. In addition, the collision size must not exceed a maximum of 511 bits.

FOIRL (Fibre Optic Inter-Repeater Link)

A FOIRL consists of two repeaters connected by a fibre optics link. Each of the two FOIRL repeaters is counted as a full repeater. Accordingly, no more than 2 FOIRLs may be configured per segment. The following functions must be satisfied by a FOIRL:

– *Signal Amplification*.

– *Retiming:*
  Removal of jitter and phase shift.

– *Signal Delay:*
  A maximum delay of 8 bit cycles (IRL without MAU) or 14 4 bits (IRL with MAU) must be adhered to.

– *Jam Generation:*
  If a collision is detected, a jam sequence must be sent within 6.5 bits (19 bits with internal MAU). As distinct from conventional repeaters, the

first 62 bits must comprise a sequence of alternating zeroes and ones, with the first bit a 1.

– Bit Error Rate:

The overall bit error rate for a FOIRL must be lower than one error in 10^{10} bits transferred.

FOMAU (Fibre Optic Media Access Unit)

A FOMAU connects the repeater unit to the actual optical fibre link. The following functions must be available:

– Sending and receiving of a serial bit stream from and to the repeater or fibre optic link.

– Collision detection.

– Jabber detection: a FOMAU should abort sending by the repeater if this lasts 20 ms > x < 150 ms.

– Detection of low light strength.

– Supports fibre links up to 1000 m.

– Reliability: MTBF > 200,000 hours.

Optical Parameters

Wavelength:
The wavelength used must be between 790 and 910 nm.
Light strength received:
At a light strength received between -9 dBm and -27 dBm the bit error rate must be < 10^{-10}.
Glass fibres:
The FOMAU as specified is capable of working with a wide range of fibre types: 50/125 µm, 62.5/125 µm, 85/125 µm and 100/140 µm. Interoperability between different cables is ensured by matching bandwidth and attenuation. The bandwidth of the cable should be > 150 MHz and the attenuation <= 4 dB/km at a wavelength of 850 nm).

Reliability

A 2-port repeater should have a MTBF of at least 50,000 hours. Each additional port must not increase the error rate by more than 3.46 x 10^{-6} errors.

11.2.6 Characteristics of Coax Cable

The mean impedance of the cable should be 50 ohms +/- 2%. Cable attenuation, measured using a 10 MHz sine wave, must not exceed 11.5 dB at a length of 500 metres (18 dB/km), or 6.0 dB (12 dB/km) if measured using a 5 MHz sine wave. Propagation speed on the cable must be at least 0.77 c. The cable sheath must be marked with coloured rings at intervals of 2.5 m +/- 5 cm. The terminating resistance must be 50 ohms +/- 1%, measured from 0 to 20 MHz.

Earthing: the sheath of the cable must be earthed at just one point. A coaxial segment must not exceed 500 metres in length (10Base5). A maximum of 100 MAUs may be connected per segment. The maximum propagation delay in a cable segment must be 2165 ns. Repeaters are required to connect segments. The maximum transmission path between two network stations consists of five segments, four repeater units, four MAUs and two AUI cables.

Since worst-case reflections of 4% arise when connecting two cable looms (one cable 49 ohms, the other 51 ohms), the following procedure should be followed when constructing networks consisting of a number of sub-networks:

1) Where possible, the entire network should consist of one homogeneous cable loom.

2) If cable segments are made up from a number of cables, all cables should be from the same manufacturer and the same production batch.

3) If a number of lengthy cable segments are used in constructing a single network segment, these should be selected in such a way that any resulting reflections stay in phase. This can be achieved be choosing lengths corresponding to odd multiples of the half-wavelength at 5 MHz before joining. This gives lengths of 23.4 m, 70.2 m and 117 m, which should be adopted as the standard lengths of cable to be used. If these lengths are kept to, any combination < 500 m can be used without fault-inducing reflections being generated.

4) A segment can be constructed from cables of different lengths if the total reflection resulting does not exceed 7%.

11.3   The IEEE 802.5/ISO IS 8802-5 standard for local networks: Token Ring access method

The following section gives details of the 1992 IEEE 802.5/ISO IS 8802-5 standard.

Design and Function

A token ring consists of stations connected by means of a transfer medium. The units of information are transferred serially, bit by bit, from one active station to the next. Each station regenerates the data and passes them on. The destination station copies the data before forwarding them, and the sending station finally removes the packet from the ring. A station acquires the right to send when it receives a token – a control signal consisting of a unique sequence of bits, which follows every transfer of information. Any station receiving a token can convert this into a start frame sequence and send it, along with the appropriate control, address and information fields, as a data packet. On completing its transmission, the station sends a new token, allowing the other stations to send data.

The maximum time a station can take between acquiring the token and releasing it again is limited by a 'Token Holding Timer'. Access to the ring can also be controlled by allocating priorities.

11.3.1 Data formats

Thee are two data types in token rings: the tokens themselves and conventional data packets (frames).

Token Format

Figure 11.19 shows a token travelling round an empty ring, as observed with a digital oscilloscope. (Altogether, three tokens are visible.)

Frame Format

The separate fields of a data packet are described in detail in Figure 11.20.

Frame Status

FS Frame Status (1 octet): this data format is used for both MAC and LLC information. The abort sequence is defined as a starting delimiter followed by an ending delimiter (Figure 11.21).

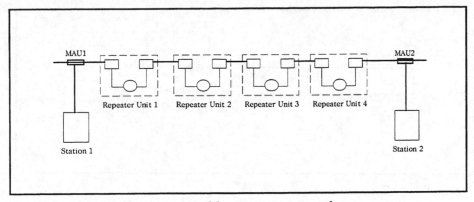

Figure 11.17   Maximum permissible transmission path

This sequence can be sent at any point in the bit stream and aborts any transfer (it is not limited to an octet boundary). If a station is sending, 'pad bits' are sent before or after a data packet, token or abort sequence to avoid an undefined transmission status. These pad bits can be of any number and consist of zeroes, ones, or any combination of zeroes and ones.

Starting Delimiter (SD)

All transfers, whether involving a token or a data packet, must begin with this sequence. If it is missing, the send is considered invalid (Figure 11.22).

Access Control (AC)

The priority bits 'PPP' indicate the priority of the token and thus provide a hierarchy of the stations allowed to use the token (Figure 11.23). There are eight priority levels, the lowest being 000 and the highest 111. The priority bits are transferred with the most significant byte first (thus, 110 has a higher priority than 011).

The token bit 'T' has the value 1 in a token and 0 in a data packet. If a station receives a token with a priority equal to or greater than the priority of a data packet waiting to be sent, it is enabled to convert the token into a start of frame sequence and to send the data.

The monitor bit 'M' prevents the permanent circulation of data packets and tokens with a priority > 0. This bit is transmitted as 0 in all frames and tokens. The Active Monitor Station checks this bit and modifies it from 0 to 1. If a data packet or a token contains a monitor bit set to 1, it indicates that this packet has already passed the Active Monitor Station once, and it is removed from the ring.

The reservation bits 'RRR' enable stations waiting to send data packets of higher priority to request a token with a specific priority.

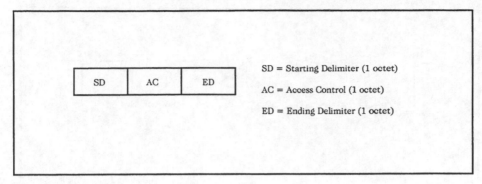

Figure 11.18 Format of a token

Frame Control (FC)

The frame type bits 'FF' in Figure 11.24 indicate the data packet type:

00 MAC frame

01 LLC frame

1X undefined

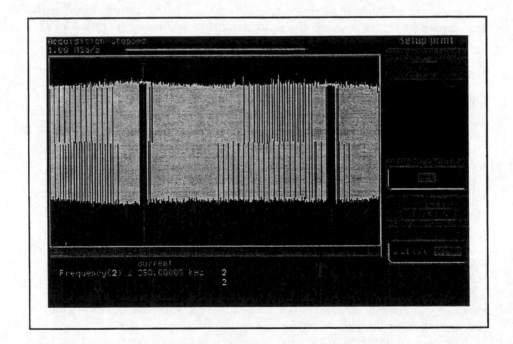

Figure 11.19 Token observed with a digital oscilloscope

For a MAC frame, the control bits are interpreted as appropriate by the stations. In LLC frames the first three control bits ZZZ are set to 0 and the other three bits are replaced by the priority of the data packet to be transmitted.

Destination Address (DA)

The destination address in Figure 11.25 identifies the station to which the packet is being sent. This field can be 16 or 48 bits long, depending on the standard implemented. The first bit defines the address as an individual (bit 1 = 0) or group address (bit 1 = 1) and the second bit (only in the case of 48-bit addresses) indicates whether the address is local (bit 2 = 1) or universal (but 2 = 0).

If the destination address field consists of 16 or 48 ones, it is a broadcast address, directed to all stations. An address consisting of 16 or 48 zeroes is defined as a null address.

Source Address (SA)

The source address identifies the sender of a packet. It must have the same length and format as the destination address. Bit 1 is always set to zero.

Information Field (INFO)

The information field can contain 0, 1 or more octets, which may be directed to the MAC or LLC level or to network management. In principle,

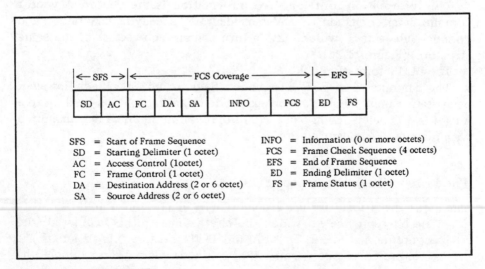

Figure 11.20　Frame Format

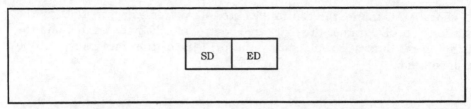

Figure 11.21 Abort Sequence

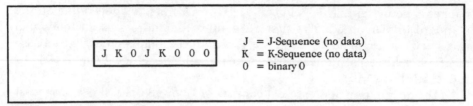

Figure 11.22 Starting Delimiter

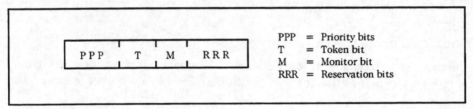

Figure 11.23 Access Control

it may contain any number of octets; however, the maximum 'token holding time' limits the time which may be taken to send a frame.

The MAC information field

The information unit for MAC information is the vector. A vector contains details of its length, a 'Vector Identifier' specifying its function and optional sub-vectors (which may in turn contain sub-vectors of the same structure) (Figure 11.26).

The LLC information field

The contents of an LLC information field are not specified. However, each station must be able to correctly receive an information field up to a length of 133 octets. Each octet within the information field is transmitted with the most significant bit first.

The Frame Check Sequence (FCS)

The frame check sequence is a sequence of 32 bits formed as follows:
- The bit sequence for which the checksum is to be calculated (the contents of the FC, DA, SA and INFO field, n bits in length) is interpreted as a polynomial $M(x)$ to the degree n-1: for example, the

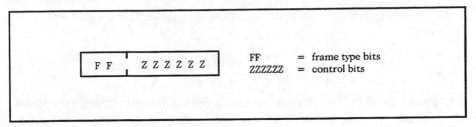

Figure 11.24   Frame Control

bit sequence 110001 has six bits and is interpreted as a polynomial with the coefficients 1,1,0,0,0,1, i.e. $X^5+X^4+X^0$).

1) The expression $X^k(X^{31}+X^{30}+...X+1)$ is formed, where k is the number of bits in the FC, DA, SA and INFO fields. Finally, the result is divided by the 'generator polynomial' $G(x)$.

2) $M(x)$ is then multiplied by x^{32} and divided by $G(x)$, with the generator polynomial defined as follows:

$G(x) = \backslash\backslash\backslash\backslash$.

– Modulo 2 is then added to the remainder of the result in each case, and the ones complement of this formed.

– The frame check sequence is transferred with the most significant bit first.

Although the checksum calculation looks complicated, it is easily implemented by hardware using a simple shift register circuit. A 32-bit CRC like the one shown here will detect all single and double errors, all errors due to an odd number of bits, all error sequences 32 bits in length or less, and with a probability of 99.99999998% all error sequences over 32 bits in length.

The Ending Delimiter (ED)

The ending delimiter (Figure 11.27) is regarded as valid by a receiving station if the first six characters, JK1JK1, are correctly received.

The intermediate frame bit indicates whether the frame is the first or nth frame in a sequence (I = 1). If the value of I in a data packet is 0, this is the last frame in a sequence.

The error detection bit is always set to 0 by the station sending the data packet, token or abort sequence.

The active stations check every frame for errors such as FCS errors, non-data signals etc. As soon as a station detects a faulty packet, the error detection bit is set to 1; otherwise it is sent on with the same value as received.

The Frame Status (FS)

The 'r' bits in Figure 11.28 are reserved for future use. They should be transmitted with the value 0. The A and C bits are also set to 0 by the station sending the data packet.

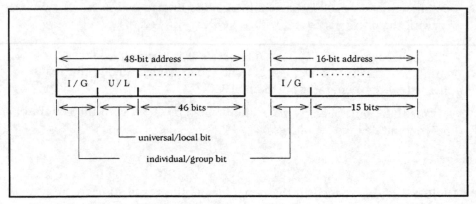

Figure 11.25   Destination Address

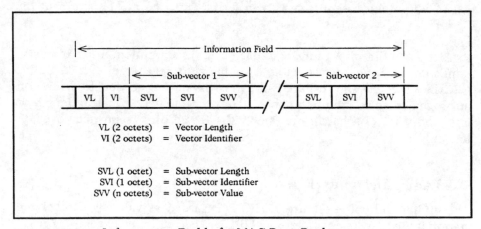

Figure 11.26   Information Field of a MAC Data Packet

If a receiving station identifies the destination address for the data packet as its own, it sets the value of the address-recognised bit to 1.

If the data packet is also copied to the station's receive buffer, the frame-copied bit is set to 1. This allows the sending station to determine which of three possibilities applies:

1) The destination station does not exist on the ring or is not active.

2) The station exists, but the data packet has not been copied.

3) The data packet has been copied into the station's receive buffer.

The A and C bits are only set if the frame satisfies the conditions for a good frame, but irrespective of the status of the error detection bits.

11.3.2 MAC frames

This section describes the contents of the various MAC frames used for ring management in token ring networks:
 − data packets with a value of hex 00 in their control field are only copied into the receive buffer if there is sufficient memory available;
 − data packets with a control field value of hex 01 are always copied into the receive buffer, even if this means that data already in the buffer are over-written;
 − − data packets with a control field value greater than hex 01 are addressed to all stations and are only copied into the receive buffer of any of the stations if there is sufficient memory available.

The Claim Token MAC Frame

If a station detects that there is no active monitor in the ring (via a timeout on the TSM timer − see also 'Timers'), it switches to Claim Token state. Whilst it is in this state, the station sends Claim Token frames and notes the source address of the Claim Token frames it receives. If it receives one of its own Claim Token frames (source address and upstream neighbour address (=SV1−1) in the Claim Token frame match its own address and upstream neighbour address) it will take over as active monitor and will send a new token.

The Duplicate Address Test MAC frame

This frame is sent by a new station in the ring as part of the initialisation procedure, and contains the station's own source address as the destination address. If the Address Recognised bit is set to 1 when the packet is received back at the sending station, this indicates that there is already a station with this address on the ring, and the station will remove itself from the ring.

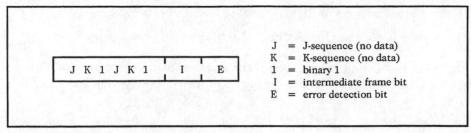

Figure 11.27   The Ending Delimiter (ED)

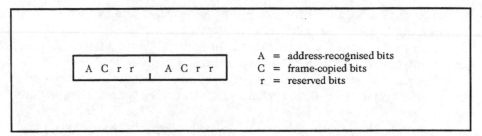

Figure 11.28   Frame Status

The Active Monitor Present (AMP) MAC Frame

This frame is sent by the active monitor either after a ring purge (see also 'Ring Purge') or on a timeout by the TAM timer (Timer, Active Monitor). On receiving the Active Monitor Present frame, all stations reset their TSM timer (Timer, Standby Monitor) to 0.

Standby Monitor Present (SMP) MAC Frame

Standby Monitor Present frames are sent by the standby monitor stations (which means all stations other than the active monitor). On receipt of an SMP or AMP with the Address Recognised bit (the A bit) and the Frame Copied bit (the C bit) both set to 0, the Queue PDU timer (TQP) is reset to zero.

As soon as the TQP timer runs out, an SMP frame is sent. (Zero A and C bits mean that the frame was sent by the upstream neighbour; it will be an SMP or AMP frame depending on whether the upstream neighbour is a standby monitor or an active monitor. The source address in the SMP/AMP frame received is therefore stored at the same time as that of the new (old) upstream neighbour. The TQP timer ensures that the sending process for the SMP or AMP frame does not occupy more than 1% of the ring's sending bandwidth.

Priority	0
Frame Control Field (FC)	00 000011 (Claim Token)
Destination address	11111111 11111111... (Broadcast)
Information` field VII	Hex1 0003 (Claim Token)
Information field SVI-1	Hex 02 (Upstream neighbour address received)
Information field SVV-1	XXXXXXXX... (Upstream neighbour address)

Beacon MAC Frame (BCN)

A beacon frame is sent when hardware errors are detected which cannot be corrected by the ring itself (e.g. breaks in the cable, a station on permanent send, jabbering etc.). The station immediately upstream of the station sending the beacon frame marks the start of the fault area, so its address is entered in the MAC information field.

Purge MAC Frame (PRG)

This frame is sent by the active monitor in one of the following situations:

Priority	0
Frame Control Field (FC)	00 000000
Destination Address	same as source address
Information Field VI	Hex 0007 (Duplicate Address Test)

1) On completion of the token claiming process and before a new token is sent.

2) Valid Transmission timer (TVX) timeout.

3) Detection of a monitor bit (in the Access Control field) with the value 1 (see Access Control Field).

11.3.3 Timers

Timer, Return to Repeat (TRR)

A timer is implemented in every station to ensure that the station returns to the signal-repeat state within a certain time. This time must be greater than the signal propagation time over the longest distance in the ring plus the aggregate delay time for all the stations. The default value is 2.5 ms.

Priority	7
Frame Control Field (FC)	00 000101
Destination Address	Broadcast
Information Field VI	Hex 0005 (Active Monitor Present)
Information field SVI-1	Hex 02 (Upstream neighbour address received)
Information field SVV-1	Upstream neighbour address

Timer, Holding Token (THT)

The THT timer limits the time for which a station can send after receiving the token. The default value is 10 ms.

Timer, Queue PDU (TQP)

The TQP timer controls the time which must elapse between receipt of an AMP or SMP frame from the upstream neighbour (A and C bits zeroed) and the sending of a SMP frame by the station itself. (This limits the load imposed on the network by these 'I am here' signals to below 1%.) Default is 10 ms.

Priority	0
Frame Control Field (FC)	00 000110
Destination Address	Broadcast
Information Field VI	Hex 0006 (Standby Monitor Present)
Information field SVI-1	Hex 02 (Upstream neighbour address received)
Information field SVV-1	Address Upstream neighbour address

Timer, Valid Transmission (TVX)

A timeout on a station's TVX timer indicates to the active monitor the absence of a valid signal. The value for this timer is the sum of THT and TRR, and is therefore set to 12.5 ms by default.

Timer, No Token (TNT)

The TNT timer implemented in every station enables the ring to be regenerated after various token errors. The value of the timer is (n THT) +

Priority	0
Frame Control Field (FC)	00 000010
Destination Address	Broadcast
Information Field VI	Hex 0002 (Beacon)
Information field SVI-1	Hex 02 (Upstream neighbour address received)
Information field SVV-1	Address of Upstream neighbour
Information Field SVI-2	Hex 01 (Beacon Type)
Information Field SVV-2	Hex 0001 (for future use)
	Hex 0002 (Permanent Non-Data J Waveform - see also Physical Level)
	Hex 0003 (No Token timer (TNT) timeout and no Claim Token frame detected)
	Hex 0004 (No Token timer (TNT) timeout during Claim Token process)
Priority	0
Frame Control Field (FC)	00 000100
Destination Address	Broadcast
Information Field VI	Hex 0004 (Purge)
Information field SVI-1	Hex 02 (Upstream neighbour address received)
Information field SVV-1	Address of Upstream neighbour

TRR, where n is the maximum number of stations on the ring. The default value is 1 s.

Timer, Active Monitor (TAM)

A timeout on a station's TAM timer causes the active monitor to send an AMP (Active Monitor Present) frame. The default is 3 s.

Timer, Standby Monitor, (TSM)

A TSM timer is implemented in every station to ensure that there is an active monitor present in the ring and that tokens are continuously received. This has a value of 7 s by default.

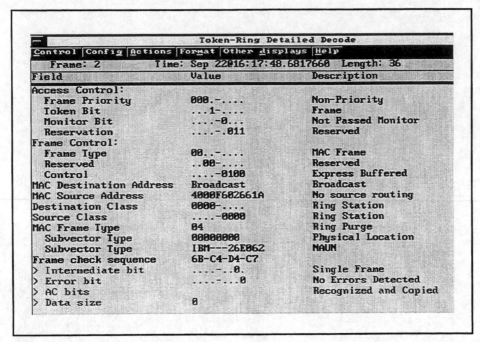

Figure 11.29   Ring purge, recorded using a protocol analyser

11.3.4 Flags

Flags are used to record the occurrence of certain events.

The 'I' Flag

The 'I' flag has its 'I' (intermediate) bit set to 1 when an ending delimiter is received. (This inidcates that the frame received is the first in a sequence.)

The SFS Flag

The SFS flag is set when a Start Frame Sequence is received.

The MA Flag

The MA flag is set when a data packet with the station's own source address is received.

11.3.5 Registers and Stacks

The Pr and Rr Registers

The value of the priority bit and the reservation bit of the last Access Control Frame received are saved in the Pr and Rr registers:
  Pr: Last Priority Value Received
  Rr: Last Reservation Value Received

The Sr and Sx Stacks

If the value of the Rr register or the priority Pm of a data packet to be sent is greater than the value in the Pr register, a token with the priority Rr or Pm is sent (depending on which has the higher priority). The priority of the token sent is saved in Sx and the value of Pr in Sr.
  – Sr: Highest Stacked Received Priority
  – Sx: Highest Stacked Transmitted Priority

11.3.6 The Latency Buffer

The latency (delay) buffer ensures that the ring keeps to a minimum propagation time of 24 bit cycles. It also compensates for any phase jitter.

11.3.7 The Token Ring Protocol

Transfer of a data packet

Access to the transfer medium is regulated by the token (Figure 11.30). The token enables the station in possession of it at any given time to send data packets (LLC, MAC or NMT frames) provided that the priority of the data to be sent is greater than or equal to that of the token received.

If the token is defective or has too high a priority, the station wishing to send can request a suitable token by entering an appropriate priority in the RRR bits of the token's Access Control Field. Once a token of this priority has been received, it can be converted into a start-of-frame sequence by setting the token bits. The station now stops repeating signals it has received and starts transmitting its own data.

Sending the token

After sending the frame(s), the sending station checks whether its own data packets – packets with its own address as the source address – have been received back (meaning that they have gone right round the ring). This is indicated by setting the MA flag. Until the MA flag is set, the station sends fill data. Only after the MA flag has been set will a new token be sent.

The station remains in transmit mode after the token has been sent until all of its packets have been removed from the ring.

Receiving data packets

Whilst the stations are repeating the incoming data stream they check whether the data packets are addressed to themselves. If these are MAC frames, all the active stations will react to them according to the instructions in the control field. If the destination address of the data packet matches the station's own, it will be copied into the receive buffer and passed through to the appropriate sub-layer.

Setting priorities

The priority bits PPP and the reservation bits RRR in the control field enable the station with the highest-priority data packets to send. Any station requesting a token with a higher priority must reset the ring to its original priority after transmitting its packets (for which the Sx and Sr stacks are used).

If a station wishes to send a packet with a priority Pm greater than 0, it begins by requesting a priority token of the desired priority. This is done by changing the RRR bits in the token's AC field to an appropriate value. Once a token of the desired priority has been received, the Pm data packets can be sent. If the station has no more packets with a priority = Pm to send and there is no reservation request (Rr register) greater than Pr, the Present Ring Service Priority, the token with a priority = Pr and a reservation value = Rr or Pm (whichever is the greater) will be sent.

If the station is still left with data packets with a priority = Pm (which could not be sent due to a timeout from the THT timer) or if there is a reservation request Rr greater than Pr, a token of priority Pm or Rr (whichever is the greater) and a reservation RRR = 0 will be sent. As the station has now increased the Present Ring Service Priority (Pr), the old value of Pr must be saved as Sr and the new Pr as Sx (Sr and Sx will be used afterwards to return the ring priority to its original level). The station has now become a 'stacking station'. The stacking station now inspects every token with a priority = Sx for the state of the reservation bits RRR and changes the priority of the token accordingly.

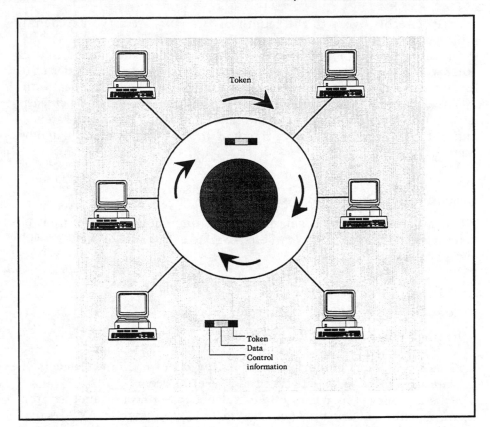

Figure 11.30

The new token is sent with a priority PPP = RRR, but not if the priority is < Sr (Sr is the original priority level). If the token's new priority PPP is greater than Sr, a new Sx of this value is written to the stack, the token's RRR bits are set to 0 and the stacking station continues with its function.

If the value of the reservation bits RRR (Rr) is < or = Sr, Sr and Sx are removed from the stack. If there are no more Sx or Sr values left on the stack (written during earlier operations), the station discontinues its stacking function.

Length of the ring

Before we go on to describe further aspects of the token ring protocol, a few remarks on the physical and effective lengths of a ring will be useful. Strictly speaking, of course, a ring is no more than a linked string of ring stations closed in a circle. Each of these stations possesses what is known as a one-bit buffer. Every incoming bit is copied to this buffer before being sent back out to the ring. (While it is in the buffer, the bit can be checked and if necessary altered.) But this also means that every station is adding exactly one bit cycle to the length of the ring. At a typical signal propagation speed of 200 m/µs (approx. 0.7c), each bit in a 4 Mbits/sec token ring thus occupies 50 metres of the ring (12.5 m at 16 Mbits/sec). In other words, every station adds an apparent 50 m to the ring. But this also implies that a ring 1000 metres long, for example, can only ever deal with 20 bits at the same time! However, the ring must be able to handle at least 24 bits (the length of a token) at the same time. This requires a 'latency buffer' to guarantee a minimum ring length of 24 bits (see also Latency Buffer).

Beaconing and Neighbour Notification

When a hardware error occurs in a token ring network, its location is determined so that the ring can be regenerated. The area of the fault will always consist of

– the station reporting the fault (the beaconing station),

– the station upstream from the beaconing station,

– the ring medium between the two stations.

To allow the area of the fault to be narrowed down, all the elements of the fault area must be known at the time the error occurs.

This is achieved by means of the 'Neighbour Notification Process': the active monitor initiates neighbour notification by sending an AMP (Active Monitor Present) broadcast. The station immediately downstream reacts as follows:

1) It resets its TSM (Standby Monitor) timer.

2) It copies the AMP broadcast frame (if possible) into its receive buffer and saves the address of its upstream neighbour (UNA).
   \ Which rather suggests that all occurrences of 'UAN' in earlier files should have been 'UNA' !!!!!!!   (Meaning 'Upstream Neighbour Address' and NOT simply 'Upstream Neighbour', as the original suggested) \

3) It sets the A and C bits to 1.

4) It sends an SMP broadcast frame. Each station in turn will receive an SMP frame of this sort with the A and C bits set to 0, which identifies the neighbour station and enables the respective UNAs to be stored. The active monitor's TAM (Active Monitor) timer is reset, as are the TSM timers in all the standby monitors. If a TSM timer runs out, the station affected starts sending Claim Token frames.

11.3.8 Signalling Specifications

The signalling between the different layers carried out by the token ring chips and described in the standard at this point is not of interest to us. However, the way error states are communicated between PHY and NMT will be briefly described here.

\ PHY and NMT are Physical Layer and um er? \

PH.CONTROL.request

Is sent to the physical layer by the NMT to log the station into the ring or remove it from the ring. The 'control action' parameters are: INSERT or REMOVE.

PH_STATUS.indication

Is used by the physical layer to inform the NMT about significant errors or status changes. The status report parameters are as follows:

– BURST_CORRECTION_START

The physical layer has begun to generate 0's and 1's and send them to its local MAC sublayer to correct a detected break in sending. (Even when no data are being sent, fill data must be transmitted to avoid the ring getting into an undefined state.)

– BURST_CORRECTION_END

The physical layer's character generation has been halted. Signals have again been detected on the ring.

– LATENCY_BUFFER_OVERFLOW

The physical layer has attempted to extend the latency buffer (see also under 'Latency Buffer') to more than 30 bits.

– LATENCY_BUFFER_UNDERFLOW

The physical layer has attempted to reduce the circulation buffer to less than 24 bits.

11.3.9 The Physical Level

This section describes the specifications for the physical layer in a token ring.

Signal Encoding

The physical level of a token ring station transmits to the transfer medium the four signal types it receives from the MAC sublayer:

0 binary 0
1 binary 1
J non-data J
K non-data K

The signals are converted to differential Manchester code (as distinct from standard Manchester code in IEEE 802.3 and 4B/5B code in FDDI) and sent. This divides each bit into two halves. The first half of the signal is then used to send the logical complement of the unit of information to be transferred, which is inverted in the second half.

In addition, the waveform of the information unit transmitted depends on the one previously transmitted: if a binary 0 is to be transmitted, the polarity of the preceding signal is reversed; if a binary 1, the polarity of the preceding signal is retained. This has three advantages:

1) The resulting signal has no DC component and can therefore immediately be coupled either inductively or capacitatively.

2) The polarity inversion in the middle of each bit implicitly carries clock information along with it. The only exceptions to this rule of division into half-bits are the J and K characters. A J signal begins with the same polarity as the preceding signal and a K signal with inverted polarity. To avoid DC components on the ring, J and K characters are usually transmitted in alternation.

3) Differential Manchester coding is less sensitive to noise than simple Manchester coding. A disadvantage, however, is that an effective data transfer rate of 4 or 16 Mbits/sec requires an actual clock speed of 8 or 32 MHz. That is, all the network components have to be set up at twice the speed. The same applies analogously to 802.3 CSMA/CD. Only in FDDI, with 4B/5B coding, is this effect avoided: here, an effective data rate of 100 Mbits/sec requires a clock speed of only 125 MHz.

Decoding signals

Incoming signals are decoded using the reverse of the algorithm described above and passed through to the MAC sub-layer. If a station detects more than four signals in succession without a polarity inversion, it will insert a polarity inversion itself at the end of the fourth signal.

Successive polarity inversions will then be transmitted until one is detected on the ring.

Similar action is taken if the clock pulse is lost or there is a latency buffer overflow or underflow. A polarity inversion is generated and sent on each bit cycle. The resulting bit stream is then passed to the local MAC sub-layer.

The Data Rate

The data rate is 1 or 4 Mbits/sec to a tolerance of +/- 0.01%.

Timing

The physical layer at each station is given the task of regenerating the timing information for the signals and keeping phase jitter to a minimum. In normal operation, a token ring will include an active monitor; all other stations will then be synchronised to the active monitor in frequency and phase. This 'phase-locked loop' is based on the following criteria:

1) The dynamic jitter of any station must not exceed 3 sigma = 10 degrees.

2) If a station logs into the ring or loses clock synchronisation, it must be able to regain phase synchronisation with the active monitor within 1.5 ms.

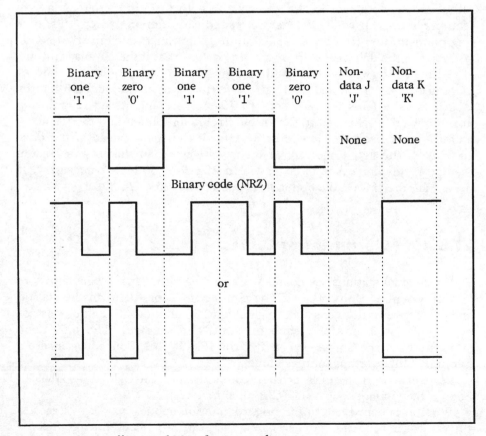

Figure 11.31   Differential Manchester coding

3) The timing must be implemented with sufficient accuracy to allow at least 250 stations and repeaters to be active on the ring at the same time.

The Latency Buffer

To ensure that the token continuously circles the ring, it must have a minimum circulation time (the time in bits it requires to complete a circuit of the ring). This time must at least equal the number of bits in the token sequence (see Data Formats: a token consists of 3 octets = 24 bits), i.e. 24 bits. As the propagation time will vary depending on the size of the ring and the number of stations, only this minimum delay time is defined and guaranteed by the active monitor.

Phase Jitter Compensation

Although the data rate is checked by the active monitor, there may be sections of the ring where the transfer speed varies minutely from this. In a ring configuration running to 250 stations, this can result in variations of +/- 3 bits in the delay time. However, this means that if the circulation time is reduced bits will be lost, and conversely, if the circulation time is increased bits will be added. To prevent this, a dynamic buffer 6 bits in length is used (this is equivalent to 12 signal elements or 12 polarity inversions). This is added to the 24-bit circulation buffer, and the resulting buffer is initialised at a length of 27 bits. If the signal speed of the data arriving at the active monitor is slightly higher than that of the master oscillator, this buffer can be extended to 28, 29 or 30 bits as necessary. If the signals are slower, the buffer is reduced to 26, 25 or 24 bits.

11.3.10 Attachment of Cables

The individual stations are coupled to the ring by means of concentrators (Trunk Coupling Units: TCUs). The connecting cable between the station and the concentrator consists of a shielded 150-ohm (+/- 15 ohms) twisted-pair cable (with one pair each for send and receive). The plug used (Medium Interface Connector, MIC) is the IBM Type 1. Concentrators are a frequent and notorious source of faults.

\ I've called Ringleitungsverteiler 'concentrators' throughout, as advised. Should they in fact have been TCUs all along? \

When it is connected to the ring, the station applies two DC voltages to the concentrator (one via each pair), with the two DC circuits connected inductively to the send and receive cables on both the station and the concentrator side (Figure 11.32). This enables AC signals (i.e. bit streams) to be transported over these DC circuits, whilst the operation of the cable pairs can at the same time be monitored (for breaks and short circuits) by measurements on the DC circuits themselves. At the same time, the DC voltage is used to control the concentrator relay, which is responsible for the mechanical connection of the station to the ring. At log-on, a voltage of between 4.1 and 7.0 volts should be applied to pins B and O (see Figure 11.32) and should result in a current of 0.65 to 2.0 mA at G and R. By-pass mode is resumed if the voltage is less than 1 V.

11.4 ANSI ASC X329.5 / ISO 9314 FDDI: THE FIBRE DISTRIBUTED DATA INTERFACE

The ANSI ASC X329.5 / ISO 9314 standard for FDDI is drawn up in four sections:
  – Section 1:
  X3.148-1988 / ISO 9314-1 1989, Token Ring Physical Layer Protocol (PHY).
  – Section 2:
  X3.139-1987 / ISO 9314-2 1989, Token Ring Media Access Control (MAC).
  – Section 3:
  X3.166-1990 / ISO 9314-3 1990, Physical Medium Dependent Layer (PMD).
  – Section 4:
  Draft Proposal, (currently) Version 7.

Station Management (SMT)

Section 1:

ANSI ASC X329.5 / ISO 9314-1 Token Ring Physical Layer Protocol (PHY)

Design and Function

FDDI is capable of setting up a high-speed connection (100 Mbits/sec) between different networks using optical fibre. Any two stations are connected via a 'primary link' (Primary In, Primary Out) and a 'secondary link' (Secondary In, Secondary Out).

There are two classes of station: Dual-Attachment Stations (DAS) and Single-Attachment Stations (SAS), the difference being that single-attachment stations can only be connected to the ring via concentrators (which are themselves always actively connected to the ring via their own

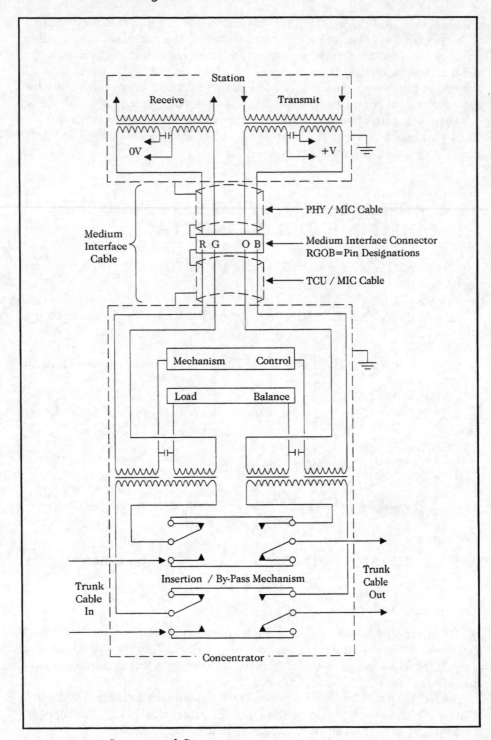

Figure 11.32   Station and Concentrator

Dual-Attach Interface, but can also link up a number of other SAS stations). The characteristics of FDDI have been calculated assuming 1000 physical stations on a ring 200 km in length (or 500 stations on a dual ring 100 km long).

The structure of FDDI is as follows:

a) The Physical Layer (PL) is made up of two sub-layers:

1) The Physical Medium Dependent Layer (PMD), which is responsible for the transport of the digital bit stream from station to station. (This includes definitions for optical drivers, receivers, cables, connectors and all other hardware-related components.)

2) The Physical Layer Protocol Layer (PHY), which takes care of the connection between the PMD and the data link layer (the PHY is synchronised to the signals and encodes or decodes the bit stream).

b) The Data Link Layer (DLL) monitors access to the medium by the individual stations and generates or verifies frame check sequences and network addresses.

c) The Station Management (SMT) looks after ring management at station level. This involves such functions as control and configuration management, error location and ring regeneration.

11.4.1 Encoding

The Code Bit

A code bit is the smallest signalling unit for the physical layer and is represented by a polarity inversion or the absence of polarity inversion.

The Code Group

A code group is a sequence of five code bits, representing a character.

The Character Set

The data link layer of each station uses fixed-length characters for communication.

Line State characters

The three line state characters are transmitted as a pad signal during breaks in transmission:

– Quiet (Q):
   The Quiet character indicates an absence of any polarity inversion.

– Halt (H):
   The Halt character indicates either control sequences or the removal of invalid characters, and at the same time keeps any DC component of the signals on the ring to a minimum.

– Idle (I):
   The Idle character indicates the normal state between two data transfers. It provides a continuous stream of pad bits used for clock synchronisation.

Control Characters

Starting Delimiter (SD)
   The starting delimiter sequence indicates the start of a data transfer sequence. Data transfer can either start when the medium is in idle state, or follow a preceding transmission, or interrupt a transmission (irrespective of character boundaries). The SD sequence consists of a series of alternating Js and Ks, which is unique even if character boundaries are disregarded (see also Figure 11.34).

Ending Delimiter (ED)
   The ending delimiter terminates every normal data transmission and consists of a 'T' character. However, the ED need not necessarily be the last character in a transfer: it may be followed by control indicators.

   These must form pairs of characters with the ED, such as an ED followed by an odd number of control indicators. If no control indicators are sent, the transmission is terminated by an ED pair (TT).

   Where there is an even number of control indicators, a further ED is added after the last control indicator. An ED cannot be decoded unless the character boundaries can be detected (unlike an SD).

Control Indicators

The control indicators specify logical states relating to the data transmission sequence. They can be changed by repeater stations without affecting the data transmitted.

Reset (R)
Indicates logical 0 state (Reset)
Set (R)

Indicates logical 1 state (Set)

Data Characters (0–F)

There are 16 data characters (Hex 0 to F), which can be sent in any sequence. The data characters are not decoded by the PHY. A correct interpretation of the data depends on correct reception of the SD sequence.

Invalid Characters (V)

Invalid characters are characters not defined as valid characters (see Figure 11.34). Receipt of invalid characters may result from various error conditions or occur during clock synchronisation sequences.

11.4.2 The various line states

The line state is monitored by the PHY and automatically passed through to the SMT if it changes, or polled by the SMT from the PHY. In addition, the PHY reports every QLS, MLS, HLS or NLS line status to the local MAC layer.

Quiet_Line_State (QLS)

The QLS is used when setting up a new physical connection: the PHY sends a continuous stream of Quiet characters. The QLS state will be adopted on any loss of signal from the PMD (Signal_Detect (off)) or (if Signal_Detect (on) – that is, if signals are being received) on receipt of 16 or 17 consecutive Q characters. The PHY quits the QLS state on receiving any character other than Q.

Master_Line_State (MLS)

The MLS state, marked by alternating Halt and Quiet characters sent by the PHY, is also used to set up physical connections. MLS state is adopted whenever 8 or 9 consecutive HQ (or QH) character pairs are received. The PHY quits the MLS state as soon as a character pair other than HQ (or QH) is received.

Halt_Line_State (HLS)

A continuous send of Halt characters (H) is another sequence used when setting up physical connections. This state is adopted on receipt of 16 or 17

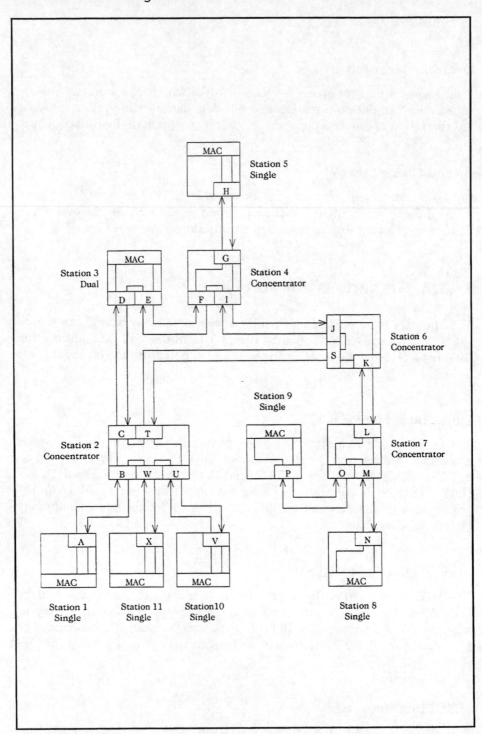

Figure 11.33 FDDI Topology (example)

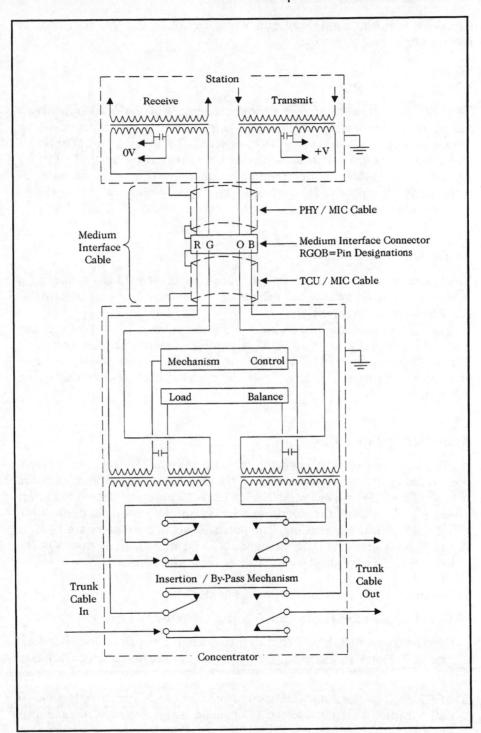

Figure 11.34   Character encoding

consecutive H characters and quit when any character other than H is received or the signal is lost.

Idle_Line_State (ILS)

The ILS, a continuous stream of Idle characters (I), is used both when setting up a new physical connection and to pad out a gap between two data packets. This state will be adopted after 4 or 5 consecutive I characters are received (this value can be increased by up to 11 bits by adjusting the elasticity buffer: minimum buffer size is 9 bits, maximum 20 bits). The PHY quits the ISL state on receiving any character other than I or losing the signal.

Active Line State (ALS)

The active line state indicates that the incoming bit stream is a sequence of MAC frames, meaning that the neighbour PHY (which has sent these data) has a connection to the ring.

The ALS is adopted on receipt of a JK character pair (=SD) or at any code bit boundary in the \?\NRZ signalling (Signal_Detect (on) and Clock_Detect Asserted, if implemented) and quit on receipt of any character other than I, n, R, S T, on loss of signal and on switching to the ILS state.

Noise_Line_State (NLS)

If the NLS is detected, it indicates that the incoming signals are noisy. If the condition persists, this means that the physical connection in question is faulty. The PHY will switch to NLS if 16 or 17 potential noise characters are received without the conditions for switching to another line state being fulfilled in the meantime. The potential noise characters are Q, H, J, K and V (or a character pair including at least one Q, H, J, K or V). The following events may also be evaluated as noise characters:

a) Elasticity Buffer Error on receipt of signal,

b) Decoding of a mixed signal pair (control indicator plus data),

c) Decoding of an n, R, S or T character (or a character pair including at least one n, R, S or T whilst Signal_Detect is (on) but the line state is not ILS or ALS.

d) If Clock_Detect (a mechanism monitoring clock synchronisation) is implemented but 'not asserted' is signalled, a signal is received and an I, n, R, S or T character is decoded (or a signal pair comprising a JK sequence or containing at least one I, n, R, S or T character).

As soon as the conditions exist for switching to a non-NLS state, the count of potential noise signals detected is reset to 0.

11.4.3 PHY Functions

Data transmission and reception; encoding

The coding used in FDDI transfers both clock information and data. Every item of information is conveyed by means of a polarity inversion or the absence of a polarity inversion. In the ideal case, every polarity inversion taking place or omitted would represent data information.

In reality, however, this is not possible – firstly, because a series of bits represented by the absence of polarity inversions would be unable to continue supplying sufficiently precise clock information, and secondly, because this would result in a sizeable DC component. For this reason, the final bit stream is given at least two polarity inversions per character sent: this limits the number of consecutive absent polarity inversions to a maximum of three, guaranteeing not only adequate clock information but also a maximum DC component of +/- 10% of the nominal value. Characters are used by the MAC layer to transfer three types of information:

– line states (e.g. QLS),

– control characters (e.g. SD, ED),

– data characters (with each data character representing four (binary) data bits: see Figure 11.34).

Each character (the character frequency being one-fifth of the base frequency of 125 MHz) is first translated by the PHY into a code group consisting of five NRZ code bits. The second step is to convert the five NRZ code bits to five NRZI code bits. On receiving the data, the PHY generates the clock from the incoming 125-MHz NRZI bit stream using a phase-locked loop circuit. This is known as the Receiver Recovery Clock (RCRCLK) and is used to synchronise the destination station to the code bit boundaries of the input signal. (The RCRCLK also generates the optional Clock_Detect signal mentioned above.)

The 125 MHz clock rate at an effective data transfer rate of 100 Mbits/sec derives from the fact that four bits of information (e.g. a hex 'F', i.e. 1111) is sent as a character five code bits long (in this case, 11101), where there must be a 0 after a maximum of three ones. This coding is also known as 4B/5B code. In fact, simple Manchester coding as used in Ethernet, or differential Manchester code in token rings, is even less efficient in operation. At data rates of 10 and 4 Mbits/sec, the actual clock rate is 20 and 8 Mbits/sec respectively.

The Elasticity Buffer

The clock frequency of the incoming bit stream (deriving from the CRCRLK) and that of the bit stream sent (supplied by the local oscillator) must not deviate from the nominal frequency by more than 0.01%. The elasticity buffer in each station is used to compensate for these frequency differences. To prevent bits being lost (if the sending frequency of a station is lower than its receiving frequency), the sending MAC layer sends at least 16 Idle characters ahead of each frame. The elasticity buffer itself must have a capacity of at least +/- 4.5 code bits.

The buffer's input clock rate corresponds to that of the RCRCLK and its output clock is taken from the local oscillator. The elasticity is calculated on the basis of 9,000 characters (the maximum frame length) or 45,000 code bits. In the worst case, the maximum permissible clock inaccuracy of 0.005% for each clock will result in a frequency difference of 0.01% or 4.5 code bits.

The rules which the elasticity buffer works to are as follows:

a) If the Idle line state gives way to an Active line state and both clocks (RCRCLK and the local clock) are working within their tolerances, the incoming NRZ bit stream, starting with a JK sequence, must be reproduced in full without adding, modifying or deleting characters, unless one of the following situations occurs:

– At least 9,000 characters have been received since the last switch to ALS (see rule b).

– At least 9 (or up to 20, according to the implementation) consecutive code bit ones are detected in the incoming NRZ bit stream (irrespective of the character boundaries) (see rules c and d).

– A second JK sequence is received between 0 and 9 code bits after receiving a JK sequence (see rule e).

– A character is received which causes ALS to be quit (see rule f).

b) If more than 9,000 characters have been received or both clocks are operating outside their tolerances, an Elasticity Buffer Error exists and characters in the incoming NRZ bit stream may be deleted, modified or inserted. This error is reported to both the MAC layer and the SMT.

c) After 9 consecutive code bit ones have been received in the NRZ bit stream, code bit ones may be deleted or inserted without the presence of an Elasticity Buffer Error (provided there are still at least 9 code bit ones in the resulting bit stream: this guarantees at least one Idle character (11111) irrespective of the character boundaries).

d) After 20 consecutive code bit ones have been received, Idle bits may be deleted or inserted without the presence of an Elasticity Buffer Error, provided that further ones continue to be received.

e) If a JK sequence is followed by a second JK sequence, up to 4 code bits may be inserted or deleted.

f) If the ring is in neither ALS nor IDL state, the incoming bit stream may be amended in any way. However, the first four consecutive invalid signals must be passed through as such.

Line State Identification

Initial line state identification begins once an NRZI signal stream has been detected. The time elapsing until the line state is reported to the SMT must not be greater than AT_Max (Maximum PHY Acquisition Time, default 100 ~s). During this interval, Line_State_Unknown or Noise_Line_State is sent to the SMT.

After the initial line state identification, a maximum time of LS_Max (Line State Change Time, default 15~s) must elapse between a change to or loss of the correct line state and a fresh Correct signal. During this interval, as before, Line_State_Unknown or Noise_Line_State is sent to the SMT.

The Local Clock

The local clock is supplied by a fixed-frequency oscillator with the following characteristics:

- fixed base frequency of 125 MHz +/- 0.005% (50 ppm),

- phase jitter above 20 kHz less than 8 degrees,

- harmonic component above 125.02 MHz less than 20 dB,

- nominal code bit time = 11.0 ns,

- nominal character time = 40.0 ns.

The Smoothing Function

The smoothing function ensures that the preamble of a frame is not reduced beyond the permissible degree after passing through a number of elasticity buffers. The smoothing function removes characters from long preambles and adds characters to short ones.

The smoothing function is capable of extending to 14 characters preambles of up to 13 characters in length or reducing to 14 characters those with a length of 15 characters or more (by adding or deleting up to 2 characters). If the MAC layer requires 11 or 12 preamble characters for error-free copying of the data, the same parameters will apply, with a threshold value of 12.

As a general rule in FDDI, the MAC layer will not copy any frames with preambles shorter than 12 characters, and will not repeat any frames with preambles shorter than 2 characters.

The Repeat Filter

Certain configurations may require the PHY to output the incoming signals directly to the ring without going via the local MAC layer (e.g. where there is a second logical ring with no local MAC).

In such a case, the Repeat Filter function prevents the spread of illegal codes and invalid line states.

The Repeat Filter amends the bit stream according to the following rules:

1) When an 'I' character is received, all following characters are converted to 'I' characters until another 'I' or a 'J' character is detected.

2) If the character immediately after a 'J' is not a 'K', it will be sent as a 'V' character.

3) If a JK sequence is followed by a K, H, V or Q, this following character will be converted to an H. The same applies to the following three characters, unless they are J or I characters. After the fourth H all following characters will be changed to I characters until a new J or I character is received.

Ring Delay

Minimum Ring Delay
To enable the ring to function without problem, every station with a MAC layer must guarantee a minimum delay of 3 octets, or two octets for stations without a MAC layer.

Maximum Ring Delay
The maximum ring delay is the total of the various delays for the individual stations plus the signal transit time on the medium. Both MAC and SMT have timers determined by this maximum ring delay. The following parameters are used in calculating this delay:

– SD_Min
   The minimum delay applied to a Starting Delimiter sequence by a station (default: 74 bits or 592 ns).

– SD_Max

The maximum delay applied to a Starting Delimiter sequence by a station. The maximum delay resulting from smoothing is two characters or 10 bits; the same applies for the elasticity buffer (+/- 4.5 bits, gives a maximum of 9 bits). Sampling and timing errors are estimated at a maximum of 4 bits. SD_Max is <= 592 ns + 4 + 80 + 80 = 756 ns.

– P_Max

Number of physical layers (PHY & PMD) on the ring. The default count is 1000, which means 500 stations for dual-attached.

– D_Max

The maximum ring delay suffered by a start delimiter sequence in the absence of signal noise. 1000 physical layers, a ring length of 100 km of dual cable and a propagation speed of 5085 ns/km give a D_Max <= (P_Max x SD_Max) + (2 x 100 x 5085) = 1.773 ms. The default value for D_Max should be smaller than 1.773 ms and is set at 1.617 ms in ISO 9314-2.

Section 2:
X3.139.1987 / ISO 9314-2:
Token Ring Media Access Control (MAC)

11.4.4 Data Formats

The MAC layer uses two types of data format (Protocol Data Units or PDUs): tokens and standard data packets (frames). A token is constructed as follows:

Tokens

A token constitutes authority to send on the ring and is passed from station to station. The preamble of the token consists of a minimum of 16 Idle characters. The length of the preamble may vary whilst the token is travelling round the ring (see Smoothing Function and Elasticity Buffer). If a valid token is received by a station, but cannot be reset for one reason or another (ring timing etc.), it will generate a new token.

Data Packets (Frames)

The frame format is used for the transfer of both MAC and LLC data. An information field may be included, but need not be. The frame length includes all fields except for the preamble. The maximum frame length is set at 9,000 characters (including 4 preamble characters). The individual fields of a data packet are shown in Figure 11.36.

Preamble (PA)

The preamble consists of at least 16 Idle characters. The length of the preamble may vary whilst the token is travelling round the ring, but a MAC layer will not copy data packets with less than 12 preamble characters in its receive buffer.

Starting Delimiter (SD)

Every valid data packet or token must start with the sequence of characters shown in Figure 11.37.

Frame Control (FC)

The frame control field specifies the data packet type:

– Frame Class bit (C):
  Frame Class bit (C) = 0: data packet is asynchronous
  Frame Class bit (C) = 1: data packet is synchronous

– Frame Address Length bit (L):
  The frame address length bit gives the length of the two MAC addresses (source address and destination address): L=0 for 16-bit addresses, L=1 for 48-bit addresses.

– Frame Format bits (FF):
  The frame format bits, together with the C, L and ZZZZ bits, indicate the frame type (see table 1).
  Control bits (ZZZZ):
  Taken together with the CLFF bits, the control bits have the following meaning:

– MAC Beacon Frame (1L00 0010):
  MAC beacon frames are sent in the event of serious hardware problems, when the ring is no longer able to regenerate itself (loss of signal, jabber frames etc.).

– MAC Claim Frame (1L00 0011):
  These frames are sent when the token is lost. If a station receives a MAC claim frame with its own address as the source address, it can re-initialise the ring and generate a new token.

– SMT Next Station Addressing Frame (0L00 1111):
  This frame is defined in detail in the SMT section of the specifications.

– LLC Frame (0L01 rPPP):

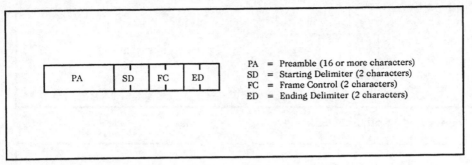

Figure 11.35 Structure of a token

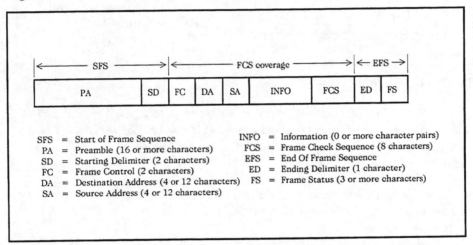

Figure 11.36 Frame Format

This LLC frame is used for asynchronous transmission. The final three bits, PPP, give the priority, with 111 the highest asynchronous priority and 0000 the lowest.

– LLC Frame (1L01 rrrr):
This LLC frame is used for synchronous transmission.

Source and Destination Address

Every data packet contains two address fields either 16 or 48 bits in length: the source and destination addresses. Stations with 16-bit addresses must be capable of operating in rings with 48-bit addresses (that is, they must be able to recognise and repeat 48-bit addresses correctly and react correctly to 48-bit address claim frames and broadcast frames). Stations with 48-bit addresses must have a fully functional 16-bit address, as well as being able to recognise other 16-bit addresses.

Destination Addresses (Figure 11.39)

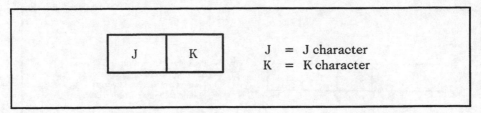

Figure 11.37   Starting Delimiter

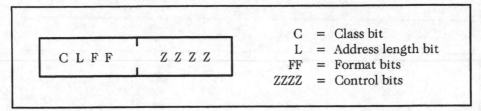

Figure 11.38   Frame Control

The first bit of the destination address distinguishes individual addresses (bit 1 = 0) from group addresses (bit 1 = 1). The second bit of the address decides whether the address will be treated as local (bit 2 = 1) or universal (bit 2 = 0).

Broadcast Addresses

Group addresses consisting entirely of ones are known as broadcast addresses and are directed to all stations.

Null Addresses

An address consisting entirely of zeroes is known as a 'null address' and is not directed to any station.

The Source Address

The source address is the individual MAC address. Bit 1 will always be set to 0.

Figure 11.40 shows an FDDI MAC packet decoded using a protocol analyser.

The INFO Field

The information field contains 0, 1 or several pairs of data characters, the significance of which is indicated by the frame control field (FC). Each character pair is transferred taking the higher-order character first. The MAC, LLC or SMT then interprets it appropriately. The length of the INFO field is variable, but the relevant data packet is limited to a length of 9,000 characters.

CLFF	ZZZZZ from		toZZZZ
0X00	0000		Void frame (logically not a frame, so ignored)
1000	0000		Non-restricted token
1100	0000		Restricted token
0L00	0001	1111	Station Management frame
1L00	0001	1111	MAC frame
1L00	0010		MAC Beacon Frame
1L00	0011		MAC Claim Frame
CL01	r000	r111	LLC frame
0L01	rPPP		Asynchronous Transfer with priority (LLC)
1L01	rrrr		Synchronous Transfer (LLC)
0L00	0001	111	SMT frame
0L00	1111		Next Station Addressing frame (SMT)
CL10	r000	r111	reserved for implementation
CL11	rrrr		for future standardisation

X	= don't care
r	= reserved and set to 0
L	= length
C	= class

The Frame Check Sequence (FCS)

The frame check sequence is a sequence of 32 bits formed as follows:
    \ I think this works out differently from the last time it was explained (?) - (pp.173-4). Hope it's meant to? \

– The bit sequence for which the checksum is to be calculated (the contents of the FC, DA, SA and INFO field, n bits in length) is interpreted as a polynomial $M(x)$ to the degree n-1: for example, the bit sequence 110001 has six bits and is interpreted as a polynomial with the coefficients 1,1,0,0,0,1, i.e. $X^5+X^4+X^0$).

1) The expression $X^k(X^{31}+X^{30}+...X+1)$ is formed, where k is the number of bits in the FC, DA, SA and INFO field.

2) $M(x)$ is then multiplied by X^{32}, added to the polynomial derived in (1) (this is the same as inverting the first 32 bits of $M(x)$), and the total is divided by $G(x)$, with the generator polynomial $G(x)$ defined as follows:

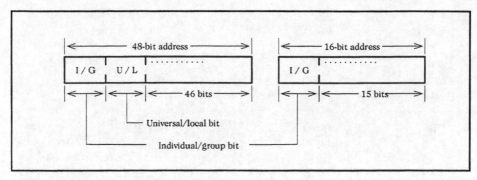

Figure 11.39   Destination Address

$G(x) = \backslash\backslash\backslash\backslash$.

The ones complement of the remainder from the division is then formed. All operations are carried out in modulo 2. The frame check sequence is transferred with the most significant bit first. Finally, the bit sequence $F(x) = x^{32}M(x)+FCS$ is sent. (Multiplying the polynomial to be checked by x^{32} simply means shifting $F(x)$ 32 places to the left to leave room for the FCS.)

The receiving station adds the $F(x)$ sequence received to X^k $(X^{32}+X^{31}+...+X^1)$, multiplies the total by X^{32} and divides the result by $G(x)$. If there has been no transmission error, the remainder from this division must always equal $C(x) = X^{32}(X^{32}+X^{31}+...+X^1)/G(x)$.

Although the checksum calculation looks complicated, it is easily implemented by hardware in token rings and Ethernet networks by means of a simple shift register circuit. A 32-bit checksum like the one used here will detect all single and double errors, all errors due to an odd number of bits, all error sequences 32 bits in length or less, and with a probability of 99.99999998% all error sequences 33 or more bits in length.

The Ending Delimiter (ED)

The ending delimiter is the closing character of a token or a frame. For a token, the ED consists of two successive 'T' characters, and for a data packet a single 'T' character.

Frame Status (FS)

The frame status field consists of a series of control indicator characters (R and S: see Figure 11.34) following the ending delimiter, and can be of any length. The first three control indicators are mandatory (E = Error Detected; A = Address Recognised; C = Frame Copied); the others are optional.

– (E): Error Detected

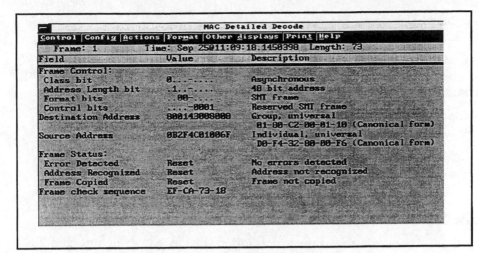

Figure 11.40   Decoding of an FDDI MAC packet

The E field is initially set to R by the sending station. If one of the repeating stations detects an error, it sets the E field to S.

– (A): Address Recognised
The A field is initially set to R by the sending station. If a station recognises the destination address of the packet as its own, it sets the A field to S.

– (C): Frame Copied
The C field is initially set to R by the sending station. If the frame is copied by a receiving station, this station then sets the C field to S.

Timers

Every station possesses three timers to control activities on the ring. The following parameters are used in calculating the timer values:

– D_Max = 1.617 ms:
default: maximum ring delay. (See ISO 9314-1)

– M_Max = 1000:
number of MAC layers on the ring.

– I_Max = 25.0 ms:
maximum station insertion time.

– A_Max = 1.0 ms:
maximum signal access time.

– Token_Time = 0.00088 ms:
transfer time for tokens (6 characters) with preambles (16 characters).

– L_Max: 0.0035 ms:
   maximum time between receipt of token and first transfer.

– F_Max = 0.361 ms:
   maximum transfer time for a frame. Calculated for a frame of 9000 characters (= the maximum frame length plus 16 preamble characters).

– Claim_FR = 0.00256 ms:
   time required to transfer a claim frame.

– S_Min = 0.3545 ms:
   regeneration time after random noise. S_Min >= F_Max+L_Max.

The Token Holding Timer (THT)

The THT controls the time for which a station can continue sending asynchronous data packets. This lasts until the THT has run out or is no longer below the priority threshold T_Pri. The THT is initialised with the value of the TRT timer when the token is received.

The Valid Transmission Timer (VXT)

Every station has a VXT to enable it to regenerate in error situations:
   TVX > Max (D_Max, F_Max)) + Token_Time + F_Max + S_Min and > 2.3 ms.
   The default value of the TVX should be at least 62,500 characters or 2.50 ms.
   \ TVX or VXT ??? \
   \ 62,500 chars or 62.5 ??? \

The Token Rotation Timer (TRT)

The TRT controls the sequence of activity on the ring during normal operation. If there is a TRT timeout or an Early Token is received (a token arriving before the TRT has run out) it is initialised with the value of T_Opr applying at any given time. In the former case, Late_Ct is also augmented by one.

   T_Opr – the operative TRT timeout value – is between the extreme values T_Min and T_Max and is set to the lowest of all available values by the stations during the Claim Token process and taken as the Target Token Rotation Time (TTRT). Because of the nature of the token protocol, it is possible in the worst case for a station to receive the token a full T_Ops period later. If the station is to ensure a guaranteed response time, it should therefore negotiate a T_Opr of 0.5 Tresp.

   \ Vacillation hereabouts between Tresp and TResp ... \

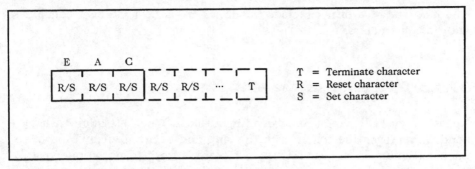

Figure 11.41 Frame Status

If T_Opr is smaller than a station's T_Min, it will not be allowed to take part in normal ring traffic.

– T_Min = 4.0 ms (default).

– T_Max = 4 x T_Init, but > 165 ms, where T_Init describes the \?\noise-free time of the ring:

– T_Init = T_React + T_Resp < 40.58 ms, where

– T_React < I_Max + D_Max + A_Max + TVX and < 30.24 ms;

– T_Resp < ((3 D_Max) + (2 M_Max . Claim_FR) + S_Min) and < 10.34 ms.

The late counter Late_Ct is set to 1 on initialisation or station reset and augmented on every TRT time out – that is, whenever a token has not been received in time. As soon as a token is received, Late_Ct is reset to 0.

To simplify fault-tracing and the localisation of errors, every MAC_Level counter keeps both an overall count and a count of the frames with one or more errors.

However, only those frames closing with a Frame Ending Delimiter (a 'T' character) are included in the count. Data packets closing in an Idle or invalid character are not counted.

– Frame_Ct:
keeps a count of all frames received.

– Error_Ct:
counts all error frames identified as such by the station itself (that is, all the frames where the Frame Status Error field (E) has been set to S by the station itself). Frames arriving with E already set to S are not counted.

– Lost_Ct:
counts all frames or tokens already in process of receipt via the MAC layer when an error occurs. The MAC layer then augments Lost_Ct and sends Idle characters to the ring in place of the remainder of the frame.

The next station will not include this frame in its Lost_Ct, as it concludes with Idle characters.

11.4.5 Operation of the MAC Layer

Access to an FDDI ring is controlled by a token. When a station wishes to send, it removes the token from the ring and begins transmission of its packets. When the transmission is complete, a fresh token is immediately sent – unlike token ring networks, where the new token is only sent after the first data packet sent has returned to the sender. (Although this mode of operation is available as an option in FDDI, it is only intended for station management purposes, as it would otherwise cause a significant reduction in performance.) In addition, every station is responsible for removing the data packets it has sent.

As soon as a station receives a data packet with its own address as the sending station, it begins re-transmitting all the remaining bits as Idle characters. As a result of this, there will be fragments on the ring consisting of PA, SD, FC, DA and SA fields followed by Idle characters. However, this will not affect the ring's efficiency, as these fragments will not fulfil certain criteria for a data packet, such as the inclusion of ending delimiters (and will therefore not be counted as error packets). Stations not sending will repeat and amplify the incoming bit stream.

An FDDI ring can operate in two different modes:

a) synchronous, with guaranteed bandwidth and response time (implementation optional).

b) asynchronous, with dynamic bandwidth sharing.

As mentioned in the section on the Token Rotation Timer (TRT) in ISO 9314-1, a Target Token Rotation Time (TTRT) is negotiated between the stations during the Claim Token process on the basis of all the token rotation times proposed, and this is then used as the operative value T_Opr for the TRT. If a token now arrives before the TRT has reached the TTRT (an early token), this token can be used for both synchronous and asynchronous transmission. If the token arrives later than this (a late token), the Late_Ct counter is augmented by one, the TRT is initialised with T_Opr, and only synchronous transfer may now be carried out. Only when the token once again reaches the station within the TTRT is Late_Ct reset to 0 so that asynchronous transfer can once again take place. This procedure guarantees a mean synchronous response time <= TTRT and a maximum of 2 x TTRT.

Synchronous Transfer

In synchronous transmission, every station has a synchronous bandwidth allocated, specified as a % of the TTRT. The bandwidth of a freshly initialised station will first be set to 0, and will be negotiated by the SMT. The total of all bandwidths allocated must not exceed the maximum available synchronous bandwidth Bsyn_max, where Bsyn_max = TTRT – (D_Max + F_Max + Token_time).

Asynchronous Transfer

There are two types of token in asynchronous Transfer:

a) Non-restricted token:
   The asynchronous bandwidth is shared by all stations.

b) Restricted token:
   The asynchronous bandwidth is allocated on request.

The ring initially operates using a non-restricted token. In this mode, priorities (T_Pri) can be issued by allocating threshold values. A non-restricted token can then be used if the priority threshold T_Pri of the station wishing to send is above the TRT. Heavy loading of the ring can thus be avoided by setting low T_Pri values for low priorities.

As soon as a station receives an early token, the current TRT value is transferred to the Token Holding Timer (THT), which starts to run. The TRT itself is initialised with T_Opr, to enable it to measure the next token rotation time relative to this.

The restricted token mode is required when a station needs to send very large quantities of data in a very short time. The station must first obtain a restricted token; it then starts data transfer, sending a restricted token when the THT runs out. The receiving station(s) accept(s) the data and return(s) the restricted token to the sending station. This exchange of restricted tokens (typically, for several TRT periods) ends once the data transfer is complete. While restricted token mode is in operation, all other asynchronous transfers are halted, but this does not affect synchronous transfers, which may use either type of token. The maximum duration of restricted token mode is negotiated by the SMT. The implementation of restricted token mode is optional.

The Claim Token Process

Every station monitors the ring to check for conditions requiring re-initialisation. Typically, this will mean inactivity (TVX timeout) or incorrect activity (TRT timeout and setting of Late_Ct). If a station discovers that re-initialisation is necessary, it sends a Claim Token frame and sets the variable Ring_Operational to 0. At the same time, all the Claim Token frames received are checked. If a frame with lower priority is received (the frame with the highest priority is the one with the lowest TTRT value or, in the case of a 'tie', with the longest and therefore highest address), a further Claim Token frame is sent; otherwise nothing is done. The ring will eventually fill with Claim Token frames from the station with the highest priority, which will then initialise the ring. To do this, it first resets T_Opr to its own TTRT, then initialises the TRT and sends a fresh non-restricted token. (In the event of a TRT timeout while the station is waiting for another station – with higher priority – to initialise the ring, it will switch to Claim Token mode, and not to Beaconing mode. This prevents the sporadic appearance of beaconing frames.)

During its first rotation, the token cannot be used by any of the stations, as the count in Ring_Operational will still be 0. It is only when the rotation is completed that Ring_Operational will rise to 1, the TRT will be initialised and Late_Ct will hold a value of 1. Synchronous transfers can start on this second rotation, and asynchronous transfers from the third.

The Beaconing Process

If the TRT runs out whilst a station is in the Claim Token process, the procedure fails and beaconing begins. In such a case, the ring has probably been physically broken and possibly globally reconfigured (making two logical rings from one, or vice-versa). Once it has gone into beaconing mode, a station will initialise its TRT and then begin continuous transmission of beacon frames.

If a station not yet in beaconing mode receives beacon frames it will repeat them.

If a station receives its own beacon frames, it will assume that the ring has been regenerated, and re-start the Claim Token Process.

Section 3:
ISO 9314-3 Physical Layer Medium Dependent (PMD)

11.4.6 The Media Interface Connector (MIC)

There are 4 MIC plug specifications:

– MIC-A:
  Primary In/Secondary Out

– MIC-B:
  Primary Out/Secondary In

– MIC-M:

    SAS inputs to the concentrator

– MIC-S:

    plugs for SAS stations to be attached to the concentrator.

The acceptable optical losses deriving from an MIC are not specified, but are limited only by the maximum overall attenuation permissible in a ring.

11.4.7 Signal characteristics

The bit error rate due to signal repetition by a station must not be greater than 2.5×10^{-10} (no greater than 1×10^{-12} if the light output is 2 dB above the minimum).

Table 2 shows the required signal characteristics at the output of an FDDI interface:

Table 3 shows the signal characteristics which an FDDI input interface must be able to process:

Signal detection

At a light output of -31 dBm or over, a signal must be recognised as valid within 100 µs. From the level of light output giving a bit error rate of 0.01 at the receiver output, or from -45 dBm (whichever be the higher), absence of signal should be indicated after a maximum of 350 µs.

The Bypass Function

The bypass function, which is optional for all stations, bridges the input and output in such a way that the structure of the dual ring is maintained (as opposed to the re-configuration resulting from a break in the line, which converts the dual ring into a single ring or a single ring into two rings). If a station is switched off or faulty, it goes into bypass mode.

Typical bypass switches are components with a high power loss. The following characteristics must be maintained:

The optical switching time is the time during which the optical primary and secondary signals are interrupted by the switching process (from the point when the signal has fallen by more than 1.5 dB from its original strength S1 to the point when it again rises to S1–1.5 dB).

The station switching time is the time required by a station from the start of the login/out process to its end (achieving 1.5 dB short of the target signal strength).

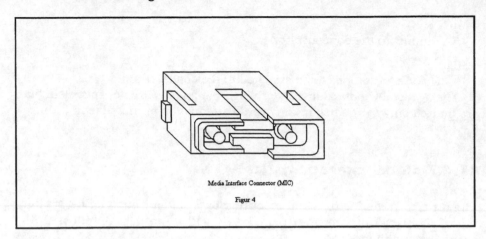

Figure 11.42

Cable specifications

The signal characteristics for FDDI are specified on the basis of multi-mode glass fibres with a core diameter of 62.5 µm and a sheath diameter of 125 µm. However, other types of optical fibre can be used provided the varying transfer characteristics are taken into account. Table 5 summarises the required characteristics for optical fibres:

It is advisable to use only one type of optical fibre in any FDDI ring. The summary in table 6 shows the theoretical power losses in dB for various combinations of fibre types:

	Min	Max	Unit
Wavelength	1270	1380	nm
Mean output	-20	-14	dBm
Rise time(10%-90%)	0.6	3.5	ns
Fall time(90%-10%)	0.6	3.5	ns

Table 2

	Min	Max	Unit
Wavelength	1270	1380	nm
Mean output	-31.0	-14	dBm
Rise time(10%-90%)	0.6	5.0	ns
Fall time(90%-10%)	0.6	5.0	ns

Table 3

Monomode Glass Fibre FDDIs

A standard for monomode optical fibres is currently being developed, and specifies the following parameters:

11.4.8 Testing methods

When testing FDDI components, attention should be given to the following:
    Measurement of optical output
    The optical output strength of a station should be measured while the station is sending a continuous sequence of HALT characters (that is, a 12.5 MHz square wave). The same applies to measurement of the optical spectrum using an optical spectrum analyser.

Section 4:
SMT Draft 7.2 – Station Management for FDDI

11.4.9 SMT draft for FDDI

The Station Management (SMT) section of the FDDI standard is still at the development stage. There is no function comparable to SMT in Ethernet or Token Ring.
    In July 1992, version 7.2 of SMT – at present the latest draft – was published. It was developed to improve the reliability of the network still further. SMT includes the following basic functions:

– SMT logs the station in and out;

	Min	Max	Unit
Wavelength	1270	1380	nm
Mean output	-31.0	-14	dBm
Rise time(10%-90%)	0.6	5.0	ns
Fall time(90%-10%)	0.6	5.0	ns

Table 4

– SMT is able to reconfigure a station's data paths (e.g. in the event of failure of a section);

– SMT checks the fibre optics links before the station logs into the ring;

– SMT controls beaconing behaviour;

– SMT reports on the station's current configuration on request;

Core diameter	62.5 µm
Sheath diameter	122.0 – 1211.0 µm
Numerical aperture	0.275
-3 dB bandwidth	500.0 MHz/km
Attenuation	11.0 dB (overall attenuation of cable including bypass switches, connectors etc.)

Table 5

Receiving fibre	Sending fibre					
	50µm	50µm	50µm	62.5µm	85µm	100µm
NA	0.20	0.21	0.22	0.275	0.26	0.29
50 µm(NA=0.20)	0.0	0.2	0.4	2.2	3.8	5.7
50 µm(NA=0.21)	0.0	0.0	0.2	1.9	3.5	5.3
50 µm(NA=0.22)	0.0	0.0	0.0	1.6	3.2	4.9
625µm(NA=0.275)	0.0	0.0	0.0	0.0	1.0	2.3
85µm(NA=0.26)	0.0	0.0	0.0	0.0	0.0	0.8
100µm(NA=0.29)	0.0	0.0	0.0	0.0	0.0	0.0

Table 6

– SMT can send Status Report Packets to localise any faults.

The SMT itself is nothing other than a software application running on the station's local operating system. It comprises four basic functions, which will now be described:

Core diameter	11.2µm – 10.5µm
Sheath diameter	125µm ± 2µm
Wavelength	1300nm
Optical attenuation	<= 0.40 dB/km (1310nm)
Maximum separation between two stations	40km

Table 7

11.4.10 ECM (Entity Co-ordination Management)

ECM controls the optical bypass system and all the SMT's other functions. That is: as soon as the FDDI station becomes active, ECM switches off the optical bypass and runs the other SMT functions.

Conversely, when the station logs out the other SMT processes are halted by ECM and the optical bypass is then activated.

In addition to these functions, the SMT draft also recommends the integration of a cable testing function in ECM. This would carry out the following tasks:

– Check all data paths within the station;

– Carry out loop-back tests of the station and its PMD interface;

– Check the parameters passed to the MAC;

– Check the MAC regeneration process (beaconing, claim token).

11.4.11 PCM (Physical Connection Management)

PCM controls the station's output and the redundant fibre routes to the neighbouring node.

Together with the neighbour station's PCM, it test the connection between the stations, checks the bit error rate (BER) and decides whether or not to set up the connection. There is one PCM per station output. 10 signalling bits are used to communicate with the neighbour station:

– Bit 0:
Always set to 0 (reserved for future applications).

– Bits 1 and 2:
Station's own output type:
00 = A,
01 = B,
10 = S,
11 = M.

– Bit 3:
Compatibility of outputs:
If both ports signal 0, the connection is not set up.

– Bits 4 and 5:
LCT (Link Confidence Test) to check the reliability of the connection: how long should the test take?
00 = short (50 ms),

01 = medium (500 ms),
10 = long (5s),
11 = extended test (50s).

The duration of the test is primarily determined by the bit error rates already encountered.

– Bit 6:
Is MAC to be used during the LCT?

– Bit 7:
Has the reliability test been passed? Was the BER low enough?
– Bit 8:
Should a MAC loop-back test be run?

– Bit 9:
Is there a MAC at the station output?

Once the PCM has attained an 'active state', the station starts sending (either QLS signals or data). Simultaneously, the PCM begins its link monitoring function as LEM (Link Error Monitor). The LEM checks the PHY module's bit error rate and deactivates it if the BER becomes too great. At a BER of 10^{-8} a warning is output, and at 10^{-7} the connection is broken.

11.4.12 CEM (Configuration Element Management)

The CEM is responsible for the configuration of the station's internal data paths, of which each station has three:

– the primary path,

– the secondary path, and

– a local path.

Each of the ports is equipped with a logical unit known as the CCE (Configuration Control Element), which guides the data via the internal paths to their destination. When the CEM alters the status of a CCE, it simultaneously deletes all data from the ring by sending ILS signals. This, of course, results in Token Claim frames from the stations on the ring.

11.4.13 Ring Management (RMT)

The RMT controls the MAC module. It only acts if a physical connection (PCM) is present and its internal data paths are allocated to the inputs and/or outputs.

The RMT has six main tasks allotted to it:

\ ... so why list EIGHT ??? \

\ Maybe #7 actually belongs as part of #6, and #8 actually belongs as a note on the end of #2 ? \

– Initialisation of the MAC after a physical connection has been set up.

– Searching for duplicate addresses before the MAC is activated, using claim and beaconing procedures. Three different methods are employed in this:

1) If the MAC receives its own claim packet after more than 2(D_max), there must be a second station with the same address. (D_max is the maximum time required for a packet to travel round the ring.)

2) If the MAC receives its own beacon packet after more than 2(D_max), there must be a second station with the same address.

3) If the MAC receives its own Claim Token packet in a TTRT (Target Token Rotation Time) varying from that used in its own Claim Token packet, there must be a second station with the same address sending Claim Token packets.

– Searching for duplicate addresses by reference to the 'A' bit in NIF packets when the MAC is active.

– Detecting and reacting to beaconing states.

– Controlling and triggering a Halt_LineState (HLS).

– Supporting and monitoring restricted tokens.

– The RMT is informed as soon as a MAC detects a restricted token, and starts a timer to monitor the time taken by the restricted-access dialogue. In the event of a timeout, a Claim Token or beaconing process is started.

– If a duplicate address is detected, the RMT can react in one of three ways:

1) Break the connection and remove the station from the ring.

2) Change the MAC address.

3) Configure the MAC in such a way that the Claim Token process is lost (by setting the TTRT to a lower value).

11.4.14 The SMT Agent

In addition to the four groups of functions described above, an SMT agent is specified to check the incoming data packets and take appropriate measures if necessary:

Neighbour Information Frame (NIF)

NIFs are used to determine the identity of the neighbour.

Status Information Frames (SIF)

SIFs are used to obtain detailed information about the status of a station. There are two types of SIF:

1) SIF Configuration Packets describe the current configuration of the station: number of inputs and outputs, number of MACs, neighbouring station to each MAC etc.

2) SIF Operation Packets describe the current operational status of a station (MAC parameters, LEM status of outputs, MAC packet counts etc.).

Echo Frame (ECF)

When an Echo Frame is received, the SMY copies the information field and sends an Echo Response Frame.

Request Denied Frame (RDF)

If the SMT receives a data packet of unknown format or in a non-supported SMT version, it sends an RDF packet. Other causes for denying receipt could include overlength packets or the absence of authorisation to receive.

Status Report Frame (SRF)

SRFs provide information on changes to the station status. The following changes are reported:

– changes to the configuration,

– interference from attempted connections,

– MAC Neighbour Change,

– MAC Frame Error condition,

– port LER condition,

– MAC frame not copied,

– duplicate MAC address,

– port elasticity buffer failure.

Two timers ensure that the ring is not flooded with status change reports:

– The Holdoff Timer prevents status change reports being sent more frequently than every two seconds.
– The Backoff Timer controls the gap between status change reports: as the reports are sent without receiving any acknowledgement from the addressee (that is, in connectionless mode), the SMT repeats the SRFs at increasing intervals (2s, 4s, 8s, 16s, 32s, 32s, 32s ...).

Parameter Management Frame (PMF)

The PMF protocol enables the network manager to read or amend certain SMT variables. This conforms to the structure of network management protocols such as SNMP or CMIP. There are four types of PMF packet:

– PMF Add,

– PMF Change,

– PMF Add,

– PMF Remove.

Extended Service Frame (ESF)

An ESF allows individual SMT packets to be defined.

Resource Allocation File (RAF)

RAFs are used to allocate synchronous bandwidths.

Neighbour Notification Protocol (NNP)

Approximately every 30 seconds, a station sends a Neighbour Notification Frame (NNF) as a broadcast. The first station to receive this packet without its 'A' bit (Address Recognized) set – that is, its neighbour – replies to this packet. There are two different ways NIFs can be sent:

1) NIF Request:
   The receiving station responds, allowing both the upstream and the downstream neighbour to be determined.

2) NIF Announcement:
   The receiving station does not respond. This allows the upstream neighbour to be determined, but cuts down on additional traffic.

```
Frame: 40          Time: Sep 25@11:10:54.2247506  Length: 77
Field                Value              Description
Frame Class          01                 Neighbor Information Frame
Frame Type           03                 Response
Version Id           1
Transaction Id       150436628
Station Id (User)    0000               User defined section
Station Id (IEEE)    00003040D334       IEEE defined section
Header Pad           00-00
Info Field Length    40                 Total length of SMT parmaters
                                        Parameters present

Parameter Decodes
-------------

Parameter            00-01              Upstream Neighbor Address
 Length              8                  Remaining parm octets
 Pad                 00-00
 Address (IEEE)      00003040D3A4       Upstream Neighbor

Parameter            00-02              Station Descriptor
 Length              4                  Remaining parm octets
 Node Class          00                 Station (no M Ports)
 MAC Count           1                  MACs present in Station
 Non-Master Count    2                  Number of A, B, or S Ports
 Master Count        0                  Number of M Ports

Parameter            00-03              Station State
Parameter            00-03              Station State
 Length              4                  Remaining parm octets
 Pad                 00-00
 Topology            10                 (See bit fields below)
  Synch Service (7.2) 00                False
  Status Reporting   ..0.-....          False
  Rooted Station     ...1-....          True
  Twisted Ring B-B   ....-0...          False
  Twisted Ring A-A   ....-.0..          False
  Unrooted Concntrtor ....-..0.         False
  Station Wrapped    ....-...0          False
 Dupl Address        00                 (See bit fields below)
  UNA Duplicate      ....-..0.          False
  My Duplicate       ....-...0          False

Parameter            20-0B              MAC Frame Status Capabilities
 Length              8                  Remaining parm octets
 Pad                 00-00
 MAC Index           00-03              FDDI Resource Index
 Pad                 00-00
 Parm Value          00                 (See bit fields below)
  Type 2 Programmable ....-.0..         False
  Type 1 Programmable ....-..0.         False
  Type 0 Programmable ....-...0         False
```

Figure 11.43   FDDI SMT decoding

```
Rooted Station        ...1-....      True
Twisted Ring B-B      ....-0...      False
Twisted Ring A-A      ....-.0..      False
Unrooted Concntrtor   ....-..0.      False
Station Wrapped       ....-...0      False
Dupl Address          00             (See bit fields below)
UNA Duplicate         ....-.0..      False
My Duplicate          ....-...0      False
-----------
Parameter             20-0B          MAC Frame Status Capabilities
Length                8              Remaining parm octets
Pad                   00-00
MAC Index             00-03          FDDI Resource Index
Pad                   00-00
Parm Value            00             (See bit fields below)
Type 2 Programmable   ....-.0..      False
Type 1 Programmable   ....-..0.      False
Type 0 Programmable   ....-...0      False
Parm Value            04             (See bit fields below)
Typ 2/Clearing (7.2)  ....-.1..      True
Typ 1/Setting (7.2)   ....-..0.      False
Typ 0/Repeatng (7.2)  ....-...0      False
----End----
```

Figure 11.43   continued

12

Network Performance

The (theoretical) efficiency of a network is described using 'queuing systems'.

According to Kleinrock (1964), the mean duration for a data packet transfer is:

$T = 1/(u\ Ci - a)$, where

– T = transfer duration (comprising queuing time plus transfer time)

– a = packets arriving for transmission, in packets/sec,

– Ci = capacity or transfer rate of communication channel in bits/sec,

– 1/u = mean packet size.

12.1 IEEE 802.5 Token Ring

Applied to an 802.5 token ring network, this formula gives a mean access time (that is, the time a station has to wait on average between giving up the token and the arrival of the next token) of:
   T-access = L/(1-a/C), where

- L = ring propagation time: time for a bit to travel round an empty ring (this is the propagation time of the signal on the medium plus a delay of one bit per station).

- a = packets arriving for transmission, in packets/sec,

- C = capacity or transfer rate of the ring in bits/sec.
   The expression a/C describes the loading of the entire ring (with n stations). The load on a single station would be a/Cn.
   The ring propagation time is calculated from the propagation speed of the signal on the medium used plus one bit per active station. A typical propagation speed is 0.7 c. A 4-Mbits/sec token ring with 100 stations and a physical length of 1000 metres thus has a ring propagation time of

- 1000/200 ~s + 0.25 ~s x 100 = 30 ~s (which would also apply to 6000 metres of plain cable).
   (At a transfer rate of R Mbits/sec, a bit will be transmitted every 1/R ~s. $0.7 \times 3 \times 10^9 = 200m/~s$)
   If the 100 stations transfer 1 Mbit/s between them, evenly shared out, the mean access time T-access is:

- T-access = 30 ~s/(1–1/4) = 40 ~s.

Thus, for a 4-Mbits/sec ring, for example, the following values result:

	Stations	100	200	400
Data;Mbits/sec	1	40µs	66.6µs	140µs
	2	60µs	110µs	210µs
	3	120µs	220µs	420µs
	3.8	600µs	1100µs	2100µs

Figures 12.1 and 12.2 illustrate how the mean access time varies with the network load carried.
   This shows that the efficiency of data transfer in a 4-Mbits/sec token ring falls off dramatically above a load of 2.5 Mbits/sec. The same feature occurs in a 16-Mbits/sec ring at around 10 Mbits/sec. A token ring should therefore always be operated below these thresholds.

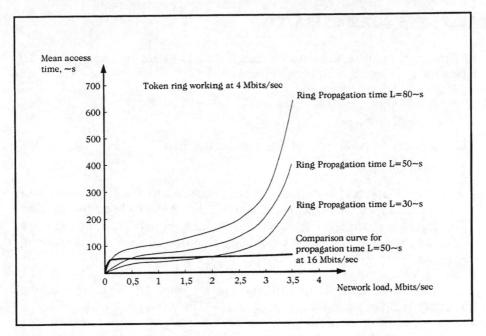

Figure 12.1   4-Mbits/sec Token ring

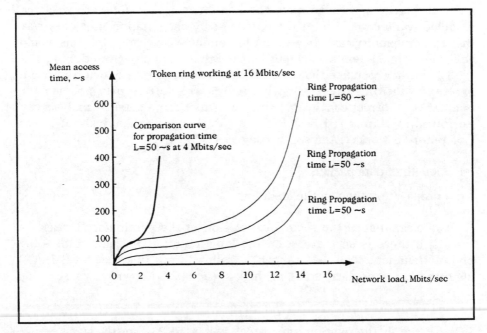

Figure 12.2   16-Mbits/sec Token ring

12.2 IEEE 802.3 CSMA/CD

In Ethernet, channel efficiency (= how well the data transfer rate of 10 Mbits/sec is being utilised) is calculated as:

$K = 1/(1+2CL/cFA)$, where

– K = channel efficiency,

– C = capacity or bandwidth of the transfer medium,

– L = cable length,

– A = probability that a station will be given authority to send during an inter-frame gap. (This means, of course, that A depends on the number of stations wishing to send as well as the probability that they are actually sending. If p is the probability that one of k stations is sending, $A = kp(1-p)^{(k-1)}$.

A is at a maximum for p = 1/k and takes a value 1/e for k approaching infinity (e is Euler's constant, approx. 2.71). The value p = 11/k leads to the simple assumption that the more stations there are on the network, the lower the probability that any one of the stations will be sending. It is precisely here that the channel efficiency achieved is at a maximum. (That is: if all stations were to have the same (notional) software package installed, which would limit the data sent by each station in such a way that the probability that they would be sending was always 1/k, this would achieve the maximum throughput for the Ethernet at any given time.)

It is further assumed that there is a constant probability of a fresh send for each station. These simplifications are sufficiently precise for qualitatively correct conclusions to be drawn. A more detailed analysis can be found in Hammond & O'Reilly's ~Performance Analysis of Local Computer Networks~, Addison-Wesley 1988.

– F = length of data packets,

– c = propagation time on the medium.

It is clear that, if the second expression in the nominator increases – that is, if there is an increase in the length and/or the bandwidth – the channel efficiency will be reduced. It follows from this that a CSMA/CD algorithm is not applicable to long, high-speed 802.3 networks, where:

– C = 10 Mbits/sec or 1.25×10^6 bytes/sec.

– 2L/c = simply the rotation time, which will be 51.2 ~s for the worst case.

– F = length of data packets, minimum 64 bytes, maximum 1518 bytes.

– and therefore $K = 1/(1+173.44/F)$ (for k >> infinity and p = 1/k).

If all stations are sending data packets with a frame length of 1024 bytes, the channel efficiency calculates at 0.85. As might be expected, packet lengths of 64 bytes are considerably less efficient, with K\eff = 0.27.

Figures 12.3 and 12.4 chart the channel efficiency of 802.3 networks with slot times of 5.12 ~s, 51.2 ~s and 100 ~s as a function of the number of stations ready to send k (where, as before, the probability that a station will be sending is taken as 1/k). In the first graph, the packet length is 1024 bytes, and in the second 64 bytes.

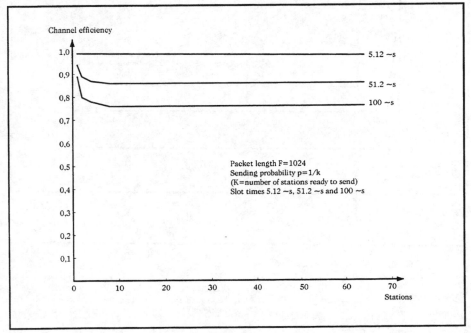

Figure 12.3

The effect of slot time and packet lengths on the channel efficiency is evident. A particularly drastic effect results from extending the network (that is, increasing the slot time) at short packet lengths. As can be seen from Figure 12.3, 40 stations can transfer data about three times more efficiently with a slot time of 5.12 ~s than at 51.2 ~s.

This demonstrates the dramatic effect the layout and design of a network can have on performance.

An assumption closer to real life is, of course, a case where the sending probability for an individual station does not fall with an increasing number of stations, but remains at least constant.

Taking as a basis a constant transfer rate of 1125 kbytes/sec = 1 Mbit/sec for each station, the sending probability for each station at a transfer speed of 10 Mbits/sec is p = 0.1.

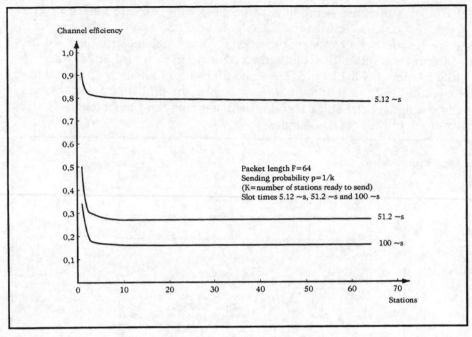

Figure 12.4

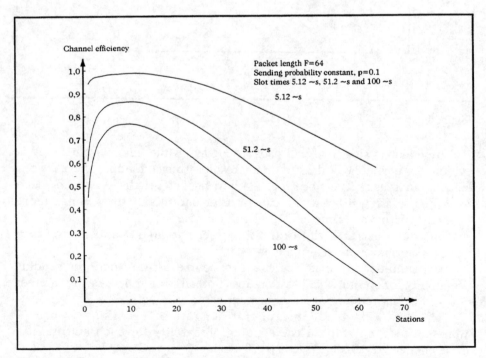

Figure 12.5

This is illustrated in figures 12.5 and 12.6, again taking packet lengths of 1024 bytes and 64 bytes.

With long packets, channel efficiency falls off abruptly with more than some 20 stations, and with as few as 15 stations when packet lengths are short.

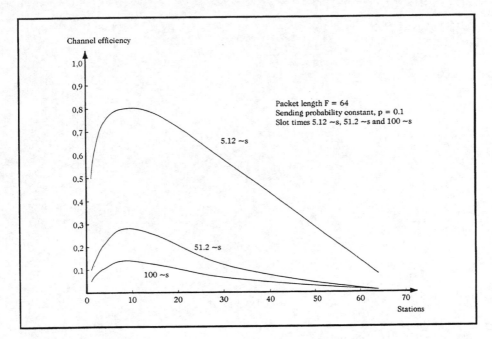

Figure 12.6

Conclusion

As well as the frame length, the performance of CSMA/CD networks is decisively affected by the cable length and the number of repeaters (or, in other words, the slot time).

The longer the cable, and the further apart the stations on the cable, the lower channel efficiency becomes, and the more frequently collisions will occur. It is clear that reducing the cable length (that is, reducing the signal delay caused by propagation on the medium and the delay attributable to any repeaters in the system) will drastically increase channel efficiency.

Appendix

	FDDI	IEEE 802.3	IEEE 802.5
Bandwidth	100 Mbits/sec	10 Mbits/sec	4 or 16 Mbits/sec
Number of stations	500	1024	250
Maximum distance between stations	2 km MMF or >20 km SMF	2.8 km	375 m in closed ring(4 Mbits/sec), otherwise 145 m.
Maximum length of network	100 km	2.8 km	varies according to configuration
Logical network structure	dual ring in tree structure	bus	single ring
Physical network structure	ring, star, hierarchical star	star, bus, hierarchical star	ring, star, hierarchical star
Medium	optical fibre	optical fibre, twisted pair, coaxial cable	twisted pair, optical fibre
Access method	Timed Token Passing	CSMA/CD	Token Passing
Acquisition of token	Token is received but not passed on	not applicable	Token converted to frame by setting status bit
Passing of token	after sending	not applicable	after deleting (own packet, 4) or after sending (16)
Data packets on network	one or more	one	one (4-Mbits/sec ring) or more
Data packets transferred per access	one or more	one	one
Maximum frame size	4,500 bytes	1518 bytes	4,500 bytes (4) or 17,800 bytes (16)

Table 1: Comparison of the various network topologies: FDDI, IEEE 802.3/Ethernet and IEEE 802.5

The first three octets of the Ethernet/802.3 hardware address are administered by the IEEE and are assigned to the various manufacturers. The remaining three octets are then available to be assigned internally by the manufacturers themselves. The following is a list of the most common manufacturers:

00 00 0C	Cisco
00 00 20	DIAB (Data Industrier AB)
00 00 22	Visual Technology
00 00 2A	TRW
00 00 5A	Schneider & koch
00 00 65	Network General
00 00 93	Proteon
00 00 9F	Ameristar Technology
00 00 A9	Network Systems
00 00 AA	Xerox, Xerox Computer
00 00 B3	CimLinc
00 00 C0	Western Digital
00 00 DD	Gould
00 01 02	BBN, BBN internal - not registered
00 17 00	Cables
00 DD 00	Ungermann Bass
00DD 01	Ungermann Bass
02 07 01	Interlan, UNIBUS or QBUS, HP-Apollo
02 04 06	BBN, BBN internal - not registered
02 60 8C	3Com: IBM-PC; Imagen; Valid
08 00 02	CMC, Massacomp, Silicon Graphics
08 00 02	Bridge
08 00 03	ACC(Advanced Computer Communication)
08 00 05	Symbolics, LISP-Computer
08 00 08	BBN
08 00 09	Hewlett Packard
08 00 0A	Nestar Systems
08 00 0A	Unisys
08 00 10	AT & T
08 00 14	Excelan, BBN Butterfly, Masscomp, Silicon Graphics
08 00 1A	Data General
08 00 1B	Data General
08 00 1E	HP-Apollo
08 00 20	Sun, Sun Computer
08 00 22	NBI
08 00 25	CDC
08 00 28	TI,Explorer
08 00 2B	DEC, UNIBUS or QBUS, VAXing, LAN bridges (DEUNA, DEQNA, DELUNA)
08 00 36	Intergraph CAE stations
08 00 39	Spider Systems
08 00 45	Xylogics
08 00 47	Sequent
08 00 49	Univation

08 00 4C	Encore
08 00 4E	BICC
08 00 5A	IBM
08 00 67	Comdesign
08 00 68	Ridge
08 00 69	Silicon Graphics
08 00 6E	Excelan
08 00 75	DDE(Danish Data Elektronik A/S)
08 00 80	Vitalink, TransLan III
08 00 80	XIOS
08 00 89	Kinetics, AppleTalk-Ethernet interface
08 00 8B	Pyramid
08 00 8D	XyVision, Xy Vision Computer
AA 00 03	DEC, global physical address for some DEC computers
AA 00 04	DEC local logical address for DECnet systems

Table 2: Comparison of the various network topologies: FDDI, IEEE
802.3/Ethernet and IEEE 802.5

Ethernet Multicast-- Addresses	Type Field	Usage
09-00-02-04-00-01	8080	Vitalink printer
09-00-02-04-04-02	8080	Vitalink management
09-00-09-00-00-01	8005	HP Probe
09-00-09-00-00-01	802.2LLC	HP Probe
09-00-09-00-00-04	8005	HPDTC
09-00-1E-00-00-00	8019	HP-Apollo DOMAIN
09-00-2B-00-00-03	8038	DEC LanBridge Traffic Monitor
09-00-2B-00-00-0F	6004	DEC Local Area Transport (LAT)
09-00-2B-00-00-00	8038	DEC LanBridge Copy Packets
09-00-2B-01-00-01	8038	DEC LanBridge Hello Packets: 1 packet/s, sent by the designated LANBridge
09-00-2B-01-00-01	8137	Novell IPX
09-00-4E-00-00-02	8080	Vitalink diagnostics
09-00-7C-02-00-05	8080	Vitalink gateway ?
09-00-7C-05-00-01	?	HP
0D-1E-15-BA-DD-06	6001	DEC Maintenance Operation Protocol (MOP); Dump/Load Assistance
AB-00-00-01-00-00	6002	DEC Maintenance Operation Protocol (MOP) Remote Console, 1 System ID packet every 8–10 minutes, by every DEC LanBridge DEC DEUNA interface DEC DELUNA interface DEC DEQNA interface (in a certain mode)
AB-00-00-03-00-00	6003	DECNET Phase IV end node Hello packets; 1 packet every 15 seconds, sent by each
AB-00-04-04-00-00	6003	DECNET host DECNET Phase IV Router Hello packets 1 packet every 15 seconds, sent byDECNET
AB-00-00-05-00-00 through AB-00-03-FF-FF-FF	?????	Reserved DEC
AB-00-03-00-00-00 through AB-00-04-00-FF-FF	6004 ????	DEC Local Area Transport (LAT) – old Reserved DEC customer private use
AB-00-04-01-xx-yy	6007	DEC Local Area VAX Cluster groups
CF-00-00-00-00	9000	Ethernet Configuration Test Protocol (Loopback)

Table 3: Ethernet multicast addresses

Ethernet Broadcast Addresses	Type Field	Usage
FF-FF-FF-FF-FF-FF	0600	XNS Packets; Hello or gateway search? 6 packets every 15 seconds per XNS station
FF-FF-FF-FF-FF-FF	0800	IP (e.g. RWHOD via UDP) as needed
FF-FF-FF-FF-FF-FF	0804	CHAOS
FF-FF-FF-FF-FF-FF	0806	ARP (for IP and CHAOS) as needed
FF-FF-FF-FF-FF-FF	0BAD	Banyan
FF-FF-FF-FF-FF-FF	1600	VALID packets, Hello or gateway search 1 packets/30 seconds per VALID station
FF-FF-FF-FF-FF-FF	8035	Reverse ARP
FF-FF-FF-FF-FF-FF	807C	Merit Internodal (INP)
FF-FF-FF-FF-FF-FF	809B	EtherTalk

Table 4: Ethernet broadcast addresses

Bytes 13 and 14 of an Ethernet V.20 packet are known as the Ethernet type field. If the value of the field is smaller than 1500 (hex 05DC), it is an IEEE 802.3 packet, and the field is interpreted as the length field.

The assignments for the Ethernet type fields are administered by XEROX. Most assignments refer to published protocols, although a few are assigned to proprietary products. A current list can be obtained from the following address:

Xerox Corporation
~Ethernet Address Administration Office~
3333 Coyote Hill Road
Palo Alto. CA 94304
USA

0000 - 05DC	IEEE 802.3	Length Field Assignments
0101 - 01FF		For experimental purposes - located in 802.3 range
0002	LLC mgmt	located in 802.3 range
0003	LLC Group	located in 802.3 range
0004	SNA path-i	located in 802.3 range
0005	SNA path-g	located in 802.3 range
000E	Proway LAN	located in 802.3 range
0011	ISO NetWare	located in 802.3 range
0019	MAP Mgmt	located in 802.3 range
0042	Spanning Tree	located in 802.3 range
004E	RS-511	located in 802.3 range
008E	Proway LAN	located in 802.3 range
00BC	Banyan Vines	located in 802.3 range
00E0	Netware	located in 802.3 range

Table 5: Ethernet V2.0 Type Field Assignments

00F0 NetBIOS	located in 802.3 range
00F1 NetBEUI	located in 802.3 range
00F4 LAN Mgmt i	located in 802.3 range
00F5 Lan Mgmt g	located in 802.3 range
00F8 RPL IBM	located in 802.3 range
00FC HP Extended	located in 802.3 range
00FE ISO Net	located in 802.3 range
0200 PUP Xerox	located in 802.3 range
0201 PUP address translation	located in 802.3 range

0600 Xerox XNS IDP
0800 IP DOD
0801 IP X.75 Internet
0802 IP NBS Internet
0803 IP ECMA Internet
0804 CHAOSnet
0805 X.25 Level 3
0806 ARP (Address Resolution protocol for
IP and   CHAOS)
0807 Xerox XNS Compatibility
081C Symbolics Private
0888 Xyplex
0889 Xyplex
088A Xyplex
0900 Ungermann Bass network debugger
0A00 PUP Xerox 802.3
0A01 802.3 PUP address translation
0BAD Banyan Systems
1000 Berkeley Trailer encapsulation
1001 Berkeley Trailer encapsulation
1001 IP - tlr 1
1002 IP - tlr 2
1003 IP - tlr 3
1003 IP - tlr 4
1005 IP - tlr 5
1006 IP - tlr 6
1007 IP - tlr 7
1008 IP - tlr 8
1009 IP - tlr 9
100A IP - tlr 10
100B IP - tlr 11
100C IP - tlr 12
100D IP - tlr 13
100E IP - tlr 14
100F IP - tlr 15

Table 5:Continued

```
1066  VALID Systems
3C01  3Com sys
3C02  3Com conn
3C03  3Com conn
3C04  3Com conn
3C05  3Com close
3C06  3Com close
3C07  3Com data
3C08  3Com broad
3C09  3Com claim
3C0A  3Com delete
3C0B  3Com rem r
3C0C  3Com rem r
3C0D  3Com reset
3C10  3Com corp
3C11  3Com corp
3C12  3Com corp
3C13  3Com corp
3C14  3Com corp
4242  PCS Basic Block Protocol
5208  BBN Simnet (BBN proprietary protocols, not registered)
6000  DEC experimental
6001  DEC MOP ( Maintenance Operation Protocol) Dump/Load Assistance
6002  DEC MOP ( Maintenance Operation Protocol) Remote Console
6003  DEC DECnet Phase IV
6004  DEC LAT (LOcal Area Transport)
6005  DEC DECnet - Diagnostic
6006  DEC DECnet Customer Use
6007  DEC LAVC
6008  DEC AMBER
6009  DEC MUMPS
7000  Ungermann Bass Download
7001  Ungermann Bass NIU
7002  Ungermann Bass Loop
7007  OS/9 Micro
7020  LRT
7021  LRT
7022  LRT
7023  LRT
7024  LRT
7025  LRT
7026  LRT
7027  LRT
7028  LRT
```

Table 5: continued

```
7030  Proteon
7034  Cabletron
8003  Cronus VLN
8004  Cronus Dir
8005  HP - Probe
8006  Nestar
8008  AT & T
8010  Excelan
8013  Silicon Graphics diagnostics type (obsolete)
8014  Silicon Graphics networks games (obsolete)
8015  Silicon Graphics reservated type (obsolete)
8016  Silicon Graphics XNS name - server, bounce server (obsolete)
8019  Apollo Domain
802E  Tymeshare
802F  Tigan, INC 802F
8035  RARP (Reverse ARP)
8036  Aeonic Sys
8038  DEC LanBridge
8039  DEC DSM
803A  DEC Aragon
803B  DEC VAXELN
803C  DEC NSMV
803D  DEC Encryption
803E  DEC DNA
803F  DEC LAN - Traffic - Monitor
8040  DEC NetBios
8041  DEC MS/DOS
8042  DEC
8044  Planning Research Corporation
8046  AT & T
8047  AT & T
8049  Experdata
805B  VMTP (Versatile Message Transaction Protocol RFC - 1045 Stanford)
805C  Stanford V Kernel Vers.6
805D  Evans & Sutherland
8060  Little Mac
8062  Counterpoint Computers
8065  University of Massachusetts
8066  University of Massachusetts
8067  Veeco Integrated Automation
8068  General Dynamics
8069  AT & T
806A  Autophon
806C  ComDesign
```

Table 5: continued

```
806D  Compugraphic Corp
806E  Landmark Graphics Corp
806F  Landmark Graphics Corp
8070  Landmark Graphics Corp
8071  Landmark Graphics Corp
8072  Landmark Graphics Corp
8073  Landmark Graphics Corp
8074  Landmark Graphics Corp
8075  Landmark Graphics Corp
8076  Landmark Graphics Corp
8077  Landmark Graphics Corp
807A  Matra
807B  Dansk Data Electronic A/S
807C  Merit Internodal
807D  VitaLink
807E  VitaLink
807F  VitaLink
8080  VitaLink Communications Bridge
8081  Counterpoint
8082  Counterpoint
8083  Counterpoint
8088  Xyplex
8089  Xyplex
808A  Xyplex
809B  AppleTalk
809B  Kinetics AppleTalk over Ethernet
809C  Datability
809D  Databitily
809E  Datability
809F  Spider Systems
80A3  Nixdorf Corp.
80A4  Siemens Gammasonics Inc
80A5  Siemens Gammasonics Inc
80A6  Siemens Gammasonics Inc
80A7  Siemens Gammasonics Inc
80A8  Siemens Gammasonics Inc
80A9  Siemens Gammasonics Inc
80AA  Siemens Gammasonics Inc
80AB  Siemens Gammasonics Inc
80AC  Siemens Gammasonics Inc
80AD  Siemens Gammasonics Inc
80AE  Siemens Gammasonics Inc
80AF  Siemens Gammasonics Inc
80B0  Siemens Gammasonics Inc
```

Table 5: continued

```
80B1  Siemens Gammasonics Inc
80B2  Siemens Gammasonics Inc
80B3  Siemens Gammasonics Inc
80C0  DCA Data (Digital Communications Associates)
80C1  DCA Data (Digital Communications Associates)
80C2  DCA Data (Digital Communications Associates)
80C3  DCA Data (Digital Communications Associates)
80C6  Pacer Software#
80C7  Applitek Corp
80C8  Integraph
80C9  Integraph
80CA  Integraph
80CB  Integraph
80CC  Integraph
80CD  Harris Corp
80CE  Harris Corp
80CF  Taylor Inst
80D0  Taylor Inst
80D1  Taylor Inst
80D2  Taylor Inst
80D3  Rosemount Corp
80D4  Rosemount Corp
80D5  IBM SNA user Ethernet
80DD  Varian Associates
80DE  Integrated Solutions TRFS (Transparent Remote File System)
80DF  Integrated Solutions
80E0  Allen Bradley
80E1  Allen Bradley
80E2  Allen Bradley
80E3  Allen Bradley
80E4  Datability
80E5  Datability
80E6  Datability
80E7  Datability
80E8  Datability
80E9  Datability
80EA  Datability
80EB  Datability
80EC  Datability
80ED  Datability
80EE  Datability
80EF  Datability
80F0  Datability
80F2  Retix
```

Table 5: continued

```
80F3  Kinetics, Apple Talk ARP (AARP)
80F2  Kinetics
80F3  Kinetics
80F7  Apollo Computer
80FF  Wellfleet Communications
8100  Wellfleet Communications
8101  Wellfleet Communications
8102  Wellfleet Communications
8103  Wellfleet Communications
8107  Symbolics (Proprietary)
8108  Symbolics (Proprietary)
8109  Symbolics (Proprietary)
8130  Waterloo Microsystems
8131  VG Laboratory Systems
8137  Novell IPX
8138  Novell
8139  KTI
813A  KTI
813B  KTI
813C  KTI
813D  KTI
8888  HP LanProbe
9000  Loopback (Configuration Test Protocol)
9001  Bridge Communications XNS Management
9002  Bridge Communications XNS/TCP IP Systems Management
9003  Bridge Communications
FF00  BBN Vital LAN Bridge cache wakeup
```

Table 5: continued

Service	Octal Value	Hex Value
Name Server	65	35
RPC Port Map	157	6F
Name Server	212	89
Datagram	213	8A
Session	1001	8B
rwho, ruptime	1002	201
syslog	1002	202
route (RIP)	1010	208
NFS daemon	4001	801

Table 6: Extended UDP Port Addresses

Service	OctalValue	Hex Value	Decimal Value
FTP	25	15	21
TELNET	27	17	23
SMTP	31	19	25
Name Server	65	35	53
RPC Port Map	157	6F	111
Name Server	211	89	137
Datagram	212	8A	138
Session	213	8B	139
Remote Exec	1000	200	512
rlogin	1001	201	513
remshell	1002	202	514
remote print	1003	203	515
rlb	2354	4EC	1260
NFT	3000	600	1536
VT	3001	601	1537
Reverse VT	3002	602	1538
PTOP	3004	604	1540
RPM	3006	606	1542
Ninstall	4071	839	2105
RFA	5000	A00	2560
RDBA	5001	A01	2561
RFA (UX)	1100	1240	4672

Table 7: Extended TCP SAPs (Service Access Points)

Notes

Notes

Notes

Notes

Notes

Notes

Notes

Notes

Notes

Notes

Notes

Notes

Notes

Notes

Notes

Notes

Notes

Notes

Notes

Notes

Notes

Notes

Notes

Notes

Notes